Praise for Diversity i

"This logical, well-structured, and timely book provides an insightful and fresh approach to understanding the cultural and gender diversity issues essential for a more effective workplace management. Its in-depth explorations of important issues and engaging organizational illustrations make this book an invaluable resource for academics and practitioners interested in understanding and creating enduring organizations."
— *Kajal Sharma, Senior Lecturer, University of Portsmouth, U.K.*

"This groundbreaking new book provides a clear, concise, and critical review of social science evidence on debates about racial, gender, and class diversity in organizations. Herring and Henderson consider the competing perspectives of organizational diversity proponents and opponents, and then provide compelling evidence in support of the business case for diversity. This critical examination is not only theoretically informed, but also bridges social science research on organizational diversity with concrete strategies useful for practitioners, managers and policy-makers."
—*Phillip J. Bowman, Professor, University of Michigan, U.S.*

"Herring and Henderson's *Diversity in Organizations* is a much-needed addition to the library of books on workplace diversity. Acknowledging the need for evidence-based information regarding the impact of diversity in the workplace, these authors carefully link their conclusions to highly rigorous data-based studies. Applying a critical lens to the diversity phenomenon, they clearly articulate the importance of acknowledging the systematic differences in treatment and life experience arising from social identity group memberships. Herring and Henderson persuasively explain the need for a very sophisticated approach to workplace diversity that considers the impact of inter-group power relationships on individuals, teams, and organizational change processes. I highly recommend this book."
—*Alison M. Konrad, Professor, Ivey Business School, Western University, Canada*

"In a groundbreaking analysis, *Diversity in Organizations* succeeds at striking a rare balance between discussing diversity in theory and in practice. In the book, Herring and Henderson outline a critical diversity perspective, which is a vast improvement over other approaches to both thinking about and doing diversity. In addition to developing this important theoretical lens, Herring and Henderson have outlined the current contours and future possibilities of diversity in a variety of organizational settings. Perhaps even more importantly, the authors use the latest research to provide cutting edge, practical strategies for achieving diversity and creating equitable and inclusive organizations. This is a must-read book for any serious student, scholar, or practitioner interested in issues of diversity."
— *Joyce M. Bell, Assistant Professor, University of Pittsburgh, U.S.*

Diversity in Organizations

Diversity in Organizations argues that ensuring a diverse workforce composition has tangible benefits for business organizations. Rather than relying on touchy-feely arguments, Herring and Henderson present compelling evidence that directly links diversity to the bottom line. However, the book goes beyond merely arguing that we should embrace diversity because it is profitable; it shows that the true power of diversity lies in its potential as a catalyst and incubator for innovation.

Critical diversity is a forceful theory that argues for the relationship between workforce composition and the business case for diversity. Contrasting critical diversity with other notions of diversity (such as colorblind, segregated, and snowflake diversity), the book offers real-life solutions to the political problems that arise from implementing diversity initiatives, and examines why some of these initiatives remain unpopular. Readers will learn:

- how and why diversity is related to business performance;
- what the impact of diversity training programs is upon productivity, business performance, and promotions;
- what the biggest mistakes in diversity management are, and how to avoid them;
- what can be done to make diversity initiatives more effective and politically palatable;
- how to measure levels of success in diversity initiatives in rigorous but non-technical ways so that managers and teams accountable for diversity practices can achieve their desired results.

The theory is presented in an accessible manner without shying away from the contentious aspects of diversity that confront our society. The book also provides concrete advice and guidance to those who seek to implement diversity programs and initiatives in their organizations, and to make their companies more competitive. Not only is it a compelling read, but students taking classes in diversity, human resource management, sociology of work, and organizational psychology will find this a comprehensive, helpful resource.

Cedric Herring is a Professor in the Language, Literacy, and Culture PhD Program at the University of Maryland, Baltimore County and formerly Professor of Sociology and Public Policy at the University of Illinois at Chicago. The author of eight books and more than 70 journal articles and book chapters, he has written on such topics as diversity, social policy, labor force issues and policy, stratification and inequality.

Loren Henderson is an Assistant Professor in the Department of Sociology and Anthropology at the University of Maryland, Baltimore County. Her research has focused on racial and gender disparities in health outcomes, race, class, gender, sexuality, and the changing meanings and controversies surrounding diversity.

Diversity in Organizations

A Critical Examination

Cedric Herring and
Loren Henderson

Routledge
Taylor & Francis Group

NEW YORK AND LONDON

First published 2015
by Routledge
711 Third Avenue, New York, NY 10017

and by Routledge
2 Park Square, Milton Park, Abingdon, Oxon OX14 4RN

Routledge is an imprint of the Taylor & Francis Group, an informa business

Library of Congress Cataloging-in-Publication Data

Herring, Cedric.
    Diversity in organizations : a critical examination / Cedric Herring & Loren
Henderson.
        pages cm
    Includes bibliographical references and index.
    1. Diversity in the workplace. 2. Personnel management. I. Henderson,
Loren. II. Title.
HF5549.5.M5H47 2014
658.3008—dc23
2013051129

ISBN: 978-0-415-74250-4
I SBN: 978-0-415-74251-1
ISBN: 978-1-315-81366-0

Typeset in Minion
by Apex CoVantage, LLC

MIX
Paper from
responsible sources
FSC
www.fsc.org   FSC® C013604

Printed and bound in Great Britain by
CPI Group (UK) Ltd, Croydon, CR0 4YY

* * *

To our mothers, Laura Washington and Fatima Sjoby

* * *

Contents

List of Figures

Acknowledgments

This book is the culmination of a journey that began several years ago. Along the way, we have benefitted tremendously from the generosity of several friends, family members, colleagues, scholars, and diversity practitioners who have provided insight, constructive criticism, enlightening conversations and debates, encouragement, and praise. We would like to thank Juan Battle, John Betancur, William Bielby, Lawrence Bobo, Phillip Bowman, Tony Brown, John Sibley Butler, Sharon Collins, Nancy DiTomaso, David Embrick, Michael Emerson, Paula England, David Fasenfest, Roberto Fernandez, Tyrone Forman, Lorena Garcia, Sydney Hart, Christopher Herring, Hayward Derrick Horton, James Kluegel, Maria Krysan, Anthony Lemelle, Jr., Sharon Mastracci, Judy Mathews, Monica McDermott, Ruby Mendenhall, Katherine Phillips, Robert Resek, Robert Rich, Vincent J. Roscigno, Moshe Semyonov, BarBara Scott, Kevin Stainback, Brett Stockdill, Melvin Thomas, Ganga Vijayasiri, and Assata Zerai for their extraordinarily helpful comments and suggestions. We acknowledge that some of the ideas in this book have been published or presented previously, at times in our collaborations with some of our friends and colleagues named above.

Our work has also benefitted from feedback provided by colleagues at various colloquia, workshops, presentations, and conferences. Earlier versions of various chapters have been presented at venues such as the American Sociological Association conference, the Association of Black Sociologists meetings, the Academy of Management conference, the Seventh Inter-American Congress on Corporate Social Responsibility, the Association of Collegiate Schools of Planning conference, and the Ford Foundation Fellows conference. In addition, parts of the book have been presented at the Workshop on the Reproduction of Race and Racial Ideologies at the University of Chicago, Rice University, the University of Notre Dame, Purdue University, the University of Wisconsin-Platteville, the University of Illinois at Chicago, the University of Illinois at Urbana-Champaign, the University of Maryland, Baltimore County, the University of Maryland, College Park, and the University of Texas. In addition, we have had the opportunity to present our ideas before government officials, corporate executives, educators, journalists, community leaders, diversity practitioners, and others who care about equity and equal opportunity. Their diverse vantage points have strengthened our work.

We have also had the good fortune of receiving support from organizations and institutions that have been quite munificent. In particular, we would like to thank the Ford Foundation and the Marion Kauffman Foundation for their generosity.

Finally, we dedicate this book to our families. In particular, we pay tribute to our mothers, Laura Washington and Fatima Sjoby. In addition, we thank Christopher, Kiara, Ashley, and Justin for their love and understanding.

Cedric Herring and Loren Henderson

1
Introduction

For several years, we have "known" that diversity is intrinsically good. It has become common for proponents of the "business case for diversity" to claim that "diversity pays."[1] For the most part, proponents of this view suggest that diversity in the corporate setting, for example, represents a compelling interest that will help meet customers' needs, enrich understanding of the pulse of the marketplace, and improve the quality of products and services offered.[2] With respect to employees, diversity brings with it different perspectives. The greater the differences among employees are, the broader their perspectives, the stronger their teams, and the better their resources for problem resolution.[3] Diversity also provides creative conflict that leads to closer examination of assumptions so that people from varied backgrounds can create complex learning environments that lead to better solutions to problems.[4] Because of the putative competitive advantages of diversity, companies increasingly have relied upon a heterogeneous workforce to increase their profits. Because diversity provides fresh ideas, strong growth, positive company images, fewer discrimination lawsuits, and an enhanced ability to hire qualified workers, businesses should be aggressive about workforce diversity.[5] In short, the rhetoric of diversity in industry suggests that a diverse workforce is good for business, and that diversity offers a direct return on investment that promises greater corporate profits and earnings.[6]

But evidence is a stubborn thing. Despite the fact that there are scores of books on the business case for diversity that have had very good sales, there are none that pass social science scrutiny in offering solid, systematic evidence to substantiate a link between the racial and ethnic composition of firms and business performance, *per se*. This lack of evidence has led to an upsurge of skeptical, anti-diversity works that suggest that the costs of diversity in the workplace outweigh its benefits.[7] They say that proponents of the diversity model too often overlook the significant costs of diversity. For example, Peter Skerry points out that research on intergroup relations consistently finds that racial and ethnic diversity are linked with conflict, especially emotional conflict among co-workers.[8] Ann Tsui, Terri Egan, and

Charles O'Reilly found that diversity can reduce the cohesiveness of the group and result in increased employee absenteeism and turnover.[9] Moreover, detractors of the diversity model suggest that the emphasis on diversity divides America into separate groups based on race, ethnicity, or gender and in so doing, suggests that some social categories are more deserving of privileges than are others.[10] There is also the argument that greater diversity is associated with worse quality because it places lower performing people in positions for which they are not suited.[11] Finally, Katherine Williams (Phillips) and Charles O'Reilly suggest that most empirical evidence shows that diversity is most likely to hinder group functioning.[12] In short, critics of the diversity model posit that group differences result in conflict and its attendant costs. For these reasons, skeptics of the business case for diversity model have questioned the real impact of diversity programs upon the "bottom line" of business organizations.

For more than 20 years, scholars have been talking up the value of research-based management and lamenting the fact that academics are not providing the kind of information and evidence that diversity managers can use in their day-to-day activities and that diversity practitioners are not using the information and research evidence that scholars have produced.[13] Unfortunately, the same thing is true in the field of human resources where there is the feeling that practitioners neither know nor follow research-based "best practices," and practitioners feel that researchers do not really provide useful advice.[14] The same is true within the growing field of diversity management.[15]

David Kravitz[16] argues that:

> academics and practitioners do not adequately grasp the other group's domain. For example, academics are often unfamiliar with the reality of diversity work in business. They are unaware of, and thus do not study, novel approaches that practitioners have developed. They do not appreciate the challenges involved in applying their findings in the workplace and often do research with little practical value. Practitioners are not blameless. They are unaware of academic research about basic human nature and about what diversity management approaches are known to work—knowledge that could increase the impact of their programs and practices. In summary, academics and practitioners do not value, appreciate, or even understand one another.

Diversity in Organizations: A Critical Examination bridges the diversity research practice gap. It does so by bringing the best practices uncovered by academic research to bear on topics that matter to practitioners who are trying to determine what they need to know and do in order to manage diversity within their organizations more effectively and profitably. But *Diversity in Organizations* is not just another atheoretical how-to book. Rather, it offers a hardheaded examination of the relationship between workforce composition and the business case for diversity. This book provides concrete evidence that diversity matters in business organizations. Rather than the kind of touchy-feely, we-wish-that-it-were-so arguments put forth by proponents of diversity in the past, it supplies data that directly links diversity to the bottom line. It provides the kind of theoretically informed, systematic analysis of data from actual business organizations that management scholars and social scientists are accustomed to seeing in their most rigorous professional journals. It puts forth a theoretical perspective—that of critical diversity—that is unapologetically pro-diversity for the right reasons. Yet, *Diversity in Organizations* presents these materials in a fashion that will make it accessible for the informed and educated person who cares about these pressing issues that confront our society and the business manager who wants to know what she needs to do in order for her company to become more competitive.

After demonstrating that diversity is beneficial, *Diversity in Organizations* shows why initiatives to promote greater diversity—like affirmative action—remain unpopular with Whites. But it does not stop there. It also offers real-life solutions to the political problems that arise from implementing diversity initiatives. It also looks at the various sources of support for, and opposition to, diversity and equal opportunity initiatives. In particular, it answers questions about why increasing proportions of the population say that they favor diversity but appear to oppose the means and goals to achieving it.

Diversity in Organizations: A Critical Examination is divided into 14 chapters. The next chapter provides explanations of some of the central concepts used by those interested in diversity issues, identifies the subject matter, and locates the work in the context of contemporary writings on diversity in employment and educational institutions. It introduces a theoretical perspective that we call "critical diversity." The chapter provides a brief historical overview of changes in the discourse and rhetoric about inclusion as it has moved from debates about affirmative action to various notions of diversity. It calls for a move away from "colorblind diversity," "segregated diversity," and "snowflake diversity" toward a "critical diversity" that must go beyond celebrating group differences to examine all forms of social inequality, oppression, and stratification that revolve around issues of difference. It lays out some concrete strategies for doing so:

1 Target goods and resources to excluded people.
2 Advocate for an expansive notion of diversity, but seek out distributive justice that will serve to assist "disprivileged" groups.
3 Shift goods and resources away from privileged groups, especially when invoking the rhetoric of diversity.
4 Reconnect diversity to affirmative action and the need to offset historical and ongoing racial and gender discrimination, segregation, and bias.
5 Remind people that diversity is consistent with legal compliance.
6 Demonstrate to organizational members that diversity is institutionally beneficial.

In Chapter 2, we argue that without linking diversity to such concerns, the usage of the term diversity is hollow.

Chapter 3 provides a comprehensive overview of the business case for diversity thesis. In doing so, it explains why a business case for diversity is necessary. It then provides an examination and critique of this perspective that critics of diversity have put forth. It provides a clear, concise explanation of diversity as a concept. It also shows how diversity compares to related concepts such as affirmative action and quotas. Perhaps most importantly, it provides evidence from a nationally representative sample of real business organizations to examine the relationship between racial and gender workforce diversity and the business case for diversity. In doing so, it provides strong support for the business case for diversity perspective. It answers questions such as: How does diversity affect the business performance of organizations? Is there any tangible evidence that there is a relationship between the racial and gender composition of the firm and its sales revenue, its number of customers, its market share, or its profitability? The results are fully consistent with the argument that racial diversity in the workforce has a positive impact upon business performance. The relationships between racial diversity and various dimensions of business performance remain even after statistical controls for such factors as legal form of organization, gender composition of the firm, organization size, organization age, type of work conducted by the organization, and region. The chapter also provides insight into how diversity managers and others can use these results to their advantage in their quest for profit, productivity, and partnerships. Indeed, the chapter explicitly discusses the "diversity-profit equation" and how it can be leveraged for organizational gain.

Chapter 4 offers an examination of organizational characteristics, recruitment and retention factors, and employment practices and job benefits that are associated with the racial and ethnic composition of for-profit and nonprofit organizations in the United States. It demonstrates that there are tangible recruitment and retention strategies that companies can employ (or avoid) that make a difference. Organizations that foster climates that are inviting to racial and ethnic minorities and actively seek to promote them have more success in retaining them. Organizations can foster climates that are inviting to racial and ethnic minorities by offering job-training opportunities for employees of color and encouraging them to keep their skills current so that they can advance. Making the job search process transparent by posting information about job vacancies and utilizing internal hiring and promotion strategies are also associated with higher percentages of racial and ethnic minorities in the workplace. Many of the effective recruitment and retention efforts go hand-in-hand with signaling the importance of fairness in employment practices and the provision of job benefits that make it easier for organizations to be inclusive. The analysis also shows that racial and ethnic diversity increases marginally as establishment size increases, with the presence of unions, formal job training, internal hiring strategies, higher percentages of women in core positions, affirmative action and Equal Employment Opportunity (EEO) departments, formal job performance evaluations, and the provision of daycare facilities and subsidies. The availability of flexible work hours is associated with lower rates of racial and ethnic diversity. The chapter also explores the centrality of having a compelling recruitment brand when trying to win over talent, especially from diverse populations.

Chapter 5 examines the pessimism and skepticism surrounding the impact of diversity training programs. It focuses on the challenges of managing diversity by pointing to the dangers of racial and ethnic heterogeneity when appropriate diversity management tools are not in place. It provides an analysis of the conditions under which diversity leads to such workplace problems as increased absenteeism and worker turnover. Importantly, it also offers ways to resolve these issues by changing the culture of organizations so that employees understand the value and importance of diversity and of focusing on the goals of the organization rather than individual needs. In short, this chapter identifies conditions and practices that create and sustain environments that are supportive of diversity. The chapter also provides information about managing diversity in work organizations, corporate governance, and the biggest mistakes to avoid in diversity management.

Chapter 6 provides an analysis of gender diversity. It shows that in the last 50 years, women have come a long way in the U.S. workplace. Women's participation in professional managerial roles has increased from 4 percent in the early 1970s to almost 50 percent today. Women have entered occupations that were previously closed to them. At the same time, women make 76 cents to the dollar of men. The number of women CEOs of *Fortune* 500 corporations can still be counted on one hand. Women account for only 12 percent of boardroom seats, and they make up only 16 percent of corporate officers. Despite women's increasing participation in the labor force, they are still concentrated in certain sectors of the labor market and within certain fields within those sectors. We show that organizations with shared governance, formalized organizational structures, transparent human resource management, and innovative management practices are more likely to have higher proportions of women. In addition to the challenges of exclusion and occupational segregation, we show that, far too often, women also confront the issue of sexual harassment in the workplace. Indeed, half of working women experience sexual harassment at some point in their careers. Thus, this chapter also examines the organizational context in which sexual harassment occurs by identifying the organizational factors that promote its occurrence and those that deter it. Interestingly, we show that organizations that have normative and structural barriers that block women's access to traditionally male occupations are often the ones that do little to deter sexual harassment in the workplace. In other words, gendered institutions that steer women into certain "female jobs" and away from "male jobs" also apparently breed organizational climates that allow sexual harassment to occur. We provide some insights into what can be done to reduce occupational segregation by gender and what can be done to reduce the incidence of sexual harassment.

Chapter 7 tackles the very difficult topic of continuing discrimination in the workplace. It shows that racial discrimination in employment is still widespread but has gone underground and become more sophisticated. The chapter also takes on the issue of occupational segregation by race and ethnicity and links it to larger issues of social inequality in American society.

The following chapter asks whether affirmative action is still needed. We examine the impact of affirmative action in redressing issues of unfair inequality. We address some of the empirical questions surrounding affirmative action policies. In doing so, Chapter 8 examines many of the myths and misconceptions about affirmative action as a policy. It asks who benefits from affirmative action. We provide evidence about the relationship of affirmative action programs to the incomes, professional statuses, work-relevant interracial perceptions and attitudes, and mobility patterns of minority and non-minority workers. The evidence suggests that affirmative action programs in the workplace are associated with higher incomes for those whom they were intended to help. Indeed, they are associated with higher incomes for racial minorities, women, and people from low-income backgrounds. Affirmative action programs accomplish these outcomes without appearing to do significant harm to the economic well-being of White males who work in such settings. Another rather clear result, however, is that affirmative action is related to increased perceptions that reverse discrimination occurs. The chapter also examines the "perils of pluralism" and asks for a critical examination of the terms of engagement between races and cultures. In staking a claim for equal opportunity, it calls for an honest and straightforward discussion about persisting racial, gender, and class inequality in America.

Chapter 9 examines the link between wealth and class diversity. This chapter provides an overview of wealth and class diversity in the United States by examining the distribution of wealth and its impact upon life chances and opportunities. It also shows how these patterns differ by race, gender, and occupational type. It shows why such disparities in wealth exist, how they are related to critical diversity, and what can be done to reduce unfair disparities in wealth and opportunity.

Chapter 10 addresses homophobia and heterosexism in organizations. Over the past decade, the number of corporations addressing the issue of sexual orientation as part of their valuing diversity initiatives has increased rather dramatically. This chapter identifies and discusses organizational best practices designed to create more inclusive, equitable, and productive workplaces for lesbian, gay, bisexual, and transgendered (LGBT) employees. It also provides some suggestions about how to allow employees to self-report themselves as LGBT and at the same time feel that they can fully participate in corporate life. It provides some strategies for creating a welcoming environment for LGBT employees.

Chapter 11 moves from the corporate world to the college campus. To some people, colleges and universities are "ivory towers" isolated from the larger society. But the reality is that academic institutions are reflections of the larger society. They struggle with many of the same social issues and prejudices. Over the last century, many academic institutions, especially the more elite ones, have gone from being the exclusive domains of mostly wealthy, White men, to including women and people of color. It is even more recent that these campuses have allowed openly gay, lesbian, bisexual, and transgender people the opportunity to express themselves freely. This chapter discusses the diversity climate on college campuses generally and what can be done to challenge racism, sexism, and heterosexism in higher education. This chapter also documents the business case for diversity in higher education by showing that greater diversity among students and faculty at research universities enhances the university's *reputational* bottom line. And this reputation is a university's bottom line.

Chapter 12 looks at the various sources of support for and opposition to diversity and equal opportunity initiatives. In particular, it answers questions about why substantial proportions of people oppose affirmative action programs. This chapter also examines intergroup attitudes, relations, and tensions, especially in the workplace. It identifies practices within business organizations that heighten or reduce work-group tensions. It also provides some guidelines for resolving workplace conflicts that arise out of group differences. The chapter pays special attention to White male angst in the workplace. It provides insight into the political aspects of diversity, and it walks readers through those elements that make diversity initiatives effective and politically palatable. The chapter concludes with a discussion of the implications of the results for debates about diversity and equal opportunity policies such as affirmative action.

Chapter 13 returns to the issue of accountability in diversity and inclusion strategies. It provides guidance so that those who are attempting to gauge their level of success in their diversity initiatives will be able to do so with rigorous but non-technical ways. It identifies ways in which organizations

can begin to hold their managers and teams accountable for diversity practices that achieve their desired results. We introduce the "Diversity Profit
Equation" and straightforward metrics that allow organizations to measure
their return on investment (ROI) in diversity. We provide details about the
Balanced Scorecard approach. This approach is the first step in positioning
diversity as a strategic initiative. The Balanced Scorecard approach offers a
way of classifying several organizational performance indicators. We provide details about the "Business Case Scorecard" in ways that are accessible
to the non-specialist.

The final chapter provides concluding remarks about critical diversity. It
also points to the future and discusses what diversity must become in the
future. It provides insights into diversity in American society in the Obama
era. It also provides guidance on some diversity issues that will become
even more important in the future, such as religious diversity in the workplace, disability, generational diversity in the workplace, and immigration
and globalization. Finally, the book concludes with advice about how to
improve your cultural competency, and how to be at the forefront of organization culture change.

Diversity in Organizations: A Critical Examination demonstrates that not
all types of diversity are created equal. While embracing the business case
for diversity, it argues that we must do more than just embrace diversity
because it is profitable. We live in an age of knowledge, and firms that succeed, especially in an era of economic uncertainty, are those that are best
able to harness the collective knowledge and talents of their employees.
These are the organizations that offer equal opportunity to all because
there is not a single person to waste.

How does *Diversity in Organizations* compare with other works on
diversity? As mentioned above, there is not another book that offers a
compelling theory that complements the business case for diversity; nor
is there one that effectively bridges the gap between forceful social science
evidence with the needs of diversity managers and executives. We believe
that *Diversity in Organizations* does both. It makes a new case for diversity
based on offering equal opportunity so that it can be more profitable for
all of the reasons that the business case makes. Although it is not a hands-
on, practical guide to the why and how-to of striving for diversity and
equity in the workplace, it does provide concrete advice and guidance to
those who seek to implement diversity programs and initiatives in their
organizations.

Similarly, while the book points out general societal trends that suggest
that the nation is becoming more diverse, unlike so many other works, it
goes the extra step to systematically demonstrate that businesses do better
by becoming more diverse themselves. Again, the emphasis is on illustrat-
ing practical ways in which organizations can address issues that arise as
they attempt to diversify. *Diversity in Organizations* demonstrates that not

having diversity can be costly because racial and sexual bias costs big bucks as a result of litigation, lowered sales, and loss of employees and customers. It relies on solid social science evidence to document this.

This is not to say that there are no other books that provide rigorous treatment of diversity and what research has to tell us about it. *The Diversity Scorecard: Evaluating the Impact of Diversity on Organizational Performance* by Edward Hubbard is a rigorous work that offers some guidelines for trying to measure diversity in order to assess its impact upon organizations. Hubbard's book is a valuable contribution to the literature about diversity. It will assist organizations in determining the return on investment of diversity programs as rigorously as they do for other parts of their business. It is not, however, very accessible to most business readers, nor does it have wide appeal to readers who are interested in issues other than methodological and measurement concerns. The same is true of Hubbard's other work entitled *How to Calculate Diversity Return on Investment.* Although Hubbard's monograph offers step-by-step methods for turning diversity initiatives and organizational data related to diversity into indicators, it is far too technical for general and business readers. This is unfortunate because it does offer a framework for demonstrating diversity's link and contribution to bottom-line performance.

In contrast, *Diversity in Organizations: A Critical Examination* offers solid social science evidence that clearly demonstrates the link between organizations' workforce compositions and their business performances. It is unique in this regard. It offers such evidence in a way that is as jargon-free and non-technical as possible so that the book will remain accessible to the non-specialist who has concern about issues of diversity, especially in business organizations. In reading this book, we hope you will agree.

Notes

1 Hubbard, 2004; Cox, 1993; and Cox and Beale, 1997
2 Hubbard, 2004
3 Cox, 2001
4 Gurin, Nagda, and Lopez, 2004
5 Williams and O'Reilly, 1998; and Florida and Gates, 2001, 2002
6 Ryan, Hawdon, and Branick, 2002
7 Skerry, 2002; Rothman, Lipset, and Nevitte, 2003a; Rothman, Lipset, and Nevitte, 2003b; Tsui, Egan, and O'Reilly, 1992; and Whitaker, 1996
8 Skerry, 2002
9 Tsui, Egan, and O'Reilly 1992
10 Wood, 2003
11 Rothman, Lipset, and Nevitte, 2003b
12 Williams and O'Reilly, 1998
13 Hambrick, 1994; and Kravitz, 2008
14 Burke, Drasgow, and Edwards, 2004; and Kravitz, 2008
15 Pendry, Driscoll, and Field, 2007; and Kravitz, 2010
16 Kravitz, 2010: 1

References

Burke, Michael J., Fritz Drasgow, and Jack E. Edwards. 2004. "Closing Science-Practice Knowledge Gaps: Contributions of Psychological Research to Human Resource Management." *Human Resource Management* 43: 299–304.

Cox, Taylor. 1993. *Cultural Diversity in Organizations: Theory, Research, and Practice*. San Francisco, CA: Berrett-Koehler.

Cox, Taylor. 2001. *Creating the Multicultural Organization: A Strategy for Capturing the Power of Diversity*. San Francisco, CA: Jossey-Bass.

Cox, Taylor and Ruby L. Beale. 1997. *Developing Competency to Manage Diversity*. San Francisco, CA: Berrett-Koehler.

Florida, Richard and Gary Gates. 2001. *Technology and Tolerance: The Importance of Diversity to High-Technology Growth*. Washington, DC: The Brookings Institution.

Florida, Richard and Gary Gates. 2002. "Technology and Tolerance: Diversity and High-Tech Growth." *Brookings Review* 20: 32–36.

Gurin, Patricia, Biren (Ratnesh) A. Nagda, and Gretchen E. Lopez. 2004. "The Benefits of Diversity in Education for Democratic Citizenship." *Journal of Social Issues* 60: 17–34.

Hambrick, David C. 1994. "Top Management Groups: A Conceptual Integration and Reconstruction of the 'Team' Label," in B. Staw and R. Sutton (Eds). *Research in Organizational Behavior*. Greenwich, CT: JAI Press.

Hubbard, Edward E. 1997. *Measuring Diversity Results*. Petaluma, CA: Global Insights.

Hubbard, Edward E. 1999. *How to Calculate Diversity Return on Investment*. Petaluma, CA: Global Insights.

Hubbard, Edward E. 2004. *The Diversity Scorecard: Evaluating the Impact of Diversity on Organizational Performance*. Burlington, MA: Elsevier Butterworth-Heinemann.

Kravitz, David A. 2008. "The Diversity-Validity Dilemma: Beyond Selection—The Role of Affirmative Action." *Personnel Psychology* 61:173–193.

Kravitz, David A. 2010. "The Research-Practice Gap in Diversity Management." *The Diversity Factor* 18 (1): 32–38.

O'Reilly, Charles A., D. E. Caldwell, and W. P. Barnett. 1989. "Work Group Demography, Social Integration, and Turnover." *Administrative Science Quarterly* 34: 21–37.

Pendry, Louise F., Denise M. Driscoll, and Susannah C. T. Field. 2007. "Diversity Training: Putting Theory into Practice." *Journal of Occupational and Organizational Psychology* 80 (1): 27–50.

Rothman, Stanley, Seymour Martin Lipset, and Neil Nevitte. 2003a. "Does Enrollment Diversity Improve University Education?" *International Journal of Public Opinion Research* 15: 8–26.

Rothman, Stanley, Seymour Martin Lipset, and Neil Nevitte. 2003b. "Racial Diversity Reconsidered." *The Public Interest* 151: 25–38.

Ryan, John, James Hawdon, and Allison Branick. 2002. "The Political Economy of Diversity: Diversity Programs in *Fortune* 500 Companies." *Sociological Research Online* (May).

Skerry, Peter. 2002. "Beyond Sushiology: Does Diversity Work?" *Brookings Review* 20: 20–23.

Thiederman, Sondra. 2003. *Making Diversity Work: Seven Steps for Defeating Bias in the Workplace*. Chicago, IL: Dearborn Trade Publishing.

Tsui, Ann S., Terri D. Egan, and Charles A. O'Reilly. 1992. "Being Different: Relational Demography and Organizational Attachment." *Administrative Science Quarterly* 37: 549–579.

Whitaker, William A. 1996. *White Male Applicant: An Affirmative Action Expose*. Smyrna, DE: Apropos Press.

Williams, Katherine and Charles A. O'Reilly. 1998. "Demography and Diversity: A Review of 40 Years of Research," in B. Staw and R. Sutton (Eds). *Research in Organizational Behavior*. Greenwich, CT: JAI Press.

Wilson, Trevor. 2000. *Diversity at Work: The Business Case for Equity*. Hoboken, NJ: John Wiley & Sons.

Wood, Peter. 2003. "Diversity in America." *Society* 40: 60–67.

2
The Critical Diversity Perspective

Over the past 40 years, the rhetoric about inclusion has changed substantially in the United States.[1] During the 1960s, African Americans and others, through the Civil Rights and Black Power movements, fought to end racial discrimination.[2] By the late 1970s and into the 1980s, there was growing recognition within the private sector that, while legal mandates were necessary, they were not sufficient for ensuring the effective management of diversity within organizations.

But a reactionary movement developed to protest what opponents of affirmative action perceived as preferential treatment, quotas, and reverse discrimination.[3] For more than two decades, affirmative action has been under sustained assault. In courts, legislatures, and the media, opponents have condemned it as an unprincipled program of racial and gender preferences that threatens fundamental American values of fairness, equality, and democratic opportunity.

The rhetoric of diversity was a neoliberal response to the reactionary backlash against affirmative action.[4] Neoliberal elites used diversity rhetoric to convey racial inclusion in language that was more politically palatable to Whites and to expand the politics and conversation about inclusion beyond concerns about race and inequality. In doing so, they transformed the terms of institutional inclusion to accommodate demands in the post-civil rights era. The new rhetoric of diversity helped to bring about the addition of some racial and ethnic minorities (e.g., Latinos and Asians), women, and other disadvantaged groups (e.g., those from underrepresented geographical locations). At the same time, elites have begun to rely on this rhetoric to accommodate and even support the inclusion of people from groups not traditionally thought of as being disadvantaged.[5]

This chapter argues that critical diversity is about embracing cultural differences that exist between groups and appreciating those differences, but critical diversity must also include examining issues of parity, equity, and inequality. It is imperative that it examines all forms of social inequality, oppression, and stratification that revolve around issues of diversity.

A theory of critical diversity includes celebrating cultural differences, but it also requires an analysis of exclusion, discrimination, and it challenges hegemonic notions of colorblindness and meritocracy.

What Is Diversity? A Brief History with Changing Meanings

For some people, the term "diversity" provokes intense emotional reactions because it brings to mind such politically charged ideas as "affirmative action" or "quotas." The idea of diversity is ambiguous. This ambiguity is expressed in the variety of the concept's definitions that exist in literature.[6] Some definitions focus narrowly on protected groups covered under the edict of affirmative action.[7] Here differences such as race, gender, ethnicity, age, national origin, religion, and disability are the focal point. Alternatively, other definitions of diversity are broadly construed and extend beyond race and gender and include all types of individual differences. These broader definitions tend to include geographic considerations, personality, sexual preferences, and a myriad of other personal, demographic, and organizational characteristics.[8] Generally speaking, the term "diversity" refers to policies and practices that seek to include people who are considered to be, in some way, different from the traditional member. Less tangibly but more centrally it means to create an inclusive culture that values and uses the talents of all would-be members.

The rhetoric about inclusion has shifted over time. Since the 1940s, the federal government has increased anti-discriminatory employment measures and enacted civil rights legislation on behalf of African Americans.[9] During the 1940s and 1950s, such efforts were through executive orders aimed at prohibiting discrimination in the federal civil service system, eliminating discrimination in the armed forces, and establishing compliance procedures in the private sector for government contractors.

In the 1960s, social movements for African-American civil rights fought to end legal racism and economic discrimination on the grounds of civil rights, justice, and equality.[10] Activists challenged widespread beliefs that certain groups—such as White people, men, the wealthy, and heterosexuals—should have privileged access to universities, workplaces, communities, voting, and other major institutions. Government officials, also facing international criticism of U.S. racial policy, institutionalized some redistributive programs and accommodationist policies of non-discrimination and affirmative action, particularly during the 1960s and 1970s.[11]

Title VII of the 1964 Civil Rights Act, for example, made it illegal for organizations to engage in employment practices that discriminated against employees on the basis of race, sex, color, and religion. Through such government action, American society made the declaration that employers must provide equal employment opportunities to people with similar qualifications and accomplishments, irrespective of their demographic characteristics.[12] In addition, Executive Order 11246 issued in 1965 required government contractors to take affirmative action to overcome past patterns of exclusion and discrimination.[13] These societal mandates eliminated formal policies that discriminated against certain classes of workers, and they raised the costs to employers who failed to implement fair employment practices. The laws remain a part of the legal responsibilities under which firms and other labor market institutions such as unions and employment agencies operate today.

Affirmative action was borne out of the racial conflict of the late 1960s and early 1970s.[14] Affirmative action consists of government-mandated or voluntary programs and activities undertaken specifically to identify, recruit, promote and/or retain qualified members of disadvantaged minority groups in order to overcome the results of past discrimination and to deter discriminatory practices in the present. The assumption is that simply removing existing impediments is not sufficient for changing the relative positions of women and people of color.[15] Affirmative action is based on the premise that to be truly effective in altering the unequal distribution of life chances, it is essential that employers and others take specific steps to remedy the consequences of discrimination.

Affirmative action came under siege not only for being politically unpopular, but also for being ineffective as a policy for reducing levels of inequality for targeted groups.[16] Some challenged affirmative action because it purportedly helps those members of minority groups who need assistance least at the same time that it does little for those who are among the "truly disadvantaged."[17] Others criticized such programs for unfairly stigmatizing qualified minority candidates who must endure the perception that they were selected or promoted only because of their institutions' need for minority representation.[18] Still others have derided affirmative action policies as "reverse discrimination" which benefits minority groups at the expense of equally or more qualified White males.[19] The attitudes of the general public on affirmative action took on even greater and more direct relevance, as referenda in several states asked voters themselves to make decisions about ending affirmative action.

By the late 1970s and into the 1980s, there was growing recognition within the private sector that, while the legal mandates were necessary, they were not sufficient for ensuring the effective management of diversity within organizations.[20] Many companies and consulting firms began to offer training programs aimed at "valuing diversity" in order to promote organizational cultures that would support workforces that are more diverse.

A reactionary movement developed to protest what opponents of affirmative action perceived as preferential treatment, quotas, and group rights.[21] Jonathan Leonard, a prominent economist, proclaimed, "affirmative action effectively passed away with the inauguration of the Reagan administration in 1981." He went on to say, "the Supreme Court decisions . . . nailed down the coffin lid."[22]

Still, elites started to frame such issues of inclusion as matters of "diversity."[23] They called for the inclusion of different types of people—disadvantaged groups such as racial minorities as well as groups not defined by their disadvantage or identity—and they portrayed this inclusion as both morally right and institutionally beneficial.

On the one hand, diversity ideology represents White elites' taming of what began as a radical fight for African-American equality.[24] On the other hand, the ideology of "diversity" was a neoliberal response to reactionary blowback against affirmative action. As Ellen Berrey suggests, neoliberal elites used diversity ideology to frame racial inclusion in language that was more politically palatable to Whites and to broaden the politics and discourse of inclusion beyond concerns about race or inequality. In doing so, they transformed the terms of institutional inclusion to accommodate demands in the post-civil rights era. Diversity rhetoric helped to encourage some institutional integration of racial minorities, women, and other disadvantaged groups. At the same time, elites have begun to rely on this ideology to accommodate and even support privileged people and to minimize the threats of integration to their own institutional interests.

Diversity ideology has become institutionalized through elites' public rhetoric. This is especially true when it comes to their descriptions and justifications, and through various structuring elements of their organizational initiatives, particularly the criteria for program participation.

Diversity was originally a concept created to justify more inclusion of people who had traditionally been left out. Back in the 1980s, it was used to make the process more inclusive of people of color, women, and other groups who had been left out of schools, universities, corporations, and other kinds of organizations.[25] Somewhere along the way, the idea got co-opted. More and more groups—for example, the left-handers of America—came to be included under the rubric of diversity. Probably one of the first categories of people to expand the notion of diversity—and rightly so—were members of the lesbian, gay, bisexual, and transgendered (LGBT) community. But with such expansion, the question then becomes "what is the rationale that undergirds" diversity? And what are the boundaries and limits of diversity? Where, exactly, does it stop? Or does it stop?

Critical Diversity

As we mentioned above, critical diversity is about more than embracing cultural differences that exist between groups and appreciating those differences. It also includes examining issues of parity, equity, and inequality in all forms. It confronts issues of oppression and stratification that revolve around issues of diversity. A theory of critical diversity includes an analysis of exclusion, discrimination, and it challenges hegemonic notions of colorblindness and meritocracy. Thus, critical diversity can be defined as the equal inclusion of people from varied backgrounds—especially those who are considered to be different from the traditional members because of exclusionary practices—on a parity basis throughout all ranks of the organization. It also refers to inclusive cultures that value and use the talents of all would-be members and includes them throughout all ranks of the organization.

Critical diversity is in stark contrast to other notions of diversity such as "colorblind diversity." A colorblind diversity understanding of the social world is based on the premise that it is sufficient to embrace cultural differences among various racial and ethnic groups without acknowledging disparities among these groups in power, status, wealth, and access. Such notions invite us to celebrate cultural events that mask social inequalities.[26] For example, universities across the nation celebrate "unity month" and other activities that point out the diversity of their faculties and student bodies. Such multicultural events might include ethnic festivals that invite people from different cultural backgrounds to showcase the food, music, clothing, etc. from their particular heritage. However, few if any of these events involve the explicit discussion of these groups and how they are discriminated against within society—let alone within the very institutions that are hosting the events. These events usually fail to highlight racial and ethnic discrimination that individual members of these groups face. They also fail to acknowledge the extent to which dominant groups benefit from such events by expropriating the very cultural items that are on display.

Another critique of colorblind diversity is that just at the point where people of color are beginning to assert themselves, their identities, their agency, and their ability to be part of the process, advocates of colorblindness make the argument that racial categories do not really exist. They suggest that race and other categories are merely socially constructed. Racial minorities just need to start feeling differently about who they think they are and what their plight is. And when they start thinking differently about who they are and what their plight is, they will see that they are not being denied privilege and access because of their group membership. By definition, they cannot be denied these things based on their group memberships because groups do not really exist as objective facts. And who really knows what determines which people—not as members of groups but as individuals—are denied access.

Kimberle Crenshaw discusses the intersectionality of these sorts of things and how, just at the point where members of groups are able to mobilize in order to make demands based on their group membership, arguments about how their groups are no more than the social construction of reality serve to undermine these very groups at critical times.[27] This suggests that some aspect of colorblind diversity is about silencing individuals who are members of groups that would serve as harsh critics of the status quo.

Perhaps one of the most insidious types of diversity is that which we call "snowflake diversity." Snowflake diversity is the idea that because all individuals—just like snowflakes—are unique, we should not pay attention to group-based differences in any meaningful way. In the case of snowflakes, generations of scientists have observed, photographed, and catalogued these tiny frozen water crystals. Their patterns adhere to the laws of physics and mathematics. Yet, no two snowflakes have ever been shown to be exactly the same. Each new snowflake is a fragile balance among factors such as temperature, the humidity, wind turbulence, and the presence of impurities in the atmosphere. Because each factor can be measured and calibrated infinitely, it is virtually impossible to predict precisely how fast a snowflake tip will grow, how narrow it will be, or how often it will branch. Therefore, with such seemingly infinite possibilities, we can understand why each snowflake ends up being truly unique.

Even though snowflakes are individual and unique, *types* of snow can be designated by the shape of the flakes, the description of how they fall, and how they collect on the ground. For example, we can classify snowflake shapes into four classes:

1   dendrites (the classic snowflakes with six points forming a star shape);
2   graupel (precipitation formed when freezing fog condenses and forms a ball of snow pellets);
3   needles (snowflakes that are acicular in shape with lengths that are much longer than their diameters); and
4   sleet (snowflakes that thaw and then refreeze when passing through sufficiently cold air).

So, even with snowflakes, going beyond their unique traits as individual flakes is useful.

So, too, is going beyond individualism when it comes to diversity. Snowflake diversity relies on the principle of "individualism." Individualism is an ideology or social outlook that stresses the worth of the individual and promotes the exercise of one's desires and goals. It is based on the notion of self-reliance that opposes external interference on one's interests by society or other institutions such as the government.

As we will show in Chapter 11, individualism is one of the culturally approved bases for many Whites to contest Blacks' attempts to gain a greater share of scarce resources. By invoking individualism, believers of snowflake diversity have a philosophy that predisposes them to oppose group-based processes and programs. Rather than seeing groups with unequal access and power, they merely see individuals, all of whom are different. Because they see individuals rather than groups, they do not really see a group basis for diversity. It makes it difficult for them to understand or see the legitimacy of group-based contests over the distribution of scarce resources between groups. However, groups come into conflict not only over actual distributions of rewards, but also over the values to be used in guiding the stratification process. As we will see throughout this book, critical diversity takes the position that paying attention to the group basis of diversity is necessary so that it can be linked to other concepts such as parity and equity.

Critical diversity is also different from what we might think of as "segregated diversity."[28] Segregated diversity exists when the entire entity (e.g., organization, community, state, or nation) becomes more diverse and differentiated within the entity but the dominant groups remain isolated from subdominant groups. Unlike a colorblind diversity perspective, segregated diversity does acknowledge the need for inclusion. Indeed, proportional representation of various groups is important to this concept, but there is no requirement for equal representation and parity throughout all ranks of the organization. In other words, we can think about racial diversity existing in a racialized social system. We can also think about gender diversity existing in a sexist social system. It is diversity, but understanding its dynamics requires examining diversity through the lens of race and gender. A concrete example of segregated diversity is the U.S. Army. The army often prides itself on being among the most diverse and inclusive institutions in American society.[29] However, the truth of the matter is that although the army has an increasing proportion of women and soldiers of color, these soldiers remain disproportionately represented in the lower ranks of the army. In the history of the U.S. Army, there is only one woman who has achieved the rank of four-star general. This disparity is the direct result of structural policies that limit women's access to higher-ranking positions. So, despite movement toward inclusion, the representation of women and people of color still reflects the longstanding hierarchical patterns that are systemic within this organization. Women and people of color are still disproportionately at the bottom. These disparities are not limited to race and gender. Indeed, by enforcing its "don't ask, don't tell" policy, until recently the U.S. Army unnecessarily discriminated against soldiers based on their sexual orientations. Such organizational segregation and exclusionary practices are the opposite of what we mean by critical diversity. Although segregated diversity does incorporate the need for proportional representation of those from diverse groups, it does not, however, redress inequality.

Skeptics of diversity are more cynical about the benefits that diversity provides.[30] Some skeptics argue that diversity leads to "process loss": inefficiencies in group process that occur when group members are involved in decision-making.[31] For example, Peter Skerry points out that research on intergroup relations consistently finds that racial and ethnic diversity are linked with conflict, especially emotional conflict among co-workers. Karen Jehn, Gregory Northcraft, and Margaret Neale found that while informational diversity positively influenced group performance, value and social category diversity diminished this effect.[32] Lisa Pelled, Kathleen Eisenhardt, and Katherine Xin found a complex link between work group diversity and work group functioning.[33] Ann Tsui, Terri Egan, and Charles O'Reilly found that diversity can reduce the cohesiveness of the group and result in increased employee absenteeism and turnover.[34] Moreover, detractors of the diversity model suggest that the emphasis on diversity divides America into separate groups based on race, ethnicity, or gender and in so doing suggests that some social categories are more deserving of privileges than are others.[35] There is also the argument that greater diversity is associated with lower quality because it places lower performing people in positions for which they are not suited.[36] Finally, Katherine Williams (Phillips) and Charles O'Reilly suggest that most empirical evidence points out that diversity is most likely to hinder group functioning.[37] In short, skeptics of diversity suggest that group differences result in conflict and process loss.[38]

Skeptics also emphasize that when we discuss "diversity," we are really just talking about race. These skeptics also suggest that our discussions of diversity should go beyond race and focus instead on class. In *The Trouble with Diversity: How We Learned to Love Identity and Ignore Inequality*, Walter Benn Michaels states that the racial identity divides that we now take for granted have really served as a diversion from our actual problem: the widening divide between rich and poor.[39] Perhaps even more provocative is his account of how America's institutions serve to undermine many of the claims of American political life.

Michaels begins with the assertion that what we call race has no objective genetic basis. This is an idea that has been well documented by biologists. Everyone has mixed genetic heritage, and even many of the traits we normally associate with "races" do not correspond as well as most people think. Nevertheless, according to Michaels, Americans have "learned to love" race and still love to talk about it, even if they reject biological notions of it. They have merely replaced biology with cultural notions or other social constructions that they reify. The paradox he points out is that while we reject racism, we embrace race. In doing so, we guard against the notion that some races are superior and others are inferior. We assert that they are merely different and to be appreciated for those differences. This approach, he suggests, invites us to ignore vast material differences that occur between groups. More to the point, these putative racial (cultural) differences mask class differences. Indeed, the problem that bothers Michaels most is "classism."

For example, he writes that elite universities are going to greater lengths to be sensitive to the needs of economically disadvantaged students. But what they have failed to notice is that there are hardly any poor students at elite institutions. The racial minority students who enter such institutions are not particularly economically disadvantaged. Yet, by providing scholarships and/or tuition waivers for the tiny percentage of such students in attendance at their institutions, these elite universities are able to convince themselves that they are on the front line of progressivism. They spend so much time talking about racial diversity that they forget that there is anything else. Michaels suggests that the yearning for a just society is what should be the goal for progressives.

Michaels holds affirmative action at universities in low esteem. He wants to get rid of race-based scholarships and worries that our racial diversity obsession "perpetuates the very concepts it congratulates itself on having escaped." But his complaint with identity politics is ultimately a different one. He insists that fighting over race and gender is not an outgrowth of leftist egalitarianism but an alternative to it. The real problem the left ought to be dealing with is what Michaels calls "class," by which he means inequalities of income and wealth. The key thing is that we should drop the language of discrimination and only talk about class inequality.

Like Michaels, William Julius Wilson explicitly argues that "race-specific" policies such as affirmative action cannot succeed in helping the "underclass" or in reducing inequality.[40] Such policies, he argues, while beneficial to more advantaged minorities, do little for those who are "truly disadvantaged" because the cumulative effects of race and class subordination passed from generation to generation are disproportionately present among the poor. These people lack the resources and skills to compete effectively in the labor market. Thus, policies based on preferential treatment of minorities linked to group outcomes are insufficient precisely because the relatively advantaged members of racial minority communities will be selected and will reap the benefits to the detriment of poor minorities. Moreover, those Whites who are rejected due to preferential programs might be the most disadvantaged Whites whose qualifications are marginal precisely because of their disadvantages.

One could make two main objections to such skeptical arguments. Both have some validity. The first is that they vastly underestimate the impact of racism and other forms of discrimination upon American life. According to Michaels, many of these issues are just economic inequality in disguise. But there is no reason why equality-lovers could not work on class-based inequality if diversity is linked to equity. Economic inequality is such a problem in the United States that any improvement would probably also advance racial diversity as well.

At times, skeptics suggest that a focus on diversity distracts the left from tackling economic injustice and class inequality.[41] Racial diversity is hardly the worst of the distractions. What would make us believe that people are more willing to eliminate inequality based on class than they are to do away with inequality based on race? People who are devoted to inequality are devoted to inequality, period. Privileged Whites want to remain privileged Whites; they do not want to give up their privilege to people of color or poor people. They do not want to remove racial, gender, class, or heteronormative inequality. They want what they consider to be a "fair advantage." We should de-emphasize the language of discrimination and focus on who is privileged and who is "disprivileged."

Who gains a "fair advantage" versus those who receive an unfair disadvantage? In the context of diversity, just about everyone claims they are receiving an unfair disadvantage. But everyone wants the right to a fair advantage—even those who are already receiving a fair advantage. There is apparently the belief that it is appropriate to make claims on more than one's fair share of any good, service, or privilege. Most people with privilege assume that it is alright to hoard opportunities in society. This notion of diversity, when critically applied, challenges the notion that it is acceptable for those with privilege to hoard more than their fair share of goods, services, or opportunities.

Still, few people challenge the lack of diversity when it comes to class. We, as a society, believe that those who are rich should have the best of the best. They should have all kinds of opportunities and should hoard opportunities even when they cannot use them. Such practices presuppose that it is perfectly acceptable for the poor to go without, even when they do not have sufficient resources and cannot compete or house or clothe themselves. Meanwhile, due to the ideology of colorblind diversity along the axis of race, most reasonable people would see such things as being totally unacceptable. In this century, most people view doling out privileges along racial and gender axes as completely unacceptable. Increasingly, people see doling out such privileges along a sexuality axis as also being unacceptable. For whatever reason, however, in our society people see allocating opportunities along the class dimension as being acceptable. Most people also believe segregation based on class lines as opposed to racial, gender, or sexuality lines is perfectly reasonable. However, critical diversity would claim that privileges continue to be unfairly doled out based on race, gender, sexuality, and class. We contend that in order to have true equality and parity, we must not only examine, but also challenge all forms of social inequality.

In most organizations that embrace and sing the praises of diversity, there is at least some degree of heterogeneity along most demographic dimensions. Far trickier, however, is achieving diversity of ideas and per-spectives. One of the chief arguments for diversity is that if we include different people from different groups we will benefit from the diversity of ideas and backgrounds. But is there really diversity in ideas, ideology, and class backgrounds? According to the homophily principle, many compa-nies try to reproduce themselves.[42] Such companies may engage in prac-tices that provide them with window dressing that allows them to claim that they have diversity. But then, they may still require that their "diverse" employees conform to the tenets and principles that they hold and cherish. If organizations operate this way, then they will get very little movement toward true ideational diversity.

Most African Americans, irrespective of their class position, would sug-gest that they have had some experience with racism because we live in a racist society.[43] They bring to the table these lived experiences. However, if we could consider class status, would we see that the racial dynamics expe-rienced by poor people of color compared with those of higher-income people of color are more harsh and severe?

We believe there is nothing intrinsically wrong with including any group under the banner of diversity. However, if diversity is changing into a "col-orblind concept," there is a problem. Why? Because a concept without boundaries and limits makes it possible for opponents of diversity to say that there are no essential elements and overall truths. There is no one meaning. It means that categories become unmeasurable. There are no restrictions. So even in identifying groups and categories, there is no "real-ness." Not only are categories socially constructed, but there is not even any genuineness. We must remember that naming and categorizing people reflects power, but it does not mean that the resulting categories have any essential realness.

Using such perspectives, diversity would be limitless—that is, it would include everybody. In doing so, however, it makes no differentiation between those who have traditionally been excluded and those who have usually had privilege. Thus, it does not really serve the interests of those who have been excluded. Instead, it might reinforce the privileges of the privileged. Consequently, we must guard against the slippery notion of diversity. We must transform it into a critical concept.

How Do We Make Diversity a More Critical Concept?

What makes diversity a critical concept and not just an elusive one? It is the idea that diversity has to be tethered to other concepts such as equity, parity, and opportunity. It must be linked to the idea of equity. There must be the notion that everyone deserves a chance—especially those who are routinely denied such opportunities. Without linking it to concerns about access, equity, parity, and opportunity, the usage of the term diversity is hollow. Without these related concepts, the very notion of diversity is meaningless because it cannot have boundaries. It can be used for any purpose— political, conservative, reactionary, racist, sexist, etc.—that anyone wants. Such usages make it possible to bastardize the term so that those who want to undermine diversity can do so by wrapping their arguments in diversity-sounding language. The military, for example, can speak of diversity while embracing a "don't ask, don't tell" policy with respect to gays in the military. It can also talk about diversity at the same time that it discriminates against women in certain combat positions that are required for upward mobility. When argued to its illogical extreme, one could even argue, on the grounds of becoming more diverse, for making greater opportunities for wealthy White men on college campuses because they are an under-represented minority group. Such examples sound ridiculous on their face; yet, opponents of true diversity have come to use the term in precisely such fashion for strategic purposes.

Proponents of unlimited inclusion under the banner of diversity are not looking at the limitations that people of color are actually facing; instead, they try to make the case that we should just include everyone. While this idea is high-minded, it misses the point that not everyone is at equal risk of being excluded to begin with. Employers and other decision-makers create boundaries for some but not for others, and definitely not for all.[44] By opening up the limited opportunities to everyone without acknowledging that some people face much greater obstacles than do others, diversity in this sense will only serve to replicate and reinforce the inequalities that already exist.

How does this self-replication and reproduction of inequality process work? We believe that it is accomplished, in part, by shifting the rhetoric of equal opportunity and turning it on its head for strategic gain. For example, those White southerners who were opposed to principles articulated by the Reverend Dr. Martin Luther King when he was alive not only say that they now embrace Dr. King and his words but also the ideal of equality of opportunity for which he lived and died.

But the truth is that such strategic thinking with respect to diversity is not really the biggest problem with its implementation. Clearly, some of the misuse of diversity is intentional. It is done by those cynical people who do not want there to be equality of opportunity. A far greater problem, however, is that many people really do believe that they are being fair and doing what is best when they invoke colorblindness or gender neutrality. For example, a 1995 *Washington Post*/Harvard/Kaiser Family Foundation Race Relations Poll asked respondents whether they believe "diversity benefits our country economically and socially, so race or ethnicity should be a factor when deciding who is hired, promoted, or admitted to college." Respondents were also given the option of saying that "hiring, promotion, and college admissions should be based strictly on merit and qualifications other than race or ethnicity." Only 15 percent of respondents said that race and ethnicity should be used as a factor.[45]

People of color who experience discrimination can spot it and detect it in an instance.[46] But these same people do not get the idea that Whites—who are so accustomed to accessing privilege—also feel discriminated against when they can no longer access that privilege. This feels like discrimination to them, if only because they feel entitled. Most people of color do not acknowledge that for White people being denied a privilege evokes real feelings. So being denied privilege feels as real as being denied opportunity feels for those people of color who are discriminated against. The loss of privilege is a real experience that Whites have. They are trying to counteract that. They experience similar physiological and psychological symptoms of stress and anxiety when they believe they are losing their privilege as those who experience discrimination.

From Colorblind Diversity to Critical Diversity: How Do We Get There from Here?

Critical diversity insists that we not only celebrate cultural differences but that we link such distinctions to concerns about equity and parity: If we believe that talent and ability are equally distributed throughout the population, and they are evenly distributed along class, racial, ethnic, and gender boundaries, then we should be able to pick people from any assortment. If talent is equally distributed and if we have true diversity, then talent would be diverse by definition. If we believe that groups are equally talented, then having diversity would maximize the use of talent. If talent is distributed in such a way that 10 percent of the people are smart and capable, and if talent is not distributed along racial or gender lines, then we should be able to pick people from any racial or gender group and get 10 percent who are talented. This logic suggests that 10 percent of people who are Latino should be just as talented and capable as 10 percent of Anglo people. But if any organization, group, employer, etc. does not include the full range of people, then that organization is not maximizing the benefits of diversity.

Unfortunately, most organizations attempt to reproduce themselves by selecting people who are similar to the members or constituencies they already have. So what we get instead of true diversity is self-replication. Even when organizations have demographic proportional representation, they are likely to have people who are similar along ideological or attitudinal lines. So, instead of getting critical diversity, what we get are members of subdominant groups who come from backgrounds that are more similar to those of the dominant group.

What steps can we take to bring about critical diversity? We believe there are several things that will make the realization of critical diversity more likely.

We believe that it is possible and necessary to target and redistribute goods and resources to people who originate from traditionally excluded, disenfranchised, or other "dispriviliged" groups that have historically been the victims of discrimination. Doing so will allow for an expansive notion of diversity, but it calls for more attention to distributive justice and its link to diversity.

Distributive justice is concerned with the equitable allocation of goods and resources among diverse members of an organization or community.[47] Achieving a fair distribution usually requires taking into account the total amount of goods and resources to be distributed, the procedure for distributing them, and the distribution patterns that result. Because societies have limited amounts of wealth and resources, the question becomes: "How should such benefits be distributed?" The critical diversity perspective suggests that such assets should be distributed in a manner so that each individual receives a "fair share." Equity and need are among the most important criteria. Different distributions advance different social goals. For a society to function effectively, it must keep its membership engaged in effective production and sustain the well-being of its members. Distributive justice based on equity gives people a sense of full-fledged membership. Moreover, equity fosters the motivation to produce and to be rewarded for one's productivity.

But distribution according to need is also necessary. It ensures that everyone's basic and essential needs will be met. Because one's race, gender, place of birth, social status, and family background influences are matters of chance over which one has no control, they should not unduly influence the amount of benefits one receives in life. The job of distributive justice is to limit the influence of chance so that goods might be distributed more fairly, especially to the benefit of those who were born into "disprivileged" circumstances or groups. So, as a guiding critical diversity principle, we should seek to target resources to people who are traditionally excluded.

In a world free of racism, sexism, colorism, religious bigotry, and heteronormativity, race, gender, color, religion, and sexuality should not be valid criteria of distribution. Unfortunately, in the real world of group-based discrimination, life experience suggests that such factors often turn out to be quite significant. In the United States, as elsewhere, issues of distributive justice are connected to concerns about systemic racism, sexism, and other forms of intolerance that raise questions about fairness and the need for forms of affirmative action and compensatory justice. Because some groups are more likely to be excluded than are others, policies that provide greater effort to include some racial, gender, religious, or sexuality groups are necessary.

We also believe that to facilitate critical diversity it is possible and necessary to redistribute goods and resources away from people who originate from privileged groups, especially when invoking the rhetoric of diversity. According to the theory of relative deprivation, a sense of injustice is aroused when individuals come to believe that their outcomes are not commensurate with the outcomes received by other people in similar situations.[48] When people have a sense that they have not received their fair share, they may challenge the system that gives rise to this state of affairs. This is especially likely to happen if a person or group's basic needs are not being met, or if there are large discrepancies between the "haves" and the "have-nots." Societies in which resources are distributed unfairly can become quite prone to social unrest. Grossly unfair distributions violate principles of equity and need and, therefore, generate conflict.

Redistribution of benefits, on the other hand, can sometimes help to relieve tensions and allow for a more stable society. Issues of distributive justice are in this way central to critical diversity. Efforts to ensure a just distribution of benefits are typically accompanied by efforts to ensure a more balanced distribution of power as well.

We further believe that to facilitate critical diversity it is possible and necessary to reconnect diversity to affirmative action and the need to offset historical and ongoing racial and gender discrimination, segregation, and bias. In other words, it is necessary to reconnect diversity to compensatory justice—the idea that people should be fairly compensated for their injuries by those who have injured them; just compensation is proportional to the loss inflicted on a person. This is precisely the kind of justice that is at stake when affirmative action is instituted in order to correct for past injustices and previous discrimination. Many Americans tend to forget that affirmative action is public policy designed to compensate the victims of past injustice. But we should recall that affirmative action was instituted to improve the employment opportunities for groups that historically had suffered discrimination in the educational sector and in the labor market. Initially, there was little resistance to such policies among those who acknowledged the existence of discrimination. However, as affirmative action became a more familiar term in legal and political debate, it also became a rallying cry for activists, a slogan for politicians, and a litmus test for both political liberals and conservatives. Research by Cedric Herring and Sharon Collins suggests that affirmative action programs in the workplace are associated with greater opportunities and better outcomes for those whom they were intended to help.[49] Indeed, they are correlated with higher incomes and higher status jobs for racial minorities, women, and people from low-income backgrounds without appearing to do significant harm to the economic well-being of White males. But we must be mindful that this is precisely why some people continue to oppose affirmative action.

We believe that to facilitate critical diversity it is possible and necessary to remind organizational members that diversity is consistent with legal compliance. Diversity has been a governmental issue since the early 1940s when President Roosevelt encouraged nondiscriminatory hiring practices among defense contractors. Since then, policy-makers have confronted pressures for greater institutional inclusion of people of color, women, members of the LGBT community, and other previously excluded or disadvantaged groups. For many years, governmental initiatives were all that were in place to direct an attempt at corporate diversity and give excluded groups opportunities to succeed. It has only been within the last few years that more and more companies have begun to realize that, as our country continues to become more diverse, their success will be tied to issues of diversity and inclusion. This becomes even more apparent when reviewing population trends that are moving toward a more diverse total population and a shrinking straight White male population that is native to this country.

Despite anti-affirmative action sentiments and misleading rhetoric and information about diversity policies, diversity and inclusion are still consistent with the law.[50] Nevertheless, in order to bring about a "color-blind" and gender-equal society, diversity efforts must be color and gender conscious. To deliver equality of opportunity, there must be calls for greater efforts to educate, recruit, train, employ, and promote only some citizens. To determine whether we are making progress, we must measure present-day employment practices against some standard of what has occurred in the past and what might be achieved in the future. And to monitor the progress of historically excluded people, critical diversity efforts must be subjected to the charge by opponents that such efforts are tantamount to "quotas" that promote "reverse discrimination" and the selection of people who are less qualified than are their straight White male counterparts.

Finally, we believe that to facilitate critical diversity it is possible and necessary to demonstrate to organizational members that diversity is institutionally beneficial. In the business world, diversity produces positive outcomes over homogeneity because growth and innovation may depend upon people from various backgrounds working together and capitalizing on their differences.[51] Although such differences may lead to some communication barriers and group conflict, diversity increases the opportunity for creativity and the quality of the product of group work. Diversity provides a competitive advantage through social complexity at the firm level when it is positioned within the proper context. In addition, linking diversity to the idea of parity—as the critical diversity approach proposed here requires—makes it easier to see that diversity pays because businesses that draw on more inclusive talent pools are more successful. Critical diversity is positively related to business success because it allows companies to "think outside the box" by bringing previously excluded groups inside the box, thereby enhancing creativity, problem solving, and performance.

Conclusion

We began this chapter with an overview of the changes in the rhetoric about inclusion as it has moved from debates about affirmative action to various notions of diversity. We argued that the discourse on diversity has been turned on its head so that it now means just about anything and everything. We called for a move away from "colorblind diversity" and "segregated diversity" toward a "critical diversity" that not only celebrates and embraces cultural differences that exist between groups, but also examines issues of parity, equity, and inequality. We also argued that it is imperative that critical scholars examine all forms of social inequality, oppression, and stratification that revolve around issues of diversity. Critical diversity must not only be about inclusion; it also requires an analysis of exclusion and discrimination. It therefore must challenge hegemonic notions of color-blindness and meritocracy.

Much of the current rhetoric surrounding diversity undermines the notion that there have been certain racial/ethnic, gender, and sexuality groups that have been denied access. Critical scholars must serve to help reverse such patterns. In this chapter, we have tried to lay out some concrete strategies for doing so. We believe that goods and resources should be targeted to excluded people. We agree with an expansive notion of diversity, but advocate that a distributive justice underpin diversity efforts that will serve to assist "disprivileged" groups and shift goods and resources away from privileged groups. We also believe that diversity and affirmative action should be reconnected to offset historical and ongoing racial and gender discrimination, segregation, and bias. By extension, the public should be reminded that diversity is consistent with legal compliance. Finally, we believe that the institutional benefits of diversity are demonstrable to organizational members.

In short, we must work toward a critical diversity that is about inclusion and is necessarily linked to access, equity, parity, and opportunity. If we had critical diversity, there would be proportional representation of people from all groups (because it occurs when we get a true reflection of the talent pool available). Without linking diversity to such concerns, the usage of the term diversity is hollow.

Notes

1 Berrey, 2011
2 Morris, 1984
3 Stryker, Scarpellino, and Holtzman, 1999
4 Berrey, 2011
5 Edelman, Riggs Fuller, and Mara-Drita, 2001
6 Ollivier and Pietrantonio, 2006
7 Kelly and Dobbin, 1998
8 Edelman and Petterson, 1999
9 Herring and Collins, 1995; Collins, 1997a; and Collins, 2002
10 Morris, 1984
11 Skrentny, 2002
12 Collins, 1997a
13 Herring and Collins, 1995
14 Skrentny, 1996; Collins, 1997b
15 Burstein, 1985
16 Ornati and Pisano, 1972; Berry, 1976; Cole, 1981; Wilson, 1987; and Loury, 1991
17 Wilson, 1987
18 Carter, 1991; Loury, 1991
19 Glazer, 1975; Sher, 1975; and Cole, 1981
20 Herring, 2009
21 Stryker, Scarpellino, and Holtzman, 1999
22 Leonard, 1990: 47
23 Downey, 1999
24 Berrey, 2011
25 Edelman et al., 2001
26 Michaels, 2006
27 Crenshaw, 1994
28 Butler, 2007
29 Moskos and Butler, 1997
30 Skerry, 2002; Rothman, Lipset, and Nevitte, 2003a; Rothman, Lipset, and Nevitte, 2003b; Tsui, Egan, and O'Reilly, 1992; and Whitaker, 1996
31 Pelled, Eisenhardt, and Xin, 1999; Pelled, 1996; and Jehn, Northcraft, and Neale, 1999
32 Jehn, Northcraft, and Neale, 1999
33 Pelled, Eisenhardt, and Xin, 1999
34 Tsui, Egan, and O'Reilly, 1992
35 Wood, 2003
36 Rothman, Lipset, and Nevitte, 2003b
37 Williams and O'Reilly, 1998
38 Herring and Henderson, 2008
39 Michaels, 2006
40 Wilson, 1987
41 Michaels, 2006
42 McPherson and Smith-Lovin, 1987
43 Herring, Thomas, Durr, and Horton, 1999
44 Edelman, Fuller, and Mara-Drita, 2001
45 *Washington Post*/Harvard/Kaiser Family Foundation Race Relations Poll, July, 1995
46 Pager and Quillian, 2005

47 Maiese, 2003
48 Gurr, 1970
49 Herring and Collins, 1995; and Herring, 1997
50 Wilson, Lewis, and Herring, 1991
51 Herring, 2009

References

Berrey, Ellen C. 2011. "Why Diversity Became Orthodox in Higher Education, and How It Changed the Meaning of Race on Campus." *Critical Sociology* 37 (5): 573–596.

Berry, Margaret C. 1976. "Affirmative Action?" *Journal of the National Association for Women Deans, Administrators, and Counselors* 39: 1–60.

Burstein, Paul. 1985. *Discrimination, Jobs, and Politics: The Struggle for Equal Employment Opportunity in the United States since the New Deal.* Chicago, IL: University of Chicago Press.

Butler, John Sibley. 2007. "Segregated Diversity and the Crisis of Race Relations Theory." Paper presented at the Association of Black Sociologists Conference, Chicago, IL.

Carter, Stephen L. 1991. *Reflections of an Affirmative Action Baby.* New York, NY: Basic Books.

Cole, Craig W. 1981. "Affirmative Action: Change It or Lose It." *EEO Today* 8: 262–271.

Collins, Sharon M. 1997a. *Black Corporate Executives: The Making and Breaking of a Black Middle Class.* Philadelphia, PA: Temple University Press.

Collins, Sharon M. 1997b. "Race Up the Corporate Ladder: The Dilemmas and Contradictions of First-Wave Black Executives," in C. Herring (Ed.). *African Americans and the Public Agenda: The Paradoxes of Public Policy.* Thousand Oaks, CA: Sage Publications: 87–104.

Collins, Sharon M. 2002. "Organizational Response to Affirmative Action," in M. Durr (Ed.). *The New Politics of Race: From DuBois to the 21st Century.* New York, NY: Greenwood Publishing: 39–54.

Crenshaw, Kimberle. 1994. "Mapping the Margins: Intersectionality, Identity Politics, and Violence against Women of Color," in M. Albertson Fineman and R. Mykitiuk (Eds). *The Public Nature of Private Violence: The Discovery of Domestic Abuse.* New York, NY: Routledge: 93–120.

Downey, Dennis J. 1999. "From Americanization to Multiculturalism: Political symbols and Struggles for Cultural Diversity in Twentieth-Century American Race Relations." *Sociological Perspectives* 42: 249–263.

Edelman, Lauren B. and Stephen Petterson. 1999. "Symbols and Substance in Organizational Response to Civil Rights Law." Special issue, The Future of Affirmative Action. *Research in Social Stratification and Mobility* 17: 107–135.

Edelman, Lauren B., Sally Riggs Fuller, and Iona Mara-Drita. 2001. "Diversity Rhetoric and the Managerialization of Law." *American Journal of Sociology* 106(6): 1589–1641.

Glazer, Nathan. 1975. *Affirmative Discrimination: Ethnic Inequality and Public Policy.* New York, NY: Basic Books.

Gurr, Ted. 1970. *Why Men Rebel.* Princeton, NJ: Princeton University Press.

Herring, Cedric. 1997. "African Americans, the Public Agenda, and the Paradoxes of Public Policy: A Focus on the Controversies Surrounding Affirmative Action," in C. Herring (Ed.). *African Americans and the Public Agenda: The Paradoxes of Public Policy.* Thousand Oaks, CA: Sage Publications: 3–24.

Herring, Cedric. 2009. "Does Diversity Pay? Race, Gender and the Business Case for Diversity." *American Sociological Review* 74: 208–224.

Herring, Cedric and Sharon Collins. 1995. "Retreat From Equal Opportunity?: The Case of Affirmative Action," in M.P. Smith and J. Feagin (Eds). *The Bubbling Cauldron,* Minneapolis, MN: University of Minnesota Press: 163–181.

Herring, Cedric and Loren Henderson. 2008. "Diversity in Illinois: Changing Meanings, Demographic Trends, and Policy Preferences," in *The Illinois Report, 2008.* Chicago and Champaign, IL: University of Illinois, Institute of Government and Public Affairs: 79–85.

Herring, Cedric, Melvin Thomas, Marlese Durr, and Hayward Derrick Horton. 1999. "Does Race Matter?: The Determinants and Consequences of Self-Reports of Discrimination Victimization." *Race & Society* 2: 109–123.

Jehn, Karen A., Gregory B. Northcraft and Margaret A. Neale. 1999. "Why Differences Make a Difference: A Field Study of Diversity, Conflict and Performance in Workgroups." *Administrative Science Quarterly* 44: 741–763.

Kelly, Erin, and Frank Dobbin. 1998. "How Affirmative Action Became Diversity Management." *American Behavioral Scientist* 41: 960–984.

Leonard, Jonathan S. 1990. "The Impact of Affirmative Action Regulation and Equal Employment Law on Black Employment." *Journal of Economic Perspectives* 4: 47–63.

Loury, Glenn C. 1991. "Affirmative Action as a Remedy for Statistical Discrimination." Paper presented at a colloquium at the University of Illinois at Chicago, IL.

Maiese, Michelle. 2003. "Distributive Justice," in G. Burgess and H. Burgess (Eds). *Beyond Intractability.* Boulder, CO: Conflict Research Consortium of the University of Colorado: 42–62.

McPherson, J. Miller, and Lynn Smith-Lovin. 1987. "Homophily in Voluntary Organizations: Status Distance and the Composition of Face-to-Face Groups." *American Sociological Review* 52: 370–379.

Michaels, Walter Benn. 2006. *The Trouble with Diversity: How We Learned to Love Identity and Ignore Inequality.* New York, NY: Metropolitan Books.

Morris, Aldon D. 1984. *The Origins of the Civil Rights Movement: Black Communities Organizing for Change.* New York, NY: The Free Press.

Moskos, Charles C. and John Sibley Butler. 1997. *All That We Can Be: Black Leadership and Racial Integration the Army Way.* New York, NY: Basic Books.

Ollivier, Michele and Linda Pietrantonio. 2006. "The Rhetoric of Openness to Cultural Diversity in Quebec." *Footnotes* July/August, American Sociological Association Newsletter.

Ornati, Oscar A. and Anthony Pisano. 1972. "Affirmative Action: Why It Isn't Working." *Personnel Administration* (September): 50–52.

Pager, Devah and Lincoln Quillian. 2005. "Walking the Talk? What Employers Say versus What They Do." *American Sociological Review* 70: 355–380.

Pelled, Lisa H. 1996. "Demographic Diversity, Conflict, and Work Group Outcomes: An Intervening Process Theory." *Organization Science* 7: 615–631.

Pelled, Lisa Hope, Kathleen M. Eisenhardt, and Katherine R. Xin. 1999. "Exploring the Black Box: An Analysis of Work Group Diversity, Conflict and Performance." *Administrative Science Quarterly* 44: 1–28.

Rothman, Stanley, Seymour Martin Lipset, and Neil Nevitte. 2003a. "Does Enrollment Diversity Improve University Education?" *International Journal of Public Opinion Research* 15:8–26.

Rothman, Stanley, Seymour Martin Lipset, and Neil Nevitte. 2003b. "Racial Diversity Reconsidered." *The Public Interest* 151: 25–38.

Sher, George. 1975. "Justifying Reverse Discrimination in Employment." *Philosophy and Public Affairs* 4: 1159–1170.

Skerry, Peter. 2002. "Beyond Sushiology: Does Diversity Work?" *Brookings Review* 20: 20–23.

Skrentny, John David. 1996. *The Ironies of Affirmative Action: Politics, Culture, and Justice in America.* Chicago, IL: University of Chicago Press.

Skrentny, John David. 2002. *The Minority Rights Revolution.* Cambridge, MA: Belknap Press of Harvard University Press.

Stryker, Robin, Martha Scarpellino, and Mellisa Holtzman. 1999. "Whither Equal Opportunity Policies? The Rhetorical Drum Beat of Quotas and the Framing of the Civil Rights Act of 1991." *Research in Social Stratification and Mobility* 17: 33–106.

Tsui, Ann S., Terri D. Egan, and Charles A. O'Reilly. 1992. "Being Different: Relational Demography and Organizational Attachment." *Administrative Science Quarterly* 37: 549–579.

Washington Post/Harvard/Kaiser Family Foundation Race Relations Poll July, 1995.

Whitaker, William A. 1996. *White Male Applicant: An Affirmative Action Expose.* Smyrna, DE: Apropos Press.

Williams, Katherine and Charles A. O'Reilly. 1998. "Demography and Diversity: A Review of 40 Years of Research," in B. Staw and R. Sutton (Eds). *Research in Organizational Behavior.* Greenwich, CT: JAI Press: 77–140.

Wilson, Cynthia, James Lewis, and Cedric Herring. 1991. *The 1991 Civil Rights Act: Restoring Basic Protections.* Chicago, IL: Urban League.

Wilson, William Julius. 1987. *The Truly Disadvantaged: The Inner City, the Underclass, and Public Policy.* Chicago, IL: University of Chicago Press.

Wood, Peter. 2003. "Diversity in America." *Society* 40: 60–67.

3

Does Diversity Pay? Beyond the Business Case for Diversity

It has become common for proponents of the "value-in-diversity" perspective to make the "business case for diversity."[1] These scholars claim, "diversity pays."[2] For the most part, proponents of this view suggest that diversity in the corporate setting, for example, represents a compelling interest that will help to meet customers' needs, enrich understanding of the pulse of the marketplace, and improve the quality of products and services offered.[3] With respect to employees, diversity brings with it different perspectives. The greater the differences among employees are, the broader their perspectives, the stronger their teams, and the greater their resources for problem resolution.[4] Diversity also provides creative conflict that leads to closer examination of assumptions so that people from varied backgrounds can create complex learning environments that lead to better solutions to problems.[5] Because of the putative competitive advantages of diversity, companies increasingly have relied upon a heterogeneous workforce to increase their profits. Because diversity provides fresh ideas, strong growth, positive company images, fewer discrimination lawsuits, and an enhanced ability to hire qualified workers, businesses should be aggressive about workforce diversity.[6] In short, the rhetoric of diversity in industry suggests that a diverse workforce is good for business and that diversity offers a direct return on investment that promises greater corporate profits and earnings.[7]

In contrast, critics of the diversity model are more skeptical about the benefits of diversity.[8] Proponents of the "diversity as process loss" perspective suggest that diversity has significant costs.[9] As we pointed out in the last chapter, research on intergroup relations consistently finds that racial and ethnic diversity is linked with emotional conflict among co-workers.[10] Similarly, while informational diversity positively influences group performance, value and social category diversity moderates this effect.[11] Also, there is a complicated link between work group diversity and work group functioning, as diversity can reduce the cohesiveness of the group and result in increased employee absenteeism and turnover.[12] Moreover, detractors of the diversity model suggest that the emphasis on diversity divides America into separate groups based on race, ethnicity, or gender and in so doing suggests that some social categories are more deserving of privileges than are others.[13] There is also the argument that greater diversity is associated with lower quality because it places lower performing people in positions for which they are not suited.[14] And, finally, there are studies that suggest that diversity is most likely to hinder group functioning.[15] In short, critics of the diversity model suggest that group differences result in conflict and its attendant costs. For these reasons, skeptics of the business case for diversity model have questioned the real impact of diversity programs upon the "bottom line" of business organizations.

But it is also possible that diversity can have dual outcomes, some of which may be beneficial to organizations and others of which may be costly to group functioning. Diversity may be valuable to organizations even when change in the composition of such organizations does not make incumbent members of these organizations feel comfortable. As Nancy DiTomaso, Corrine Post, and Rochelle Parks-Yancy point out, "research generally finds that heterogeneity on most any salient social category contributes to increased conflict, reduced communication, and lower performance, at the same time that it can contribute to a broader range of contacts, information sources, creativity, and innovation." Ironically, research on this issue also shows that "homogeneity on most any salient social category contributes to greater liking and trust, better coordination, increased communication, and higher performance, but also to limitations in adaptability and innovation."[16] Such results suggest that diversity may be both conducive to productivity and counterproductive in work group processes.

Because many of the claims and hypotheses about the impact of diversity have gone unexamined empirically, it is not clear what effect, if any, diversity has on the overall functioning of organizations, especially businesses. It is possible that diversity has many benefits as the value-in-diversity perspective suggests. It is also plausible that any benefits of diversity are more than offset by significant costs that have been identified by the diversity as process loss perspective. It is also reasonable to believe that diversity is associated with the twin outcomes of group-level conflict and increased performance at the establishment level. Although the current research cannot adjudicate all of the claims of the proponents and skeptics of the business case for diversity,[17] the growing heterogeneity of the United States warrants a serious examination of the impact of diversity. Using data from the 1996–1997 National Organizations Survey, this chapter offers an examination of the relationship between racial and gender workforce diversity and such business performance indicators as sales revenue, number of customers, relative market share, and relative profitability.

Overview of the "Value-in-Diversity" Perspective

Although we provided our definition of diversity in Chapter 2, there is no consensus on that definition, and that lack of consensus and uncertainty is expressed in the multiplicity of the concept's meanings that exist in literature. For some people, the term provokes intense emotional reactions because it brings to mind such politically charged ideas as "affirmative action" or "quotas," in part because some definitions focus narrowly on protected groups covered under the pronouncements of affirmative action. Here differences such as race and gender are the focal point. Alternatively, other designations of diversity are largely formulated to extend beyond race and gender to include all types of individual differences. These broader definitions tend to include ethnicity, age, religion, disability status, geographic considerations, personality, sexual preferences, and a myriad of other personal, demographic, and organizational characteristics. Thus, diversity can be an all-inclusive term that incorporates people in many different classifications. Generally speaking, the term "diversity" refers to policies and practices that seek to include people who are considered to be, in some way, different from the traditional member. More centrally, it means to create an inclusive culture that values and uses the talents of all would-be members.

The politics surrounding inclusion have shifted dramatically over the past 50 years.[18] Title VII of the 1964 Civil Rights Act made it illegal for organizations to engage in employment practices that discriminated against employees based on race, color, religion, sex, and national origin. Through this action, the government mandated that employers must provide equal employment opportunities to people with similar qualifications and accomplishments. In addition, in 1965 Executive Order 11246 required government contractors to take affirmative action to overcome past patterns of discrimination. These directives eradicated policies that formally permitted discrimination against certain classes of workers. They also increased the costs to organizations that failed to implement fair employment practices. The laws remain a part of the legal responsibilities under which business organizations and other establishments operate today.

By the late 1970s and into the 1980s, there was growing recognition within the private sector that while the legal mandates were necessary, they were not sufficient for ensuring the effective management of diversity within organizations. Alexandria Kalev, Frank Dobbin, and Erin Kelly conducted a study of private sector establishments from 1971 to 2002.[19] They found that diversity programs designed to establish organizational responsibility for diversity were more efficacious in increasing the share of White women, Black women, and Black men in management than were efforts to change organizational cultures by reducing managerial bias through diversity training or efforts to reduce social isolation through mentoring of women and racial and ethnic minorities. They also found that employers who were subject to federal affirmative action edicts were likely to have diversity programs with stronger effects.

During the 1990s, diversity rhetoric shifted to emphasize the "business case" for workforce diversity.[20] Essentially, the argument made was that to manage diversity effectively is a business necessity not only because of the nature of labor markets, but also because a more diverse workforce— relative to a homogeneous one—produces better business results. Exploiting the nation's diversity was viewed as key to future prosperity. Ignoring the fact that discrimination limits the potential of the society because it leads to under-utilization of pools of talent was no longer practical or feasible in an increasingly diverse society. Diversity campaigns, thus, became part of the attempt to strengthen the US and move beyond its history of discrimination by providing greater access to previously excluded groups to educational institutions and workplaces.[21] The new imperative for diversity advocates was to find evidence to support the "business case" argument that diversity expanded the talent pool and, thereby, strengthened America's institutions. So, even if the shift from affirmative action to diversity might be considered a "taming" of what began as a radical fight for equality,[22] in the 21st century, workforce diversity has become an essential business concern.

Mechanisms by which Diversity May Affect Business Outcomes

But if diversity affects business outcomes, how does it do so? Scott Page suggests that groups that display a range of perspectives outperform groups of like-minded experts.[23] Diversity yields superior outcomes over homogeneity because progress and innovation may depend less on lone thinkers with high intelligence than on diverse groups of people working together and capitalizing on their individuality. The best group decisions and predictions are those that draw on unique qualities. Similarly, J. Stuart Bunderson and Kathleen Sutcliffe show that teams composed of individuals with a breadth of functional experiences may be better able to overcome communication barriers because team members can relate to one another's functions while still realizing the performance benefits of diverse functional experiences.[24] Katherine Williams (Phillips) and Charles O'Reilly argue that diversity increases the opportunity for creativity and the quality of the product of group work.[25] Sen and Bhattacharya propose that factors such as consumers' perceptions of firms' commitment to corporate social responsibility are related to their purchasing practices.[26] Similarly, Black, Mason, and Cole found that consumers have strongly held in-group preferences when a transaction involves significant customer–worker interaction.[27] Nancy DiTomaso and her colleagues suggest that diversity may contribute to greater creativity because homogeneous groups are less innovative than heterogeneous ones.[28] Finally, Orlando Richard argues that cultural diversity provides a competitive advantage through social complexity at the firm level when it is positioned within the proper context.[29] Collectively, these factors suggest mechanisms by which diversity potentially makes differences in business performance. Irrespective of the specific processes, it is possible that diversity has a positive impact upon organizations' functioning, net of any internal work–group processes that may be impeded by the existence of diversity.

Although the sociological literature on diversity continues to grow,[30] to date, there has been little systematic research conducted in actual organizations that addresses the impact of diversity upon the financial success of business organizations. Few studies have utilized quantitative data and objective performance measures from real organizations to assess hypotheses. One exception includes a study that compared companies with exemplary diversity management practices to those that had paid legal damages to settle discrimination lawsuits. The results of this study showed that the exemplary firms performed better as measured by their stock prices.[31]

A second exception includes a series of studies that found no significant direct effects of either racial or gender diversity on business performance.[32] Gender diversity had positive effects on group processes while racial diversity had negative effects. The negative relationship between racial diversity and group processes was, however, largely absent in groups that had received high levels of training in career development and diversity management. This same research team also found that racial diversity was positively associated with growth in branches' business portfolios. Racial diversity was also associated with higher overall performance in branches that enacted an integration-and-learning perspective on diversity. In addition, they found that employee participation in diversity education programs had a limited impact upon performance. Finally, this group found no support for the idea that diversity that matches a firm's client base increased sales by satisfying customers' desires to be served by those who physically resemble them.[33]

Demographic Diversity and Organizational Functioning

Those studying demographic diversity have usually taken one of two approaches in their treatment of the subject. One approach has been to treat it broadly, making statements about heterogeneity or homogeneity in general, rather than about a particular type.[34] The second approach has been to treat each demographic diversity variable as a distinct theoretical construct based on the argument that different types of diversity may produce different outcomes.[35] Instead of assuming that all types of diversity produce similar effects, these researchers build their models around specific types of demographic diversity.[36] Indeed, Smith, DiTomaso, Farris, and Cordero argue that scholars should not lump women and racial minorities together as a standard approach to research.[37] Doing so, they argue, is problematic because issues such as favoritism and bias are significantly affected by the relative number, power, and status of various groups within organizations, and such variations may be masked by aggregating them together.

As the demography of the workforce continues to change and employers remove obstacles that once prevented access to women and people of color, diversity in business organizations has increasingly become an important topic. The results of research on heterogeneity in groups suggest that diversity offers both a great opportunity for organizations as well as an enormous challenge. Research suggests that more diverse groups have the potential to consider a greater range of perspectives and to generate more high-quality solutions than less diverse groups.[38] Yet, studies suggest that the greater the amount of diversity in a group or an organizational subunit, the less integrated the group is likely to be[39] and the higher the level of dissatisfaction and turnover.[40] Diversity, thus, appears to be a paradoxical double-edged sword that increases the opportunity for creativity as well as the likelihood that group members will be dissatisfied and fail to identify with the organization. Thus, examining demographic factors will make clearer what relationship, if any, diversity has to organizational functioning, especially in business organizations.

Alternative Explanations

In attempting to assess the relationship between diversity and business outcomes, the literature suggests that there are several organizational factors that could make a difference in for-profit business establishments. Moreover, such workplaces are appropriate sites for examining questions about diversity, as it is these organizational entities in which decisions about employment are made, and these organizational sites act as settings in which work is performed.[41] Moreover, organizational processes perpetuate segregation and influence the character of jobs and workplaces.[42]

Several organizational characteristics potentially affect the amount of racial and gender diversity of organizations and the business performance of such organizations. According to the institutional perspective in organizational theory, for example, organizational behavior is a response to pressures from the institutional environment.[43] The institutional environment of an organization is the regulative, normative, and cultural-cognitive institutions affecting the organization, such as the current law and social attitudes.[44] According to this formulation of organizational behavior, adoption of new organizational practices is often an attempt to gain legitimacy in the eyes of important constituents and not necessarily an attempt to gain greater efficiency.[45] Based on institutional theory, for-profit businesses that are accountable to a larger public may be more sensitive to public opinion on what constitutes legitimate organizational behavior. Thus, publicly held for-profit businesses should have employment practices that are more subject to public scrutiny. They should employ relatively more minorities than private-sector employers to the degree that they are under greater pressure to achieve racial and ethnic diversity, as public sentiment views such policies as a necessary element of legitimate organizational governance.[46]

There are also reasons to believe that size matters. In particular, organizational size is positively related to sophisticated personnel systems,[47] which may contribute to diversity in the workplace. But at the same time, if some organizations, when left to their own devices, have a preference for hiring Whites over racial minorities, larger size and slack resources gives them more ability to indulge preferences for White workers.[48] When they are large enough, organizations that are concerned about due process and employment practices will institute specific offices and procedures for handling employee complaints.[49] These establishments will also make greater efforts at prevention and redress because there are direct legal obligations on them. Antidiscrimination laws make discrimination against minorities and women potentially costly, but not all establishments are subject to these laws. Federal law banning sex discrimination in employment exempts firms with fewer than 15 workers, and enforcement efforts have often targeted large firms.[50] Moreover, affirmative action regulations apply only to firms that do at least US$50,000 worth of business with the federal government and have at least 50 employees.[51] Thus, establishment size may be related to vulnerability to equal employment opportunity and affirmative action regulations, which in turn should be related to increased racial and ethnic diversity. Indeed, research by Harry Holzer has shown that affirmative action implementation has led to gains in the representation of African Americans and White women in firms required to practice affirmative action.[52]

Art Stinchcombe also introduced reasons for the age of an organization to matter. In particular, he proposed the concept of "liability of newness" that states that organizational mortality rates decrease with organizational age.[53] Thus, younger organizations are more prone to mortality than older organizations, and they will approach threats to their existence differently. It is possible, therefore, that organizations of different ages will vary in their responses to racial and gender diversity concerns.

The labor pools from which establishments hire may be important factors that may be related to the effects of diversity on business outcomes. The sex and racial composition of regional labor markets may influence an establishment's composition as well as its relative success.[54] However, regional differences in residential segregation may obscure regional effects of demographic composition.[55]

Similarly, there are reasons to believe that the industrial sector will be related to levels of diversity and business performance. In particular, organizations in the service sector will be more proactive with regard to racial and gender diversity than those that produce tangible goods, as their performance depends to a greater extent on public goodwill. But there are also reasons to believe that the economic sector in which businesses operate can matter, as service-sector establishments are more likely than manufacturing and public service establishments to exclude Blacks—especially Black men—by utilizing personality traits and appearance as job qualifications.[56]

Overall, the search for evidence that directly assesses the business case for diversity has proved elusive. In its most basic form, the business case for diversity perspective predicts that there is a diversity return on investment.[57]

How Diversity Is Related to Business Performance

How is diversity related to the business performance of organizations? Is there any tangible evidence that there is a relationship between the racial and gender composition of the establishment and its sales revenue, its number of customers, its market share, or its profitability? Before examining the particular theoretical expectations advanced in the business case for diversity perspective, a descriptive overview of the characteristics of the organizations in the sample is in order.

Figure 3.1 illustrates the distribution of business establishments with low, medium, and high levels of racial and gender diversity. It shows that 30 percent of businesses in the sample are classified as having low levels of racial diversity, 27 percent have medium levels of diversity, and 43 percent have high levels of racial diversity. It also shows that 28 percent of establishments have low levels of gender diversity, 28 percent have medium levels of diversity, and 44 percent have high levels of gender diversity.

Figure 3.2 shows that average sales revenues are associated with higher levels of racial and gender diversity. The mean revenues of organizations with low levels of racial diversity are roughly US$52 million, compared with $384 million for those with medium levels of racial diversity, and $761 million for those with high levels of racial diversity.

The chart shows that the same general pattern holds true for sales revenue by gender diversity. The average revenues of firms with low levels of gender diversity are roughly US$45 million, compared with $299 million for those with medium levels of gender diversity, and $644 million for those with high levels of gender diversity.

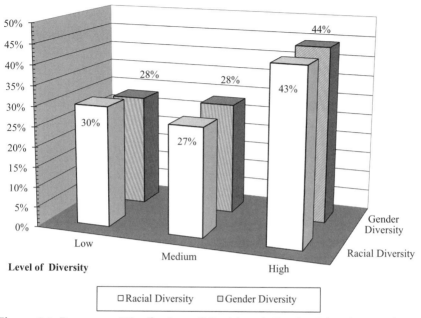

Figure 3.1 Percentage Distribution of Racial and Gender Diversity Levels in Establishments

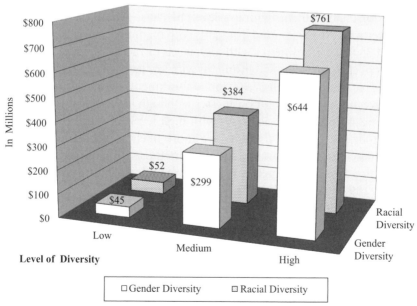

Figure 3.2 Average Sales Revenues by Level of Racial and Gender Diversity

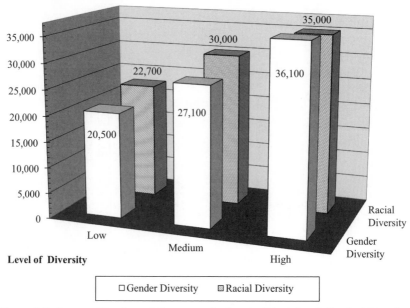

Figure 3.3 Average Number of Customers by Level of Racial and Gender Diversity

Figure 3.3 shows that higher levels of racial and gender diversity are also associated with greater numbers of customers, as the average number of customers for establishments with low levels of racial diversity is 22,700. This compares with 30,000 for establishments with medium levels of racial diversity and 35,000 for businesses with high levels of racial diversity. The mean number of customers for establishments with low levels of gender diversity is 20,500. This compares with 27,100 for establishments with medium levels of racial diversity and 36,100 for businesses with high levels of racial diversity.

Figure 3.4 shows that businesses with high levels of racial (60 percent) and gender (62 percent) diversity are more likely to report higher than average percentages of market share than are those with low levels of racial and gender diversity (45 percent) and those with medium levels of racial diversity (59 percent) and gender diversity (58 percent).

Figure 3.5 shows that the same is generally true in terms of reporting higher than average profitability. Less than half (47 percent) of establishments with low levels of racial diversity report higher than average profitability. This compares with more than six in ten of those establishments with medium levels (63 percent) and high levels (61 percent) of racial diversity. Establishments with high levels of gender (62 percent) diversity are more likely to report higher than average profitability than are those with low levels of gender diversity (45 percent) and those with medium levels of gender diversity (58 percent).

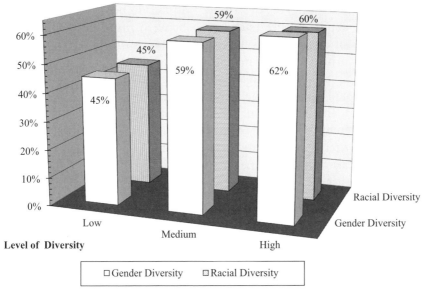

Figure 3.4 Percentage of Firms with Above Average Market Share by Level of Racial and Gender Diversity

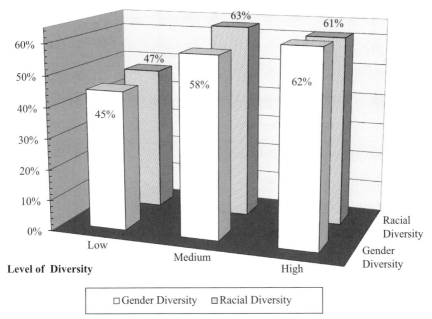

Figure 3.5 Percentage of Firms with Above Average Profitability by Level of Racial and Gender Diversity

Although interesting, the descriptive statistics do not provide complete information about the net relationship between diversity and business performance of organizations. In order to address this issue more rigorously, we performed multivariate statistical analysis. Our analysis examined the relationship between racial and gender diversity in establishments and (the logarithm of) sales revenue, number of customers, estimates of relative market shares, and estimates of relative profitability, net of other factors. Figure 3.6 presents a summary of our results. As Figure 3.6 illustrates, we found that the relationship between diversity and sales revenues is positive.

Figure 3.7 also shows that racial diversity is significantly related to the number of customers. As the racial and gender diversity in establishments increases, their number of customers also increase.

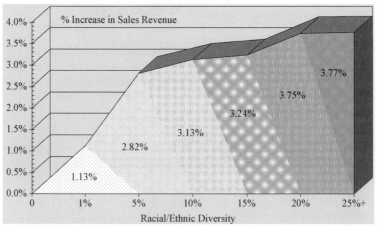

Figure 3.6 Percentage Increases in Sales Revenue for Given Amounts of Racial/Ethnic Diversity

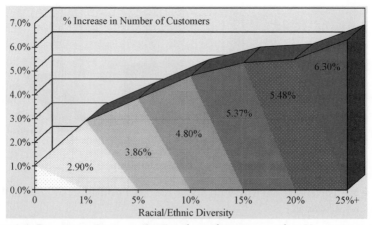

Figure 3.7 Percentage Increases in Number of Customers for Given Amounts of Racial/Ethnic Diversity

The relationship between number of customers and diversity is statistically significant for both racial diversity and gender diversity. Moreover, the relationship between racial and gender diversity and estimates of relative market shares indicates that diversity and estimates of greater market shares are positively related. As the racial and gender diversity in establishments increases, estimates of relative market share also increase significantly. The relationship is statistically significant for racial diversity and marginally significant for gender diversity. Finally, the relationship between racial and gender diversity and relative profitability is such that as diversity increases, estimates of relative profitability also increase. The results are statistically significant for both racial diversity and gender diversity.

But do these results hold up once alternative explanations are taken into account? Overall, the multivariate analysis provides strong support for the business case for diversity perspective. The results are consistent with all but one of the hypotheses suggesting that racial and gender diversity are related to business outcomes. The relationships between diversity and various dimensions of business performance remain even after statistical controls for factors associated with alternative explanations such as legal form of organization, company size, establishment size, organization age, industrial sector, and region. Indeed, racial diversity was consistently among the most important predictors of business outcomes, and gender diversity was a strong predictor of such outcomes in three of the four indicators.

Conclusion

The main objective of this chapter was to examine the impact of racial and gender diversity upon business performance. It began with two competing views about the effects of diversity. The "value-in-diversity" perspective makes the business case for diversity and argues that a diverse workforce, relative to a homogeneous workforce, produces better business results. In particular, a central claim of the perspective is that diversity is good for business because it offers a direct return on investment that promises greater corporate profits and earnings.

In contrast, "diversity as process loss" perspective is skeptical of the benefits of diversity and points out why diversity is counterproductive. This view suggests that, in addition to dividing the nation, the emphasis on diversity introduces conflict and other problems that detract from an organization's ability to be effective and profitable. In short, this view suggests that diversity impedes group functioning and, thus, will have negative effects on business performance.

A third, paradoxical view of diversity suggests that greater diversity is associated with more group conflict and better business performance.

This is possible because diverse groups are more prone to have conflict, but such conflict forces groups to go beyond easy solutions that occur when like-minded people come together; rather, diversity leads to contestation of different ideas, more creativity, and superior solutions to problems. Homogeneity, in other words, may lead to greater group cohesion but also less adaptability and innovation. Heterogeneity, in contrast, may be associated both with more group-based conflict and greater creativity and higher performance. Thus, diversity, although possibly associated with more conflict and process loss, is also associated with creativity and greater value.

Using data from a national sample of for-profit business organizations (the National Organizations Survey), our analysis focused on eight hypotheses that are consistent with the value-in-diversity (business case for diversity) perspective. These indicators included both "objective" and perceptual indicators. Although some detractors may view the perceptual indicators as problematic, it is important to keep in mind that this mixture of indicators is a strength. It is highly unlikely that these different kinds of indicators have the same set of unobserved processes or sources of measurement error that might produce spurious results. The multivariate statistical analysis provided support for seven of the eight hypotheses: diversity is associated with increased sales revenue, more customers, greater market share, and greater relative profits. Such results clearly run counter to the expectations of skeptics who believe that diversity (and efforts to achieve it) would be harmful to business organizations. These results are, moreover, consistent with arguments that suggest that a diverse workforce is good for business and that diversity offers a direct return on investment that promises greater corporate profits and earnings. In addition, the statistical models help to rule out alternative and potentially spurious explanations that offer the most obvious threats to causal inference.

How is diversity related to the bottom-line performance of organizations? Despite the assertion put forth by critics of the business case that diversity is linked with conflict, lower group cohesiveness, increased employee absenteeism and turnover, and lower quality and performance, there is now tangible evidence that there is a positive relationship between the racial and gender diversity of establishments and their business functioning.

It is likely that diversity produces positive outcomes over homogeneity because growth and innovation may depend on people from various backgrounds working together and capitalizing on their differences. Although such differences may lead to some communication barriers and group conflict, diversity increases the opportunity for creativity and the quality of the product of group work. Diversity provides a competitive advantage through social complexity at the firm level when it is positioned within the proper context. In addition, linking diversity to the idea of parity makes it easier to see that diversity pays because businesses that draw on more inclusive talent pools are more successful. So, despite the potentially negative impact of diversity upon internal group processes, diversity has a net positive impact upon organizations' functioning. The results presented in this research effort are currently the best available, and they are based on a nationally representative sample of business organizations.

As we mentioned earlier, diversity was originally a concept created to justify more inclusion of people who had traditionally been left out. It was used to make the process more inclusive of people of color, women, and other groups who had been left out of schools, universities, corporations, and other kinds of organizations. Our research suggests that diversity—when tethered to concerns about parity—is linked to positive outcomes, at least in business organizations. The findings presented here are consistent with arguments that suggest that diversity is related to business success because it allows companies to "think outside the box" by bringing previously excluded groups inside the box. In doing so, it enhances creativity, problem solving, and performance. Future research will need to uncover the mechanisms and processes involved in the diversity-business performance nexus.

Notes

1 Cox, 1993; and Thomas, 2003
2 Hubbard, 2004; Cox, 1993; Cox and Beale, 1997; Richard, 2000; Smedley, Butler, and Bristow, 2004
3 Hubbard, 2004
4 Cox, 2001
5 Gurin, Nagda, and Lopez, 2004
6 Williams and O'Reilly, 1998; and Florida and Gates, 2001, 2002
7 Ryan, Hawdon, and Branick, 2002
8 Skerry, 2002; Rothman, Lipset, and Nevitte, 2003a; Rothman, Lipset, and Nevitte, 2003b; Tsui, Egan, and O'Reilly, 1992; and Whitaker, 1996
9 Pelled, Eisenhardt, and Xin, 1999; Pelled, 1996; and Jehn, Northcraft, and Neale, 1999
10 Skerry, 2002
11 Jehn, Northcraft, and Neale, 1999
12 Tsui, Egan, and O'Reilly, 1992
13 Wood, 2003
14 Rothman, Lipset, and Nevitte, 2003
15 Williams and O'Reilly, 1998
16 DiTomaso, Post, and Parks-Yancy, 2007: 488
17 Although it is possible to derive propositions from arguments put forth by those who are skeptical of the "business case for diversity" thesis, works in this skeptical vein typically provide *critiques* of more optimist views of diversity rather than systematic, alternative theoretical formulations. When skeptics do put forward testable hypotheses, they tend to focus on intermediary processes and mechanisms rather than the diversity-business "bottom line" linkage, *per se*. The primary goal in citing such skeptics is to establish that there are reasons to be skeptical about the diversity → business performance linkage.

18 Berrey, 2007
19 Kalev, Dobbin, and Kelly, 2006
20 von Eron, 1995; Hubbard, 1997, 1999; Berry, 2007; and Bell and Hartmann, 2007
21 Alon and Tienda, 2007
22 Berry, 2007
23 Page, 2007
24 Bunderson and Sutcliffe, 2002
25 Williams and O'Reilly, 1998
26 Sen and Bhattacharya, 2001
27 Black, Mason, and Cole, 1996
28 DiTomaso, Post, and Parks-Yancy, 2007
29 Richard, 2000
30 Alon and Tienda, 2007; Kalev, Dobbin, and Kelly, 2006; Bell and Hartmann, 2007; Berry, 2007; DiTomaso, Post, and Parks-Yancy, 2007; and Embrick, 2011
31 Wright et al., 1995
32 Reported by Kochan et al., 2003
33 Although it would be preferable to model an array of internal processes in organizations in order to establish how diversity affects business performance (e.g., functionality of work teams, marketing decisions, innovation in production or sales, etc.), it is not possible to do so with data from the National Organizations Survey because such indicators are not available in the dataset. These topics do, however, offer potentially fruitful paths for subsequent research efforts.
34 Hambrick and Mason, 1984
35 Hoffman and Maier, 1961; and Kent and McGrath, 1969
36 Zenger and Lawrence, 1989
37 Smith et al., 2001
38 Hoffman and Maier, 1961; Cox, Lobel, and McLeod, 1991; Watson, Kumar, and Michaelsen, 1993
39 O'Reilly, Caldwell, and Barnett, 1989
40 Jackson et al., 1991; Wagner, Pfeffer, and O'Reilly, 1984
41 Reskin, McBrier, and Kmec, 1999; and Baron and Bielby, 1980
42 Tomaskovic-Devey, 1993b
43 Stainback, Robinson, and Tomaskovic-Devey, 2005
44 Scott, 2003
45 Di Maggio and Powell, 2003
46 Edelman, 1990
47 Pfeffer, 1977
48 Cohn, 1985; and Tolbert and Oberfield, 1991
49 Gwartney-Gibbs and Lach, 1993; and Welsh, Dawson, and Nierobisz, 2002
50 Reskin, McBrier, and Kmec, 1999
51 Reskin, 1998
52 Holzer, 1996
53 Stinchcombe, 1965
54 Blalock, 1957
55 Jones and Rosenfeld, 1989
56 Moss and Tilly, 1996
57 Hubbard, 2004

References

Alon, Sigal and Marta Tienda. 2007. "Diversity, Opportunity, and the Shifting Meritocracy in Higher Education." *American Sociological Review* 72: 487–511.
Baron, James N. and William T. Bielby. 1980. "Bringing the Firm Back In: Stratification, Segmentation, and the Organization Of Work." *American Sociological. Review* 45: 737–765.
Bell, Joyce M. and Douglas Hartmann. 2007. "Diversity in Everyday Discourse: The Cultural Ambiguities and Consequences of 'Happy Talk.'" *American Sociological Review* 72 (6): 895–914.

Berrey, Ellen C. 2011. "Why Diversity Became Orthodox in Higher Education, and How It Changed the Meaning of Race on Campus." *Critical Sociology* 37 (5): 573–596.

Black, Genie, Kevin Mason, and Gene Cole. 1996. "Consumer Preferences and Employment Discrimination." *International Advances in Economic Research* 2: 137–145.

Blalock, Herbert M. 1957. "Percent NonWhite and Discrimination in the South." *American Sociological Review* 22: 677–682.

Bratter, Jenifer and Tukufu Zuberi. 2001. "The Demography of Difference: Shifting Trends of Racial Diversity and Interracial Marriage, 1960–1990." *Race and Society* 4: 133–148.

Bunderson, J. Stuart and Kathleen M. Sutcliffe. 2002. "Comparing Alternative Conceptualizations of Functional Diversity in Management Teams: Process and Performance Effects." *Academy of Management Journal* 45: 875–893.

Cohn, Samuel. 1985. *The Process of Occupational Sex-Typing: The Feminization Of Clerical Labor In Great Britain.* Philadelphia, PA: Temple University Press.

Cox, Taylor. 1993. *Cultural Diversity in Organizations: Theory, Research, and Practice.* San Francisco, CA: Berrett-Koehler.

Cox, Taylor. 2001. *Creating the Multicultural Organization: A Strategy for Capturing the Power of Diversity.* San Francisco, CA: Jossey-Bass.

Cox, Taylor and Ruby L. Beale. 1997. *Developing Competency to Manage Diversity.* San Francisco, CA: Berrett-Koehler.

Cox, Taylor H., Sharon A. Lobel and Poppy Lauretta McLeod. 1991. "Effects of Ethnic Group Cultural Differences on Cooperative and Competitive Behavior on a Group Task." *Academy of Management Journal* 34: 827–847.

Di Maggio, Paul and Walter Powell. 2003. "The Iron Cage Revisited: Institutional Isomorphism and Collective Rationality in Organizational Fields," in M.J. Handel (Ed.). *The Sociology of Organizations: Classic, Contemporary, and Critical Readings.* London: Sage Publications: 243–253.

DiTomaso, Nancy, Corinne Post, and Rochelle Parks-Yancy. 2007. "Workforce Diversity and Inequality: Power, Status, and Numbers." *Annual Review of Sociology* 33: 473–501.

Edelman, Lauren B. 1990. "Legal Environments and Organizational Governance: The Expansion of Due Process in the American Workplace." *American Journal of Sociology* 95: 1401–1440.

Ely, Robin J. and David A. Thomas. 2001. "Cultural Diversity at Work: The Effects of Diversity Perspectives on Work Group Processes and Outcomes." *Administrative Science Quarterly* 46: 202–228.

Embrick, David G. 2011. "The Diversity Ideology in the Business World: A New Oppression for a New Age." *Critical Sociology* 37 (5): 541–556.

Embrick, David G. Forthcoming. "What Is Diversity? Re-examining Multiculturalism, Affirmative Action, and the Diversity Ideology in Post-Civil Rights America." *Sociology Compass.*

Florida, Richard and Gary Gates. 2001. *Technology and Tolerance: The Importance of Diversity to High-Technology Growth.* Washington, DC: The Brookings Institution.

Florida, Richard and Gary Gates. 2002. "Technology and Tolerance: Diversity and High-Tech Growth." *Brookings Review* 20: 32–36.

Gurin, Patricia, Biren (Ratnesh) A. Nagda, and Gretchen E. Lopez. 2004. "The Benefits of Diversity in Education for Democratic Citizenship." *Journal of Social Issues* 60: 17–34.

Gwartney-Gibbs, Patricia A., and D.H. Lach. 1993. "Sociological Explanations for Failure to Seek Sexual Harassment Remedies." *Mediation Quarterly* 9: 365–374.

Hambrick, Donald C., and Phyllis A. Mason. 1984. "Upper Echelons: The Organization as a Reflection of Its Top Managers." *Academy of Management Review,* 9: 193–206.

Hoffman, L. Richard and Norman R.F. Maier. 1961. "Quality and Acceptance of Problem Solutions by Members of Homogeneous and Heterogeneous Groups." *Journal of Abnormal and Social Psychology* 62: 401–407.

Holzer, Harry J. 1996. *What Employers Want.* New York, NY: Russell Sage Foundation.

Hubbard, Edward E. 1997. *Measuring Diversity Results.* Petaluma, CA: Global Insights.

Hubbard, Edward E. 1999. *How to Calculate Diversity Return on Investment.* Petaluma, CA: Global Insights.

Hubbard, Edward E. 2004. *The Diversity Scorecard: Evaluating the Impact of Diversity on Organizational Performance.* Burlington, MA: Elsevier Butterworth-Heinemann.

Jackson, Susan E., Joan F. Brett, Valerie I. Sessa, Dawn M. Cooper, Johan A. Julin and Karen Peyronnin. 1991. "Some Differences Make a Difference: Individual Dissimilarity and Group

Heterogeneity as Correlates of Recruitment, Promotions, and Turnover." *Journal of Applied Psychology* 76: 675–689.

Jackson, Susan E., K.A. May, and K. Whitney. 1995. "Understanding the Dynamics of Diversity in Decision Making Teams," in R.A. Guzzo and E. Salas (Eds). *Team Decision Making Effectiveness in Organizations*. San Francisco, CA: Jossey-Bass: 204–261.

Jehn, Karen A., Gregory B. Northcraft, and Margaret A. Neale. 1999. "Why Differences Make a Difference: A Field Study of Diversity, Conflict, and Performance in Workgroups." *Administrative Science Quarterly* 44: 741–763.

Jones, Jo Ann and Rachel A. Rosenfeld. 1989. "Women's Occupations and Local Labor Markets: 1950 to 1980." *Social Forces* 67: 666–692.

Kalev, Alexandria, Frank Dobbin, and Erin Kelly. 2006. "Best Practices or Best Guesses? Assessing the Efficacy of Corporate Affirmative Action and Diversity Policies." *American Sociological Review* 71: 589–617.

Kalleberg, Arne L., David Knoke, and Peter Marsden. 2001. *National Organizations Survey (NOS), 1996–1997* (Computer file). ICPSR version. Minneapolis, MN: University of Minnesota Center for Survey Research (producer), 1997. Ann Arbor, MI: Inter-University Consortium for Political and Social Research (distributor), 2001.

Kent, R.N. and J.E. McGrath. 1969. "Task and Group Characteristics as Factors Influencing Group Performance." *Journal of Experimental Social Psychology* 5: 429–440.

Kochan, Thomas, Katerina Bezrukova, Robin Ely, Susan Jackson, Aparna Joshi, Karen Jehn, Jonathan Leonard, David Levine, and David Thomas. 2003. "The Effects of Diversity on Business Performance: Report of the Diversity Research Network." *Human Resource Management* 42: 3–21.

Milliken, Frances J. and Luis L. Martins. 1996. "Searching for Common Threads: Understanding the Multiple Effects of Diversity in Organizational Groups." *Academy of Management Review* 21: 402–433.

Moss Philip and Chris Tilly. 1996. "Soft Skills and Race: An Investigation Of Black Men's Employment Problems." *Work and Occupations* 23: 252–276.

O'Reilly, Charles A., D.E. Caldwell, and W.P. Barnett. 1989. "Work Group Demography, Social Integration, and Turnover." *Administrative Science Quarterly* 34: 21–37.

Page, Scott E. 2007. *The Difference: How the Power of Diversity Creates Better Groups, Firms, Schools, and Societies*. Princeton, NJ: Princeton University Press.

Pelled, Lisa Hope. 1996. "Demographic Diversity, Conflict, and Work Group Outcomes: An Intervening Process Theory." *Organization Science* 7: 615–631.

Pelled, Lisa Hope, Kathleen M. Eisenhardt, and Katherine R. Xin. 1999. "Exploring the Black Box: An Analysis of Work Group Diversity, Conflict and Performance." *Administrative Science Quarterly* 44: 1–28

Pfeffer, Jeffery. 1977. "Toward an Examination of Stratification in Organizations." *Administrative Science Quarterly* 22: 553–567.

Reskin, Barbara F. 1998. *The Realities of Affirmative Action in Employment*. Washington, DC: American Sociological Association.

Reskin, Barbara F., Debra B. McBrier, and Julie A. Kmec. 1999. "The Determinants and Consequences of Workplace Sex and Race Composition." *Annual Review of Sociology* 25: 335–361.

Richard, Orlando C. 2000. "Racial Diversity, Business Strategy, and Firm Performance: A Resource-Based View." *The Academy of Management Journal* 43: 164–177.

Rothman, Stanley, Seymour Martin Lipset, and Neil Nevitte. 2003a. "Does Enrollment Diversity Improve University Education?" *International Journal of Public Opinion Research* 15: 8–26.

Rothman, Stanley, Seymour Martin Lipset, and Neil Nevitte. 2003b. "Racial Diversity Reconsidered." *The Public Interest* 151: 25–38.

Ryan, John, James Hawdon, and Allison Branick. 2002. "The Political Economy of Diversity: Diversity Programs in *Fortune* 500 Companies." *Sociological Research Online* (May).

Scott, W. Richard. 2003. *Organizations: Rational, Natural, and Open Systems*. Upper Saddle River, NJ: Prentice Hall.

Sen, Sankar C. and B. Bhattacharya. 2001. "Does Doing Good Always Lead to Doing Better? Consumer Reactions to Corporate Social Responsibility." *Journal of Marketing Research* 38: 225–243.

Skaggs, Sheryl L. and Nancy DiTomaso. 2004. "Understanding the Effects of Workforce Diversity on Employment Outcomes: A Multidisciplinary and Comprehensive Framework," in N. DiTomaso and C. Post (Eds). *Diversity in the Workforce*. Stamford, CT: JAI Press.

Skerry, Peter. 2002. "Beyond Sushiology: Does Diversity Work?" *Brookings Review* 20: 20–23.

Smedley, Brian D., Adrienne Stith Butler, and Lonnie R. Bristow. (Ed.). 2004. *In the Nation's Compelling Interest: Ensuring Diversity in the Health-Care Workforce*. Washington, DC: The National Academies Press.

Smith, D. Randall, Nancy DiTomaso, George F. Farris, and Rene Cordero. 2001. "Favoritism, Bias and Error in Performance Ratings of Scientists and Engineers: The Effects of Power, Status, and Numbers." *Sex Roles* 45: 337–358.

Stainback, Kevin, Corre L. Robinson, and Donald Tomaskovic-Devey. 2005. "Race and Workplace Integration: A Politically Mediated Process?" *American Behavioral Scientist* 48: 1200–1228.

Stinchcombe, Arthur L. 1965. "Social Structure and Organizations," in J.G. March (Ed.). *Handbook of Organizations*. Chicago, IL: Rand-McNally: 142–193.

Thomas, R. Roosevelt. 2003. *Building a House for Diversity: How a Fable about a Giraffe and an Elephant Offers New Strategies for Today's Workforce*. Atlanta, GA: AMACOM.

Tolbert, Pamela S. and Alice Oberfield. 1991. "Sources of Organizational Demography: Faculty Sex Ratios in Colleges and Universities." *Sociology of Education* 64: 305–315.

Tomaskovic-Devey, Donald. 1993a. "The Gender and Race Composition of Jobs and the Male/Female, White/Black Pay Gaps." *Social Forces* 92: 45–76.

Tomaskovic-Devey, Donald. 1993b. *Gender and Racial Inequality at Work: The Sources and Consequences of Job Segregation*. Ithaca, NY: ILR Press.

Tomaskovic-Devey, Donald and Sheryl Skaggs. 1999. "Degendered Jobs? Organizational Processes and Gender Segregated Employment." *Research in Social Stratification and Mobility* 17: 139–172.

Tsui, Ann S., Terri D. Egan, and Charles A. O'Reilly. 1992. "Being Different: Relational Demography and Organizational Attachment." *Administrative Science Quarterly* 37: 549–579.

von Eron, Ann M. 1995. "Ways to Assess Diversity Success." *HR Magazine* (August): 51–60.

Wagner, Gary W., Jeffrey Pfeffer, and Charles A. O'Reilly. 1984. "Organizational Demography and Turnover in Top-Management Groups." *Administrative Science Quarterly* 29: 74–92.

Watson, Warren E., Kannales Kumar, and Larry K. Michaelsen. 1993. "Cultural Diversity's Impact on Interaction Process and Performance: Comparing Homogeneous and Diverse Task Groups." *Academy of Management Journal* 36: 590–602.

Welsh, Sandy, Myrna Dawson, and Annette Nierobisz. 2002. "Legal Factors, Extra-Legal Factors, or Changes in the Law? Using Criminal Justice Research to Understand the Resolution of Sexual Harassment Complaints." *Social Problems* 49: 605–623.

Whitaker, William A. 1996. *White Male Applicant: An Affirmative Action Expose*. Smyrna, DE: Apropos Press.

Williams, Katherine and Charles A. O'Reilly. 1998. "Demography and Diversity: A Review of 40 Years of Research," in B. Staw and R. Sutton (Eds). *Research in Organizational Behavior*. Greenwich, CT: JAI Press.

Wood, Peter. 2003. "Diversity in America." *Society* 40: 60–67.

Wright, Peter, Stephen P. Ferris, Janine S. Hiller, and Mark Kroll. 1995. "Competitiveness through Management of Diversity: Effects on Stock Price Valuation." *Academy of Management Journal* 38: 272–287.

Zenger, Todd R. and Barbara S. Lawrence. 1989. "Organizational Demography: The Differential Effects of Age and Tenure Distributions on Technical Communication." *Academy of Management Journal* 32: 353–376.

Zuberi, Tukufu. 2001. "The Population Dynamics of the Changing Color Line in the USA," in E. Anderson and D. Massey (Eds). *Problem of the Century: Racial Stratification in the United States at Century's End*. New York, NY: Russell Sage Foundation.

4

Achieving Workplace Diversity

As the population of the United States continues to become more diverse, employers have come to realize that their success may be tied to the diversity of their workforce and practices.[1] In particular, the recruitment, promotion, and retention of employees of color are increasingly important to success in business organizations.[2] Although there are several moral and social arguments for recruiting diverse employees, the most compelling reasons to pursue a diverse workforce for many employers is that excellence in diversity recruiting relates to more customers, better service, and better performance. There is a global battle for talent, and any company that restricts its search for talent in any way—by race, gender, national origin, sexual orientation, or any other factor—gives its competitors who do not restrict their talent searches in such ways the clear edge that they can use as a competitive advantage. Such arguments resonate with employers of all sizes and industries. And recent research on the link between diversity and the bottom line has provided evidence supporting such thinking.[3]

Proponents of diversity suggest that in the corporate setting, diversity represents a compelling interest that will help meet customers' needs, enrich understanding of the pulse of the marketplace, and improve the quality of products and services offered.[4] With respect to employees, diversity brings with it different perspectives. Because of the clear competitive advantages of diversity, employers increasingly have relied on a diverse workforce to improve their performance. Because diversity provides fresh ideas, strong growth, positive company images, fewer discrimination lawsuits, and an enhanced ability to hire qualified workers, employers should be aggressive about workforce diversity.[5]

Diversity is not just about hiring minorities. It also involves cultivating and retaining talent from as broad a talent pool as possible. Successful organizations place emphasis on getting talented people and then providing the working conditions and best practices that will allow them to flourish within supportive environments. Although there are several case studies that document best practices that have worked within particular firms,[6] there is little quantitative work that shows which organizational factors, working conditions, and employment practices lend themselves to recruiting and retaining a racially diverse workforce.

This chapter offers such a systematic examination of some of the factors that matter in attempts to increase racial and ethnic diversity in organizations. Using data from the National Organizations Survey, it offers a systematic examination of the organizational characteristics, working conditions, and employment practices that are associated with the racial and ethnic composition of for-profit and nonprofit organizations in the US. It also provides Denny's Restaurants as an example of what organizations can do to turn around their lackluster diversity records.

Literature Review

Recruitment is critical to having a diverse workforce and having multicultural leaders of an organization. Such diversity in organizations is often vital to attracting the increasing number of consumers from diverse backgrounds in the United States. But knowing how to reach talented diverse people is challenging for both beginners and experienced people from many companies, especially those in industries that are not attuned to the benefits of diversity.

Attracting the best employees during times of economic uncertainty can be a double-edged sword for organizations and job seekers. When unemployment rates are high and climbing, some companies can more easily choose from a larger pool of potentially qualified job applicants. This is what makes it an employer's market. Meanwhile, the Great Recession put more multicultural talent in the job market. This provides diversity-savvy companies a critical opportunity to recruit these workers before other companies can recruit them. But with the glut of qualified workers and slow growth in the creation of new jobs, finding the right people for the right jobs has become increasingly difficult. The good news for companies seeking new talent is that they can take advantage of economic uncertainty that has their competitors sitting on the sidelines while they recruit from a diverse talent pool. After all, top talent with diverse backgrounds brings a wider perspective and deeper connection to emerging markets.

Although there is an emerging consensus that employers value diversity,[7] there is less agreement about the factors that are important to achieving racial and ethnic diversity in the workforce. In the past, the success or failure of corporate-diversity initiatives was measured using "soft" data, such as whether or not a given workplace fostered diversity through "ethnic" lunch days. Today, that sort of diversity awareness clearly is deficient when compared with the hard metrics that support a business case for diversity. While measurements such as the percentage increase of multi-cultural employees or the total number of diverse executives can shed light on certain aspects of a company's diversity commitment, there is a growing science developing to gauge the actual bottom-line contribution of diversity. Still, little practical research is available to guide organizations on how to become more diverse. In lieu of such research guidance, some employers have been told to "demonstrate sincerity of intentions" as a strategy to attract, hire, and retain the right people to become more diverse.

While the first step to developing a successful strategy to attract top-tier multicultural talent may be as simple as declaring an intention to seek out a diverse workforce and then executing on that promise, other things are also important. Having a pro-diversity reputation goes a long way. Having a reputation as an employer of choice for people of color, women, and gays and lesbians will greatly facilitate reaching out to and attracting diverse job applicants. Studies show that solid reputations invariably yield positive bottom-line results, while poor reputations can hinder financial returns.

In addition to demonstrating sincere intentions, we believe there are organizational factors, recruitment and retention strategies, and employment practices and procedures that make a difference in the racial and ethnic composition of nonprofit organizations and for-profit business establishments. Moreover, we believe that such workplaces are appropriate sites for examining questions about diversity, as it is these organizational entities in which decisions about employment are made, and these organizational sites act as settings in which work is performed.[8] Moreover, it is organizational processes that perpetuate segregation and influence the character of jobs and workplaces.[9]

Some Organizational Factors

Several organizational characteristics potentially affect the amount of racial and ethnic diversity of organizations. According to the institutional perspective in organizational theory, for example, organizational behavior is a response to pressures from the institutional environment.[10] The institutional environment of an organization is the regulative, normative, and cultural-cognitive institutions affecting the organization, such as the current law and social attitudes.[11] According to this formulation of organizational behavior, adoption of new organizational practices is often an attempt to gain legitimacy in the eyes of important constituents and not necessarily an attempt to gain greater efficiency.[12] Based on institutional theory, nonprofit organizations and for-profit businesses that are accountable to a larger public may be more sensitive to public opinion on what constitutes legitimate organizational behavior. Thus, nonprofit organizations and publicly held for-profit businesses have employment practices that are more subject to public scrutiny. They often employ relatively more minorities than private-sector employers to the degree that they are under greater pressure to achieve racial and ethnic diversity, as public sentiment views such policies as a necessary element of legitimate organizational governance.[13]

Organizational size is positively related to sophisticated personnel systems,[14] which may contribute to diversity in the workplace. But at the same time, if some organizations, when left to their own devices, have a preference for hiring Whites over racial minorities, larger size and slack resources gives them more ability to indulge preferences for White workers.[15]

As we mentioned previously, Art Stinchcombe proposed the concept of "liability of newness"[16] that states that organizational mortality rates decrease with organizational age. Thus, younger organizations are more prone to mortality than older organizations, and they will approach threats to their existence differently. It is possible, therefore, that organizations of different ages will vary in their responses to racial and ethnic diversity concerns. Moreover, it is plausible that organizations that were founded during periods of EEO (Equal Employment Opportunity) enforcement (i.e., the post-1960s era) are more prone to be concerned about issues of diversity.[17]

Historically, labor unions have used exclusionary tactics to protect the wages and working conditions of their members who have been overwhelmingly White and male.[18] In recent history, however, organizations that have unions have been positively associated with procedural justice[19] and greater inclusion of racial and ethnic minorities.[20] There is reason to believe, therefore, that organizations that show a greater commitment to labor rights through the presence of labor unions will also be more proactive with regard to racial and ethnic diversity.

Similarly, organizations in the service sector are typically more proactive in their racial and ethnic diversity efforts than are those that produce tangible goods. This is true because their performance depends on public goodwill to a greater extent. But service-sector establishments are more likely than manufacturing and public service establishments to exclude Blacks, especially Black men, by utilizing personality traits and appearance as job qualifications.[21]

Recruitment and Retention Factors

Companies that have successfully recruited top diverse talent frequently are faced with the additional challenge of retaining these valuable and highly sought-after employees. There are several reasons to believe that the racial and ethnic composition of establishments is related to their recruitment and retention practices. Don Tomaskovic-Devey and Sheryl Skaggs suggest that gender composition of establishments is a function of the result of a series of organizational changes involving new approaches to recruitment, selection, promotion, career development, and job analysis and classification.[22] They found that organizational social divisions of labor moved from gender-segregated to marginally integrated when organizations have difficulty finding sufficient employees for jobs with many incumbents. By extension, it is likely that employers who use progressive recruitment practices and consequently hire greater percentages of women may also achieve greater racial and ethnic diversity. But employers who are openly reluctant to hire women will probably also be averse to hiring racial and ethnic minorities.[23]

Recruitment through informal networks reproduces an establishment's composition because workers usually tell people who are similar to them about jobs.[24] So, employers who make their recruitment efforts more transparent and open by publicizing job vacancies are likely to have greater levels of racial and ethnic diversity. More generally, any recruitment and retention practices that alert racial and ethnic minorities about job vacancies should serve to increase their representation within establishments that try to ensure that such groups are actively included in such information dissemination.

Establishments that have successfully recruited diverse workers are frequently faced with the additional challenge of retaining them. Employee turnover has serious fiscal implications that often are not immediately apparent. For example, because the average cost-per-hire for a salaried employee was estimated at more than US$10,000 in 2010, it is also in organizations' best interests to retain their recruits. Moreover, losing a single employee can cost companies as much as four times that employee's annual salary. The costs include paying temporary hires to fill a position, advertising costs to find a qualified replacement, and the time spent training a new worker. Multiply that figure by a high rate of turnover, and the potentially huge financial toll on corporations is clear.

An organization's "culture" of promoting from within is often related to its ability to retain racial and ethnic minority employees. Organizations that actively seek to promote racial and ethnic minorities from within their establishment should also have relatively more success in retaining them. Moreover, practices such as offering opportunities for employees to keep their skills current so that they can advance. Such practices not only help in retention efforts, they also serve to cultivate and broaden the internal talent pool that might serve as a basis for expanding diversity.

Employment Practices and Job Benefits

When they are large enough, organizations that are concerned about due process and employment practices will often institute specific offices and procedures for handling employee complaints.[25] These establishments will also make greater efforts at prevention and redress because there are direct legal obligations on them. Antidiscrimination laws make discrimination against minorities and women potentially costly, but not all establishments are subject to these laws. Federal law banning sex discrimination in employment exempts firms with fewer than 15 workers, and enforcement efforts have often targeted large firms.[26] Moreover, affirmative action regulations apply only to firms that do at least US$50,000 worth of business with the federal government and have at least 50 employees.[27] Thus, establishment size may be related to vulnerability to equal employment opportunity and affirmative action regulations, which in turn should be related to increased racial and ethnic diversity. Indeed, research by Harry Holzer has shown that affirmative action implementation has led to gains in the representation of African Americans and White women in firms required to practice affirmative action.[28]

More generally, an organization's culture can either encourage inclusion and diversity or undermine it. Employers can create work environments that signal their commitment to diversity. For example, perceptions that job promotions are implemented fairly are likely to be associated with higher proportions of racial and ethnic minorities (who would avoid employers who have negative reputations in this regard). Such even-handed practices can be signaled by the availability of written job descriptions and formal job performance evaluations. Also, Denise Narcisse has shown that jobs that offer stability and security are often more attractive to racial and ethnic minorities.[29] These characteristics are associated with employers who offer due process rather than arbitrariness and unpredictability.

In addition to these traits, it is possible that incentives to learn new skills, the ability to participate in job rotation, and the opportunity to share in group-based incentives will be attractive options that will increase the levels of racial and gender diversity within establishments.

Finally, there are additional job benefits that should be attractive to most employees, but especially female employees: the availability of onsite or employer-subsidized childcare and the option of employees working flexible work hours. Again, employers who use such progressive practices to recruit and retain women may also hire and retain greater percentages of racial and ethnic minorities.

We will report the results from our analysis of the relationship of racial and ethnic diversity to organizational factors, recruitment and retention factors, and employment practices and job benefits with data from the National Organizations Survey. We also review the case of Denny's Restaurant to show how that organization used many of the strategies that we identify to go from a laggard to a leader in diversity.

Achieving Workplace Diversity with Organizational Factors, Working Conditions, and Employment Practices

Are organizational factors, working conditions, and employment practices associated with the racial and ethnic composition of for-profit and nonprofit organizations? Are such factors related in the same way to the amount of racial and ethnic diversity in core positions as they are to establishments' overall amounts of racial and ethnic diversity?

Figures 4.1 to 4.3 illustrate how organizational characteristics, recruitment and retention factors, and employment practices and job benefits are related to the racial and ethnic composition of establishments. The overall percentage of racial and ethnic minorities working for all establishments is approximately 24 percent. So, as a rule of thumb, any factor that is associated with more than 25 percent minorities in an establishment is related to higher than average levels of racial and ethnic diversity. Any factor that is associated with less than 23 percent minorities is associated with lower than average levels of racial and ethnic diversity.

Figure 4.1 shows that establishments in the nonprofit sector, on average, have higher rates of racial and ethnic diversity (30 percent) than do their

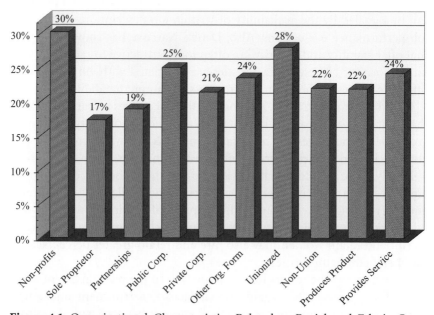

Figure 4.1 Organizational Characteristics Related to Racial and Ethnic Composition of Establishments

for-profit counterparts. But there are also apparent differences in levels of racial and ethnic diversity among different types of for-profit businesses. In particular, 17 percent of sole proprietorships, 19 percent of partnerships, and 21 percent of private corporations are racial minorities. In contrast, 25 percent of publicly held corporations are racial minorities, and 24 percent of those in other organizational forms are racial minorities. These patterns are fully consistent with the argument that nonprofit organizations and publicly held for-profit businesses have employment practices that are more subject to public scrutiny and, thus, more likely to achieve racial and ethnic diversity.

Figure 4.1 also shows that establishments with labor unions have higher levels of racial and ethnic diversity than those without such unions (28 versus 22 percent). This pattern is consistent with the idea that organizations that show greater commitment to labor rights through the presence of labor unions will also be more proactive with regard to racial and ethnic diversity. Finally, this chart suggests that there are few differences in the levels of racial and ethnic diversity between goods producers (22 percent) and service providers (24 percent).

Figure 4.2 presents the relationship between racial and ethnic diversity and various recruitment and retention factors. It shows that establishments with "easy to fill" positions are more diverse than are those with "hard to fill" positions (27 versus 19 percent). This finding is contrary to the expectation that organizations that have difficulty finding sufficient employees for jobs

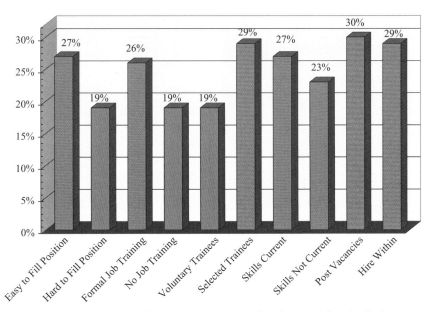

Figure 4.2 Recruitment and Retention Factors Related to Racial and Ethnic Composition of Establishments

are more likely to turn to minority employees. But the results are consistent with the proposition that practices such as offering job-training opportunities for employees and encouraging them to keep their skills current so that they can advance would be appealing to racial and ethnic minorities. Establishments that offer formal job training are more diverse than those that do not offer such opportunities (26 versus 19 percent). Establishments that select job trainees rather than let them self-select are also more diverse (29 versus 19 percent). And those employers who encourage employees to keep their skills current are slightly more diverse than those who do not encourage skills currency (27 versus 23 percent).

Consistent with the idea of transparency and rewarding racial and ethnic minorities already with the company, Figure 4.2 also shows that establishments that post information about job vacancies are more diverse than average (30 percent), as are those that hire from within (29 percent). These results are consistent with the idea that organizations that actively seek to promote racial and ethnic minorities from within their establishment should also have relatively more success in retaining them.

Figure 4.3 illustrates the relationship between racial and ethnic diversity and various employment practices and job benefits. This chart suggests that establishments that have affirmative action or EEO departments are generally more diverse than are those organizations without such entities. It also shows that those organizations where there is the

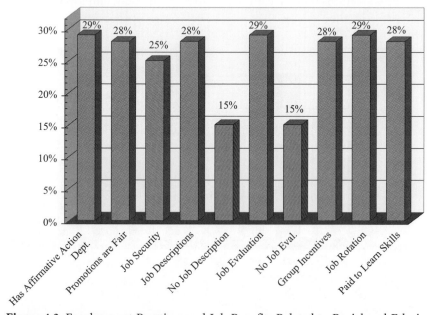

Figure 4.3 Employment Practices and Job Benefits Related to Racial and Ethnic Composition of Establishments

belief that promotions are handled fairly are also more diverse, on average. Establishments that offer job security are slightly more diverse than those that do not offer such security. The notion of even-handedness that written job descriptions and formal job performance evaluations signal also appear to make a difference, as those establishments with written job descriptions are more diverse than those without such job descriptions (28 versus 15 percent), and those with formal job evaluations are more diverse than those without such evaluations (29 versus 15 percent). This graph also shows that group incentives, the ability to participate in job rotation, and financial incentives to learn new skills are associated with higher than average levels of racial and ethnic diversity within establishments. It also shows that the provision of daycare facilities or subsidies is associated with greater racial and ethnic diversity. Contrary to expectations, it shows that establishments that offer flexible work hours have lower levels of diversity than those that do not offer such flexibility (22 versus 29 percent).

Multivariate analysis shows that organizations with low diversity were:

- smaller;
- less likely to be unionized;
- more likely to have been established after the 1960s;
- less likely to offer formal job training;
- less likely to encourage their employees to keep their skills current;
- less likely to post job vacancies;
- less likely to hire from within the establishment;
- less likely to have affirmative action departments;
- less likely to have formal job performance evaluations;
- less likely to pay their employees to learn new skills;
- less likely to offer daycare facilities or subsidies;
- likely to haves smaller percentages of female employees in core positions.

When we examined the relationship between diversity and these factors in a multivariate framework, the results showed that diversity increases under the following conditions:

- as establishment size increases;
- with the presence of unions;
- when there is formal job training;
- when there are internal hiring strategies;
- when there are higher percentages of women in core positions;
- when organizations have affirmative action or EEO departments;
- when there are formal job performance evaluations;
- when organizations provide daycare facilities and subsidies.

Denny's Restaurants: From Laggards to Leaders in Diversity

What are the differences between organizations that are successful in their efforts to achieve workplace diversity and those that are unsuccessful? To illustrate more concretely how organizations' efforts and characteristics make a difference in achieving workplace diversity, we will use the case of Denny's Restaurants.

During the early 1990s, Denny's was embroiled in a series of discrimination lawsuits that involved discrimination against African Americans. Thousands of Black customers across the nation were systematically refused service, forced to wait longer than their White counterparts, or required to pay more for their food and service than White customers. In 1994, Denny's settled a class action lawsuit for US$54.4 million. The settlement was the largest and broadest under federal public accommodations laws established to end segregation in restaurants and public spaces.

But to make matters worse, Denny's also discriminated in its recruitment and employment of African Americans, both as workers and as franchise owners. For example, in 1993 there was only one African American-owned Denny's franchise out of more than 1,000 in the nation. There were no minority supplier contracts. There were no diversity considerations in their strategic marketing. There were no targeted efforts. The company was losing more than US$100 million per year in potential sales by ignoring African American consumers. After the $54.4 million settlement, Denny's created a diversity training program for all employees.

If we fast-forward 20 years, we see that Denny's is now ranked among the top ten leaders in corporate diversity by *Fortune* magazine in its annual ranking of "America's 50 Best Companies for Minorities." More than 45 percent of Denny's employees are minorities; 44 percent of Denny's board of directors comprises minorities or women; and 46 percent of Denny's senior management team is made up of minorities or women. African Americans own 57 Denny's restaurants. Minority franchisees own 44 percent of all Denny's franchise restaurants. Denny's contracts with minority suppliers have grown to more than US$100 million annually, which represents 17 percent of total annual food and non-food purchases. Moreover, African-American businesses account for the majority of Denny's minority contracts.

How did Denny's make such a turnaround? We believe that Denny's was successful because of its recruitment and retention efforts aimed at reaching out to minorities. Also, it reinforced its commitment to diversity through education and training. All 70,000 Denny's company and franchise employees, management and non-management, have completed diversity training. All Denny's managers are required to participate in a full-day diversity training session. In addition, every year, every employee is evaluated against a set of key competencies. "Valuing and Managing Diversity" is within that set of competencies for both management and non-management employees. Annual merit increases are tied directly to these competency areas; and in the late 1990s, 25 percent of senior management's annual bonuses were tied to the company's diversity progress.

Moreover, Denny's sought to create and maintain an inclusive, high-performance organization based on the belief that diversity could become a source of richness, creativity, and innovation. The company implemented a fourfold approach to achieving this goal:

1 Educate and train the workforce, at all levels, to value and manage diversity.
2 Systematically eliminate all structures (i.e., systems, practices, policies, and processes) that impede inclusion and create structures that foster diversity.
3 Monitor, measure, and report results on a regular basis to the highest levels of the organization.
4 Tie reward and recognition systems to diversity progress.

Such efforts are fully consistent with critical diversity, and they are in keeping with the strategies and characteristics we outlined above.

So what are the factors that prevent some organizations from achieving workplace diversity? This chapter moves us closer to understanding some of the constraints that hinder nonprofit organizations and businesses from becoming diverse. Several "hard to change" organizational characteristics matter to an establishment's racial and ethnic diversity: an organization's for-profit or nonprofit status, its legal form of incorporation, and whether it is unionized or not. There is little that organizations can do about such things to make themselves more attractive to recruiting or retaining people of color. Still, they can realize that they are probably similar to their competitors, who will often find themselves similarly situated.

There do, however, appear to be tangible recruitment and retention strategies that companies can employ (or avoid) that make a difference. Offering job training opportunities for employees of color and encouraging them to keep their skills current so that they can advance appears to pay dividends. Establishments that offer formal job training are more diverse than those that do not offer such opportunities, and those that proactively select people of color for job training rather than let employees self-select are also more diverse. And those establishments that reward people of color to keep their skills current have the opportunity to do even better, as employers who encourage employees to keep their skills current are more diverse than those who do not pursue such efforts. Also, establishments can take advantage of transparency. The results show that establishments that do things as simple as posting information about job vacancies and use internal hiring strategies (and presumably promote from within) are more diverse. Again, establishments can use such strategies, especially with employees of color to enhance their diversity. These results are consistent with the idea that organizations that foster climates that are inviting to racial and ethnic minorities and actively seek to promote them have more success in retaining them.

Many of these recruitment and retention efforts go hand-in-hand with signaling the importance of fairness in employment practices and the provision of job benefits that make it easier for establishments to be inclusive. Several due process issues and working conditions matter to a company's racial and ethnic diversity: The presence of an affirmative action department; job security; written job descriptions; formal performance evaluation processes; group incentives; job rotation; incentives to learn new skills; and the availability of daycare facilities or subsidies appear to pay dividends in terms of achieving racial and ethnic diversity.

In short, an important key to achieving workplace diversity appears to be creating attractive positions and opportunities for professional development. Minority candidates, like their majority counterparts, place utmost emphasis on the opportunity itself. Organizations can signal a concern for opportunity and commitment to diversity by putting employment practices and benefits in place.

Notes

1 Darity, Guilkey, and Winfrey, 1996; Farley, 1990; Harris and Farley, 2000; and Denton and Tolnay, 2002
2 Richard, 2000; and Ely and Thomas, 2001
3 Herring, 2009; Richard, 2000; Goncalo and Staw, 2006; Ely and Thomas, 2001; and van der Vegt, Bunderson, and Oosterhof, 2006
4 Hubbard, 2004
5 Williams and O'Reilly, 1998; and Florida and Gates, 2001, 2002
6 Cole, 2003; and Conklin, 2001
7 Frankel, 2003
8 Reskin, McBrier, and Kmec, 1999; and Baron and Bielby, 1980
9 Tomaskovic-Devey, 1993b
10 Stainback, Robinson, and Tomaskovic-Devey, 2005
11 Scott, 2003
12 Di Maggio and Powell, 2003
13 Edelman, 1990
14 Pfeffer, 1977
15 Cohn, 1985; and Tolbert and Oberfield, 1991
16 Stinchcombe, 1965
17 Tomaskovic-Devey and Skaggs, 1999
18 Wong and Chen, 1998
19 Deery and Iverson, 2005
20 Weyher and Zeitlin, 2005

21 Moss and Tilly, 1996
22 Tomaskovic-Devey and Skaggs, 1999
23 Neckerman and Kirschenman, 1991; and Kennelly, 1999
24 Kalleberg et al., 1996
25 Gwartney-Gibbs and Lach, 1993; and Welsh, Dawson, and Nierobisz, 2002
26 Reskin, McBrier, and Kmec, 1999
27 Reskin, 1998
28 Holzer, 1996
29 Narcisse, 2006

References

Baron, James N. and William T. Bielby. 1980. "Bringing the Firm Back In: Stratification, Segmentation, and the Organization Of Work." *American Sociological Review* 45: 737–765.

Cohn, Samuel. 1985. *The Process of Occupational Sex-Typing: The Feminization of Clerical Labor in Great Britain.* Philadelphia, PA: Temple University Press.

Cole, Yoji. 2003. "Who's White, Who's Black, Who's Brown, Who's Yellow? Why Do We Care So Much?," in *The Business Case for Diversity, Fourth Edition.* New Brunswick, NJ: Allegiant Media: 35–39.

Conklin, Wendy. 2001. "Conversations with Diversity Executives." *Diversity Factor* 10: 5–14.

Darity, William, Jr., David K. Guilkey, and William Winfrey. 1996. "Explaining Differences in Economic Performance among Racial and Ethnic Groups in the U.S.A.: The Data Examined." *American Journal of Economics and Sociology* 55: 411–435.

Deery, Stephen J. and Roderick D. Iverson. 2005. "Labor-Management Cooperation: Antecedents and Impact on Organizational Performance." *Industrial and Labor Relations Review* 58: 588–609.

Denton, Nancy A. and Stewart E. Tolnay. 2002. "Introduction: Multicultural Insights from the Study of Demography," in N. A. Denton and S. E. Tolnay (Eds). *American Diversity: A Demographic Challenge for the Twenty-First Century.* Albany, NY: State University of New York Press: 1–21.

Di Maggio, Paul and Walter Powell. 2003. "The Iron Cage Revisited: Institutional Isomorphism and Collective Rationality in Organizational Fields," in M. J. Handel (Ed.). *The Sociology of Organizations: Classic, Contemporary, and Critical Readings.* London: Sage Publications: 243–253.

Edelman, Lauren B. 1990. "Legal Environments and Organizational Governance: The Expansion of Due Process in the American Workplace." *American Journal of Sociology* 95: 1401–1440.

Ely, Robin J. and David A. Thomas. 2001. "Cultural Diversity at Work: The Effects of Diversity Perspectives on Work Group Processes and Outcomes." *Administrative Science Quarterly* 46: 202–228.

Farley, Reynolds. 1990. "Blacks, Hispanics, and White Ethnic Groups: Are Blacks Uniquely Disadvantaged?" *American Economic Review* 80: 237–241.

Florida, Richard and Gary Gates. 2001. *Technology and Tolerance: The Importance of Diversity to High-Technology Growth.* Washington, DC: The Brookings Institution.

Florida, Richard and Gary Gates. 2002. "Technology and Tolerance: Diversity and High-Tech Growth." *Brookings Review* 20: 32–36.

Frankel, Barbara. 2003. "How Do Most Americans Perceive Corporate Diversity?: They're Confused, Poll Finds," in *The Business Case for Diversity, Fourth Edition.* New Brunswick, NJ: Allegiant Media: 23–25.

Goncalo, Jack A. and Barry Staw. 2006. "Individualism-Collectivism and Group Creativity." *Organizational Behavior and Human Decision Processes* 100: 96–109.

Gwartney-Gibbs, Patricia A. and D. H. Lach. 1993. "Sociological Explanations for Failure to Seek Sexual Harassment Remedies." *Mediation Quarterly* 9: 365–374.

Harris, David R. and Reynolds Farley. 2000. "Demographic, Economic, and Social Trends," J. S. Jackson (Ed.). *New Directions: African Americans in a Diversifying Nation.* Washington, DC: National Policy Association: 125–142.

Herring, Cedric. 2009. "Does Diversity Pay? Race, Gender and the Business Case for Diversity." *American Sociological Review* 74: 208–224.

Holzer, Harry J. 1996. *What Employers Want.* New York, NY: Russell Sage Foundation.

Hubbard, Edward E. 2004. *The Diversity Scorecard: Evaluating the Impact of Diversity on Organizational Performance.* Burlington, MA: Elsevier Butterworth-Heinemann.

Kalleberg, Arne L., David Knoke, Peter V. Marsden, and Joel L. Spaeth. 1996. *Organizations in America: Analyzing Their Structures and Human Resources Practices*. Thousand Oaks, CA: Sage.

Kennelly, Ivy 1999. "That Single-Mother Element: How White Employers Typify Black Women." *Gender and Society* 13: 168–192.

Lach, D. H. and Patricia A. Gwartney-Gibbs. 1993. "Sociological Perspectives on Sexual Harassment and Workplace Dispute Resolution." *Journal of Vocational Behavior* 42: 102–115.

Moss, Philip and Chris Tilly. 1996. "Soft Skills and Race: An Investigation of Black Men's Employment Problems." *Work and Occupations* 23: 252–276.

Narcisse, Denise Ann. 2006. *The Employment Attitudes and Decision of African American Professional Women*. PhD Dissertation, University of Illinois at Chicago, Department of Sociology.

Neckerman, Katherine and Joleen Kirschenman. 1991. "Hiring Strategies, Racial Bias, and Inner-City Workers: An Investigation Of Employers' Hiring Decisions." *Social Problems* 38: 433–447.

Pfeffer, Jeffery. 1977. "Toward An Examination of Stratification in Organizations." *Administrative Science Quarterly* 22: 553–567.

Reskin, Barbara F. 1998. *The Realities of Affirmative Action in Employment*. Washington, DC: American Sociological Association.

Reskin, Barbara F., Debra B. McBrier, and Julie A. Kmec. 1999. "The Determinants and Consequences of Workplace Sex and Race Composition." *Annual Review of Sociology* 25: 335–361.

Richard, Orlando C. 2000. "Racial Diversity, Business Strategy, and Firm Performance: A Resource Based View." *Academy of Management Journal* 43: 164–177.

Scott, W. Richard. 2003. *Organizations: Rational, Natural, and Open Systems*. Upper Saddle River, NJ: Prentice Hall.

Stainback, Kevin, Corre L. Robinson, and Donald Tomaskovic-Devey. 2005. "Race and Workplace Integration: A Politically Mediated Process?" *American Behavioral Scientist* 48: 1200–1228.

Stinchcombe, Arthur L. 1965. "Social Structure and Organizations," in J. G. March (Ed.). *Handbook of Organizations*. Chicago, IL: Rand-McNally: 142–193.

Tolbert, Pamela S. and Alice Oberfield. 1991. "Sources of Organizational Demography: Faculty Sex Ratios in Colleges and Universities." *Sociology of Education* 64: 305–315.

Tomaskovic-Devey, Donald. 1993a. "The Gender and Race Composition of Jobs and the Male/Female, White/Black Pay Gaps." *Social Forces* 92: 45–76.

Tomaskovic-Devey, Donald. 1993b. *Gender and Racial Inequality at Work: The Sources and Consequences of Job Segregation*. Ithaca, NY: ILR Press.

Tomaskovic-Devey, Donald and Sheryl Skaggs. 1999. "Degendered Jobs? Organizational Processes and Gender Segregated Employment." *Research in Social Stratification and Mobility* 17: 139–172.

van der Vegt, Gerben S., J. Stuart Bunderson, and Aad Oosterhof. 2006. "Expertness Diversity and Interpersonal Helping in Teams: Why Those Who Need the Most Help End Up Getting the Least." *Academy of Management Journal* 49: 877–893.

Welsh, Sandy, Myrna Dawson, and Annette Nierobisz. 2002. "Legal Factors, Extra-Legal Factors, or Changes in the Law? Using Criminal Justice Research to Understand the Resolution of Sexual Harassment Complaints." *Social Problems* 49: 605–623.

Weyher, L. Frank and Maurice Zeitlin. 2005. "Questioning 'Supply and Demand': Unions, Labor Market Processes, and Interracial Inequality." *Labor History* 46 (1): 19–36.

Williams, Katherine and Charles A. O'Reilly. 1998. "Demography and Diversity: A Review of 40 Years of Research," in B. Staw and R. Sutton (Eds). *Research in Organizational Behavior*. Greenwich, CT: JAI Press.

Wong, Kent and May Chen. 1998. 'The Challenge of Diversity and Inclusion in the AFL-CIO,' in G. Mantsios (Ed.). *A New Labor Movement for the New Century*. New York, NY: Monthly Review Press.

Zellner, Arnold. 1962. "An Efficient Method of Estimating Seemingly Unrelated Regressions and Tests for Aggregation Bias." *Journal of the American Statistical Association* 57: 348–368.

5

Training for Business Success: How Diversity Training Improves Productivity, Performance, and Fair Promotions

There is a great deal of pessimism about the impact of diversity. Some critics have declared that diversity training programs do not work. This chapter offers an examination of the relationship between the presence of diversity management and training in business organizations and assessments of business performance, business productivity, and fairness in job promotion processes. It shows how, even after taking several organizational characteristics into account, companies that have diversity training are more likely than are their counterparts without diversity training programs to report better productivity. Similarly, business organizations with diversity training programs are more likely than are other business organizations to report higher business performance than their competitors. Also, companies with diversity training are more likely than are companies without diversity training programs to report that their employees believe procedures for determining promotions are fair and equitable.

Diversity as a business necessity has taken on a life of its own.[1] Many companies have crafted broad business cases, created diversity leadership teams, and started diversity initiatives. These efforts, however, have had varying amounts of success. Some organizations and companies introduced programs aimed at addressing workplace diversity in the early 1990s. But many of these efforts failed to move beyond a "political correctness" agenda and, in many cases, had negative outcomes among workforce members. Failure to truly link diversity efforts to core organizational management issues proved to cast diversity programs as special ventures outside of central management concerns.[2]

Diversity as a business enhancement tool is relatively new. There is a steep learning curve, and like other long-term efforts to bring about change, there are considerable challenges, pitfalls, and problems.[3] So, despite a growing body of work that documents that diversity pays,[4] there is a great deal of pessimism about the impact of diversity. In part, because of the varying degrees of success, some have raised questions about whether diversity matters. Critics are skeptical about the benefits of diversity.[5] They believe that proponents of diversity efforts too often overlook the major costs of diversity. There is also the suggestion that more diversity is associated with inferior quality because it gives positions to less qualified people or puts people in jobs for which they are not prepared or suited.[6] In short, critics of diversity suggest that group differences result in group conflict and its attendant costs. As a consequence, skeptics have questioned the true impact of diversity training programs upon business organizations. Indeed, some critics have gone as far as to declare that diversity training programs do not work.[7] Thus, one can legitimately question what effect, if any, diversity management has on assessments of business performance, assessments of business productivity, and assessments of fairness in the job promotion process.

Diversity Training and Managing Diversity

Diversity training refers to all the strategies that enable us to develop diversity consciousness. Through diversity training, we develop awareness, understanding, and a variety of skills in the area of diversity. In this book, we refer to such skills as diversity skills. Among these are flexible thinking, communication, teamwork, and leadership skills, as well as the ability to overcome personal and social barriers. Diversity training takes many forms. It is something we can initiate and control, such as reading a book, volunteering to help others in need, attending a workshop, and exchanging ideas about diversity issues with thousands of people over the Internet. Diversity training usually focuses on "managing diversity" (i.e., how relationships among different people can be improved and understood to better the organization as a whole).[8] It is more than just an acquired skill. It involves creating an environment that allows all employees to contribute to organizational goals and to experience personal growth. The key is to help employees reach their full potential by creating an environment that will allow them to be motivated, productive, and beneficial for the organization.

Why do people at all levels and in all positions need diversity skills? How do these skills affect productivity? Why do CEOs of large and growing companies believe diversity is essential to their ongoing success? At the organizational level, the advantages of having a diversity-conscious workforce are clear. Diversity consciousness generates innovative responses to challenges. In dealing with technological advances and social and economic changes, there is less reliance on tradition and more of a focus on creative problem solving. In the business world, the outcome is typically better products and services, new customers, and expansion of existing markets. For example, companies often change their marketing strategies as they become more aware of the buying power of different types of minorities.

Effective diversity training also helps with bringing about better communication. It is not enough to have employees with diverse talents and backgrounds. With better communication skills and a stronger commitment to the group, teams are better able to maximize their collective talent. When they put team goals first, they can reach consensus on their goals and roles. Without effective communication, teamwork suffers and talent is wasted. An example of this is "groupthink," which occurs when team members go along with other members of the group without thinking critically about how best to achieve the goals and expectations of the group. This, in turn, can limit understanding of an issue in its full complexity. Groupthink is a great challenge for homogeneous groups. When group members share similar backgrounds and beliefs, group cohesion and conformity can become ends in themselves. People often fail to think critically and independently, as they are eager to agree with what appears to be the consensus of the group. In contrast, diverse groups in which some members think outside the box may come up with solutions to problems that are fundamentally different. Critical diversity, then, will make group members more likely to express ideas that may run counter to groupthink. With effective diversity training, team members are more likely to express different ways of approaching problems without feeling that their contributions will be dismissed as being far-fetched and idealistic. In groups lacking diversity or effective diversity training, members may end up going along with the group because they do not want to "rock the boat." Unfortunately, this group dynamic is all too common in work teams, and it often produces mediocre or insufficient solutions to difficult problems.

Effective diversity training also makes it more likely that organizations will be able to recruit and retain top diverse employees. Those organizations with the best reputations for attracting and maintaining inclusive and talented members will be at an advantage in terms of recruiting and keeping the best talent. The consequences of limiting the talent pool are obvious. Organizations that do not make room for the full spectrum of talent often deny themselves some of the best members.

Organizations with critical diversity and effective diversity training are also less likely to incur the costs of discrimination. Discrimination is very expensive. It creates conflict, siphons off people's talents and energies, and leads to the underutilization of human potential. It deprives companies of the talent and diversity they need to compete effectively.

Effective diversity training can also lead to greater productivity. When employees feel valued, they usually are more productive. This is the rationale behind "managing diversity." Managing diversity does not imply control or manipulation; rather, it means creating an environment that enables everyone to contribute his or her full potential. People who develop their diversity consciousness are more valued employees. They can help members of any organization work together to improve the quality of their product or service. This, in turn, will increase profits. Therefore, the importance of diversity consciousness is not some "feel good" issue. It relates directly to the "bottom line"—productivity and profit.

Diversity Training in the Workplace

Diversity training consists of activities aimed at promoting awareness, knowledge, and building the skills necessary for operating in a diverse environment. The style and content of such activities often depends on organizations' definitions of diversity and their commitment to effective training. Diversity training activities might include demonstrating to managers how to construct and fairly conduct performance evaluations of employees from different cultures. It might also include cross-cultural programs that assist employees who are attempting to understand customs that differ from their own.

Today, diversity training has become an important administrative function in companies seeking to respond to change. New government legislation and demographic changes in the available labor pool have led large organizations to include women and people of color and to reconcile intergroup tensions.

Diversity trainers use their expertise in conflict resolution, in preparing organizations for increases in racial, ethnic, cultural, and gender diversity, and in preparing employees for international work. They also help organizations to safeguard against harassment and unfair employment lawsuits, and to take advantage of employee diversity to increase productivity. They may also conduct cultural audits, help manage sexual attraction and romantic relationships in the workplace, and develop competencies needed to exploit the international marketplace. It is conceivable, however, that diversity training can cause more harm than good to an organization or its individual employees.

Organizations managing successful diversity initiatives conduct diversity training. Such training can vary greatly. Some critics see diversity training as little more than "political correctness" and a feel-good activity that does little to expose behaviors and issues related to oppression and discrimination at the individual, interpersonal, group, and organizational levels. At their best, however, diversity training programs should help participants understand themselves and others, and to build skills to address issues that are sometimes uncomfortable. Diversity training should not humiliate or shame people into acting. Rather, through a well-designed methodology, it should allow them to understand the fundamental flaws of oppressive behavior for themselves and those who are oppressed. Such interventions, when correctly structured, are initiatives aimed at improving organizational effectiveness and efficiency. They seek to identify and implement diversity efforts that will improve the organization and create management accountability for diversity issues. A variety of interventions can be introduced to include human resource, strategic planning, and management initiatives. Human resource interventions may involve revising job descriptions, reviewing job application processes, or adjusting job evaluation systems.

Incorporating diversity in the workplace involves more than internal policy changes. It also involves an ideological shift in the acceptance of a diverse workforce. It is essential that employers are willing to establish their work environments in ways that allow their employees to exercise their true talents, contribute to the goals of the organization, and maximize their personal potential as workers.

Incorporating and maintaining a diverse workplace requires employers to expand their ability to enhance the relationships between individuals from different cultural, political, and racial backgrounds. Understanding how employers manage diversity is significant. Given the aggravation that many employees feel about affirmative action—this includes both those with positive and negative feelings toward affirmative action—and the cultural climate that makes it possible for employees to express pride in their race and cultural beliefs, it is essential that within a global economy, organizations manage diversity effectively.[9]

There are two basic assumptions that underlie the notion that organizations must manage diversity well. First, when organizations manage diversity effectively, this truly provides an economic and competitive edge in the marketplace. Second, if individuals remain resistant to the idea of a diverse workforce, this can lead to breakdowns in group cohesion and productivity. Therefore, the effective management of workplace diversity should lead to greater tolerance, productivity, and an increase in overall organizational profitability.[10]

In *Managing Diversity: The Courage to Lead,* Elsie Cross draws on her experience to describe what a company needs in order to develop effective diversity strategies—and why some strategies work better than others.[11] She points out that after the publication of the Hudson Institute report, *Workforce 2000,* many organizations and consultants who had not recognized that these were important issues, or that their importance had increased exponentially as a result of significant changes in national demographics, began to explore the meaning of "managing diversity" and to develop "diversity programs." As the needs of organizations grew, the number of consultants and trainers eager to address these needs also increased rapidly. The popular press got wind of some of the less impressive approaches and began to attack the entire enterprise.

By the late 1990s, the idea of managing diversity had become so confused that we often regretted having begun to use the term in the first place. What are some of the elements of this general confusion? One common theme in some approaches is that "diversity is about all kinds of difference." As we suggested in Chapter 2, in our view, this takes us down a dead-end road. Surely, the goal of management, in general, is just that: "managing all kinds of difference." But what we need from a field that is called "managing diversity" are theories and factually based best practices that help organizations to reduce discrimination and enable employees who are increasingly diverse by race, gender, sexual orientation, and ability to work together effectively. Managers not only need to be competent in basic management skills, they need to learn how to apply those skills competently.

Because managers in this country have been overwhelmingly White, male, straight, and from the middle or upper classes, management theory and practice have not usually addressed issues of race, gender, sexual orientation, class, and so forth. It was often expected that women and people of color would serve in the lower ranks of the organization, and that those people who made their way up through the hierarchy would be other White men. Managing middle-class, straight White men, therefore, might have seemed like a realistic approach to managing. But now, most organizations realize that they need to reach out to people who are not middle-class, straight White men. They recognize the need to hire, train, develop, and promote people who come from various backgrounds. Thus, those in positions of authority within organizations need to learn how to avoid discriminating against, harassing, demeaning, or overlooking those who differ from themselves. They must learn to recognize that the "differences," although observable in gender and skin color, are differences in experiences—not in innate intellectual, mechanical, spatial, or other abilities.

As Cross points out, "because we are all human, and, in our humanity, more alike than different, those who are in leadership positions must learn how to see the sameness, while at the same time not attempting to overlook or downplay the importance of the differences in our experiences."[12]

What happens when people who have no experience and no training in working with people who are different from them—and who have negative feelings and attitudes about their differences—become responsible for managing in heterogeneous settings? They usually will behave and manage in ways that are familiar to them. For example, a typical response might be that the White male manager who is confronted with the responsibility of managing women or people of color (or gays and lesbians or people with disabilities) will not want to acknowledge differences. This may be true even though every minute that he is in the presence of someone different— a Black woman, for example—he will be aware of the differences. He will assume that the appropriate behavior in this situation is for him to pretend that he is "color blind" and "gender neutral" and that he can and should treat this woman in the same way that he treats another White man. This seems to him like the fair, principled, and logical way to behave. But taking this attitude—pretending—means that this manager has no way of understanding that there may be dynamics between him and the other person that would create negative feelings in her. He will not understand that he has expectations about that person's behavior—about that person's very being—that he communicates very clearly, even while he is trying to be impartial and fair. If he is working hard to pretend that there is no difference, he is likely to be patronizing or even demeaning. At some level, he almost certainly assumes that she is less capable than he is—and less capable than the other White men with whom he is accustomed to working.

What do managers need to know and do in order to create the harmonious, productive workplaces that organizations want? At a minimum, they need to understand the sociopolitical and historical realities of discrimination and oppression. They also need knowledge of how organizations work and how they can change. It is also useful for them to have experience and competence in helping organization members learn. They need an understanding of themselves and how they relate to others, especially across differences of race, gender, sexual orientation, and ability. It is important to stress that all of these are subjects that can be learned. Diversity training can offer such skills.

Often, the person chosen to head up an organization's diversity effort is not likely to have direct access to power, authority, and the ability to influence decisions that directly affect the organization's financial performance. But it is clear that the person who leads in this effort should understand what the business goals of the organization are. They should understand why it is important to their company to resolve its problems concerning racism, sexism, heterosexism, and so forth. The organization needs someone with a solid understanding of the historical and sociopolitical facts of oppression and discrimination that undergird many diversity efforts, as well as someone who understands how organizations work and the functions and goals of the organization.

People are not blank slates when they come to organizations. They bring their experiences, knowledge, and the influences of their world. Around such sensitive issues as race, gender, and sexuality, it is important that diversity training be guided by a qualified diversity trainer who knows about group dynamics and intergroup relations. These are not skills and experiences that can be acquired by just reading about them. They must also be learned within group settings, and they are enhanced when they are guided by experienced trainers who are tuned in to the difficulties surrounding diversity. Such learning also requires more than logic and intellect. It also requires learning about how we relate to each other. It requires that we go deeper and draw on emotions and feelings.

Learning about Race, Gender, and Other Diversity Topics

The general principles of successful diversity training could be applied to just about any management situation. Everyone needs to be educated and aware of the realities of our society. We all need to know how complex organizations work. And we all need to be familiar with ways of assisting members of organizations in their efforts to gain new information, insights, and skills. But when we are dealing with subject matter and problems caused by oppression and discriminatory behavior, we have to understand the role of our own attitudes, prejudices, and behaviors about race, gender, sexuality, and other forms of difference. Often, coming to grips with these feelings calls for the ability to cope with additional sentiments such as shame and guilt. It also requires that we confront hierarchy, power, and conflict over differences. Unfortunately, these are often deep-rooted psychological issues that are more potent and troubling than any other issue with which managers must deal. And guiding people through such processes of self-examination requires trainers who have already made a great deal of progress on their own journeys toward self-consciousness. Such training also calls for people who are excellent at helping others. Not only is this kind of diversity difficult to master, but it is hard to find.

Few business schools offer courses or even workshops that prepare their students with such skills. While they may occasionally offer courses on organizational behavior or group dynamics, they seldom take the additional step of helping their students become proficient in interpersonal awareness. Such awareness is necessary for applying the principles of group dynamics as they relate to issues of race, gender, sexuality, and other types of difference.

Does Employee-Targeted Diversity Training Really Work?

Given the multiple benefits of having an integrated, well-run and diverse workplace, employers should be flocking toward enhancing their diversity.[13] It appears to be common knowledge within mainstream businesses that increasing diversity is good for the overall profitability of companies.[14] Still, companies must figure out ways to manage diversity effectively inasmuch as research continues to support the notion that racial and ethnic diversity are associated with higher rates of conflict between employees, greater reports of employee absenteeism, and reduced group functioning.[15] Overall, those who are critical of theories that suggest that workplace diversity increases economic profitability continue to remain skeptical that diversity initiatives have any real, positive impact upon creating or maintaining the economic performance of business organizations.

Often, those who provide diversity training help their organizations by initially preparing them for shifting proportions in the racial, cultural, and gender climate of their companies. They then use their expertise to help employers to protect themselves against lawsuits and harassment. These efforts guard against liabilities that would serve to deplete profits. Still, despite good intentions, diversity training can have negative consequences. For example, if diversity training programs are poorly managed or if their trainers are poorly prepared, such efforts can lead to emotional distress or inadvertently increase racial and ethnic stereotypes. This could leave both employers and employees with a strong distaste for increasing diversity.

But it is also quite possible that diversity training programs can result in positive outcomes. They may lead to productivity gains because they bring talented people together to work more effectively and productively. Such training programs may also cause co-workers to appreciate the efforts of others who differ from themselves but who, nevertheless, make contributions to the organization. Such efforts may also help employees to better understand how and why various contributions to an organizational effort are to be rewarded.

So, what effect, if any, does diversity management have on assessments of business performance, assessments of business productivity, and assessments of fairness in the job promotion process? Figure 5.1 shows that companies that have diversity training (68 percent) are more likely than are other companies (57 percent) to report higher productivity than their

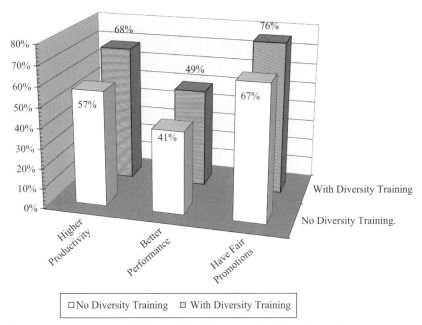

Figure 5.1 Percentage of Firms with Higher Productivity, Better Business Performance, and Fair Promotions by Presence of Diversity Training Programs

competitors. Similarly, business organizations with diversity training programs (49 percent) are more likely than are other business organizations (41 percent) to report better business performance than their competitors. Finally, this chart shows that companies with diversity training (76 percent) are more likely than are companies without diversity training programs (67 percent) to report that their employees believe procedures for determining promotions are fair and equitable.

The results in Figure 5.1 suggest that diversity training programs are associated with such positive outcomes as enhanced business performance, greater business productivity, and assessments of fairness in the job promotion process.

These statistics, however, do not provide much information about the net impact of diversity training upon assessments of business performance, productivity, or the promotion process of organizations. In order to address this issue more rigorously, we again carried out multivariate analysis. Our multivariate analysis examined the relationship between the presence of diversity training programs in firms and assessments of business performance, business productivity, and fairness in the job promotion process.

We found that, net of the size of the organization, the age of the organization, the percentage of workers who were minority, the percentage of workers who were female, and whether the organization was a private corporation, on average, organizations with diversity training programs were more likely than those without such programs to report that they performed better than their competition. Similarly, after taking into consideration the size of the organization, the age of the organization, the percentage of workers who were minority, the percentage of workers who were female, and whether the organization was a private corporation, on average, organizations with diversity training programs were more likely than those without such programs to report that they had higher productivity than their competition. And, finally, after taking into consideration the other factors, companies with diversity training are more likely than are companies without diversity training programs to report that their employees believe procedures for determining promotions are fair and equitable. These results suggest that even after taking other factors into consideration, diversity training programs are associated with such positive outcomes as enhanced business performance, greater business productivity, and assessments of fairness in the job promotion process.

Conclusion

This chapter began with an overview of some of the debates about the nature and effectiveness of diversity training programs. It put forward the proposition that there is a great deal of pessimism about the impact of diversity because of the varying degrees of success in implementing diversity initiatives. Some skeptics have raised questions about whether diversity matters. Moreover, some critics have argued that diversity training programs do not work. Using data from the National Organizations Survey, this chapter offered an examination of the relationship between the presence of diversity management and training in business organizations and assessments of business performance, business productivity, and fairness in the job promotion process. These results from multivariate statistical analysis suggest that even after taking other factors into consideration, diversity training programs are associated with such positive outcomes as enhanced business performance, greater business productivity, and assessments of fairness in the job promotion process. Such results go a long way toward dispelling the notion that diversity training programs do not matter.

This chapter shows that diversity training programs can lead to positive outcomes. They may increase productivity because they bring diverse people together who differ in the talents that they bring to the workplace. Diversity training may enable such people to work together more effectively and productively. Training programs may also lead employees to appreciate the efforts of their co-workers who make different kinds of contributions to the organization. Such efforts may also help employees better understand how and why various contributions to an organizational effort are to be rewarded and, therefore, to have a better sense of how promotions in the company work and why they are fair and equitable.

Some companies already understand that diversity training can be crucial to their bottom lines. Generally, those companies accord diversity directors the same respect that line executives receive. Typically, they also hold these directors to the same kind of accountability. However, in companies where diversity training is erroneously defined as lawsuit-prevention, it may be more difficult to establish the motive behind a diversity director's position. What does an effective diversity director do? Is it necessary that she or he understands the corporate leadership's mission? And is she or he able to implement diversity in the strategic, bottom-line daily business decisions? We believe that diversity training must be tied to issues of fairness and equity. But in today's competitive work environment, highlighting the link between diversity training and business acumen is also critical.

Notes

1 Metzler, 2003
2 Lewis, 1998
3 Metzler, 2003
4 Herring, 2009; Richard, 2000; Goncalo and Staw, 2006; Ely and Thomas, 2001; Chicago United, 2005; and van der Vegt, Bunderson, and Oosterhof, 2006
5 Skerry, 2002; Rothman, Lipset, and Nevitte, 2003a; Rothman, Lipset, and Nevitte, 2003b; Tsui, Egan, and O'Reilly, 1992; and Whitaker, 1996

6   Rothman, Lipset, and Nevitte, 2003b
7   Van Kerckhove, 2007
8   Roosevelt, 1991
9   Roosevelt, 1991
10 Collins and Herring, 2008
11 Cross, 2000
12 Cross, 2000: 138
13 Williams and O'Reilly, 1998; and Florida and Gates, 2001, 2002
14 Ryan, Hawdon, and Branick, 2002
15 Skerry, 2002; Tsui, Edan, and O'Reilly, 1992; and Williams and O'Reilly, 1998

References

Chicago United. 2005. *Chicago United's Board Trend Analysis: What Happens to Corporations When Boards are Diverse?: A Review of Eight Corporate Boards of Directors.* Chicago, IL: Chicago United.

Collins, Sharon and Cedric Herring. 2008. "Managing Diversity to Improve Employees' Understanding of Diversity Initiatives in the Workplace." Unpublished Manuscript.

Cross, Elsie Y. 2000. *Managing Diversity: The Courage to Lead.* Westport, CT: Praeger Publishers.

Ely, Robin J. and David A. Thomas. 2001. "Cultural Diversity at Work: The Effects of Diversity Perspectives on Work Group Processes and Outcomes." *Administrative Science Quarterly* 46: 202–228.

Florida, Richard and Gary Gates. 2001. *Technology and Tolerance: The Importance of Diversity to High-Technology Growth.* Washington, DC: The Brookings Institution.

Florida, Richard and Gary Gates. 2002. "Technology and Tolerance: Diversity and High-Tech Growth." *Brookings Review* 20: 32–36.

Goncalo, Jack A. and Barry Staw. 2006. "Individualism-Collectivism and Group Creativity." *Organizational Behavior and Human Decision Processes* 100: 96–109.

Herring, Cedric. 2009. "Does Diversity Pay?: Racial and Gender Composition and the Business Case for Diversity". *American Sociological Review* 74: 208–224.

Lewis, Richard, Jr. 1998. "Why Diversity Is Important to Organizations?" Unpublished Manuscript.

Metzler, Christopher. 2003. "Ten Reasons Why Diversity Initiatives Fail." *The Diversity Factor* 11: 2.

Richard, Orlando C. 2000. "Racial Diversity, Business Strategy, and Firm Performance: A Resource Based View." *Academy of Management Journal* 43: 164–177.

Roosevelt, Thomas, Jr., 1991. "The Concept of Managing Diversity." *The Best of the Bureaucrat* 2: 41–44.

Rothman, Stanley, Seymour Martin Lipset, and Neil Nevitte. 2003a. "Does Enrollment Diversity Improve University Education?" *International Journal of Public Opinion Research* 15: 8–26.

Rothman, Stanley, Seymour Martin Lipset, and Neil Nevitte. 2003b. "Racial Diversity Reconsidered." *The Public Interest* 151: 25–38.

Ryan, John, James Hawdon, and Allison Branick. 2002. "The Political Economy of Diversity: Diversity Programs in *Fortune* 500 Companies." *Sociological Research Online* (May).

Skerry, Peter. 2002. "Beyond Sushiology: Does Diversity Work?" *Brookings Review* 20: 20–23.

Tsui, Ann S., Terri D. Egan, and Charles A. O'Reilly. 1992. "Being Different: Relational Demography and Organizational Attachment." *Administrative Science Quarterly* 37: 549–579.

van der Vegt, Gerben S., J. Stuart Bunderson, and Aad Oosterhof. 2006. "Expertness Diversity and Interpersonal Helping in Teams: Why Those Who Need the Most Help End Up Getting the Least." *Academy of Management Journal* 49: 877–893.

Van Kerckhove, Carmen. 2007. "Diversity Training Doesn't Work. Here's Why." Unpublished Manuscript.

Whitaker, William A. 1996. *White Male Applicant: An Affirmative Action Expose.* Smyrna, DE: Apropos Press.

Williams, Katherine and Charles A. O'Reilly. 1998. "Demography and Diversity: A Review of 40 Years of Research," in B. Staw and R. Sutton (Eds). *Research in Organizational Behavior.* Greenwich, CT: JAI Press.

6

Gendered Jobs and Opportunities

In popular language, the "good old boys" club has come to describe a system of social cronyism that is used to exclude those who are not part of the inner circle of friends or acquaintances of decision-makers. Historically, such good old boys clubs excluded women and people of color. The basic idea behind such exclusion was that, in offering better deals to friends, good old boys could reinforce traditional power dynamics and facilitate the success of their friends and acquaintances over others.[1]

While it is clear that the good old boys club still exists, some would argue that women have come a long way in the last 50 years. For example, they comprised less than 5 percent of those in professional-managerial roles in the early 1970s; today, women make up nearly 50 percent of those in professional-managerial positions. However, women still make only 76 cents to the dollar of men, and they constitute 12 percent of boardroom seats and 16 percent of corporate officers. Women are still much more likely than are men to be the victims of sexual harassment on the job, as half of working women report experiencing sexual harassment at some point.[2] Moreover, despite women's increasing participation in the labor force, they are still concentrated in certain sectors of the labor market and within certain fields within those sectors.[3] The finer the distinctions in occupational categories researchers use, the more gender segregation they find.[4] Attempts to explain these patterns of occupational segregation by gender have focused on both "supply-side" and "demand-side" factors.[5] While it is probably true that both socialization[6] and employers' "tastes for discrimination"[7] play roles in these patterns, the relative importance of these factors is not clear.

It may be true that men and women are socialized to rank various job attributes differently, but research shows that women's work role motivations have begun to converge toward those of men.[8] So what about when men and women give the same priority to the same job attributes? Do they then end up in the same kinds of jobs? In this chapter, we examine the role that five general work attributes play in determining whether men and women will work in female-typed, male-typed, or sex-balanced occupations. In addition, because there have been changes in the social and structural arrangements in the labor market over the last few decades, we also examine changes in the way that job attributes have influenced the kinds of occupations in which men and women work.

The existence of occupational segregation is not new, as it has been reported to exist at least since the work of Edgeworth.[9] Still, while there is an extensive literature on the effects of such occupational segregation,[10] far less analysis exists on the causes of occupational segregation by gender in the labor market; therefore, far less information is available about what can be done to rectify it.

In this chapter, we review some of the leading explanations for gender segregation in the workplace and in organizations more generally. We explain why the workplace and opportunities in American society more generally are gendered. We also examine some of the implications of these gendered patterns for such outcomes as sexual harassment in the workplace. Finally, we offer some recommendations for reducing workplace segregation and related problems such as sexual harassment.

Overview of Existing Theoretical Formulations: Human Capital Theories

During the last three decades, several studies have explored why it is that women participate in the labor force as they do.[11] These analysts differ over what they see as being the central basis for decisions about how and why men and women participate in the labor market.

"Human capital" theory is a conceptual framework that looks at the rational use of human resources. The concept of human capital refers to the productive capabilities of human beings. It is the skills or productive capacities that people have. More specifically and precisely, human capital embraces the abilities and expertise of men and women that have been acquired at some cost and that can command a price in the labor market because they are useful in the productive process.

Researchers using the human capital perspective often contend that the concentration of women in low-paying jobs is a process of self-selection.[12] Individual employees, according to this explanation, "have a set of indifference surfaces between wages and non-pecuniary job characteristics."[13] Workers possess utility functions in which job attributes such as wages, intrinsic rewards, and working conditions enter the process of preparation for and selection of occupations.[14] The economy, in turn, provides a means by which workers can obtain employment in firms that provide them with job characteristics that most appeal to them, whether they care more about working conditions, intrinsic rewards, or wages. Workers' decisions depend on such economic considerations as the market value of their work and the value they place on their time outside the market.[15] The value of their labor in the marketplace is determined by how much they have invested in themselves in terms of such human capital attributes as schooling, job training, and healthcare. If, on the one hand, people value their time outside the labor market more than the wages they would receive in the market, they will pursue duties that will permit them to have greater scheduling flexibility or leisure time. If, on the other, they care more about maximizing monetary income, they will devote most of their time to activities in the paid labor market doing those kinds of assignments that will bring financial gratification. For the most part, this model assumes that a person's decision to supply labor is fundamentally economically based, though some will at times trade "monetary" income for "psychic" or other kinds of income.

A basic assumption made by human capital and other supply-side theorists is that women are more likely than are men to self-select into occupations that facilitate departure and re-entry into the job market because of home responsibilities. Solomon Polachek's human capital explanation of women's labor force choices, for example, suggests that women self-select themselves into occupations with characteristics which will enable them to move in and out of the labor market with minimal opportunity costs.[16] The implication here is that women are more likely to look for jobs that allow them greater flexibility so they can accommodate their domestic responsibilities. Thus, the human capital model suggests that, given the constraints of family responsibilities and the trade-off between psychic and monetary income, women will choose those occupations that are relatively easy to re-enter after labor force withdrawals, provide flexible work hours, and have little in the way of wage penalties for intermittent labor force participation. Men will be less likely to choose such occupations. Thus, proponents of the human capital model maintain that wage and other sex-based inequalities would be greatly reduced if more similarities existed between men and women in their job characteristic preferences.[17]

Structural Explanations of Labor Market Outcomes

There are, of course, other explanations of the differences in men's and women's labor market participation. Indeed, it could be argued that it is not self-selection *per se* that is the ultimate source of the linkage between gender and job type. Instead, it is possible that "gender structuring" of jobs, employers' stereotypical beliefs about appropriate "men's jobs" and "women's jobs," employers' "tastes for discrimination," "statistical discrimination," "labor market segmentation," institutional and organizational practices, and other mechanisms all act to steer women into stereotypical "women's jobs" and men into stereotypical "men's jobs."

"Gender structure" models, for example, argue that there is a "gender-structuring" of organizations that affects the contours and dynamics of internal labor markets, evaluation criteria, distributional processes, and disparate treatment of male and female incumbents in jobs.[18] Because organizational practices help define gender relations, organizations are gendered. Men's outlooks act as the basis for both formal and informal organizational structures, and hierarchical arrangements in organizations help to validate masculine styles of authority. Moreover, there are aspects of personnel practices within business organizations that systematically devalue women in the workplace, generate gender bias in performance evaluations, and define skill and merit in ways that are antithetical to the interests of most women. So, patriarchal assertions about the gendered division of labor guide organizational routines and accompany expectations about work performance. These pronouncements and expectations, in turn, serve to reinforce the idea that women should be encouraged to do certain kinds of jobs and prevented from doing others.

The main source of occupational segregation in the labor market, then, is discrimination against women. The subordinate position of women in this society benefits men who thereby obtain greater economic, political, and social power. These economic advantages lead to differences in power and prestige that justify and make it possible for the next round of economic inequality. Men, therefore, have a vested interest in maintaining their gendered advantages. They are not just passive recipients of organizational advantages; rather, they actively reproduce their dominance on a daily basis. As a result, inequalities between men and women are perpetuated long after they serve any functional purpose.

There are other factors that are potentially related to sex segregation in the labor market. For example, "labor market discrimination" theories provide reasons for believing that race and ethnicity are important determinants of occupational sex-type, as racial and ethnic minorities are posited to have less access to higher status (typically male) occupations.[19] Similarly, "labor market segmentation" theories suggest that women are less likely than men to be employed in the high-wage, good-benefits manufacturing sector and more likely to work in the service sector.[20] "Family structure" explanations also provide reasons for believing that married men and women, as well as those with young children, will have labor force commitments that differ from those of their unmarried and childless counterparts.[21] In addition, "role theory" provides reasons for anticipating that the work roles of people's mothers will influence the kind of work their offspring will pursue.[22] There are also reasons to believe that over the past two decades, there has been a decline in patriarchal ideologies and other mechanisms used to restrict the access of women to certain jobs.[23] Finally, it is possible that such factors as class, region, and religion will influence the kinds of occupations men and women undertake. In our analysis, we provide statistical controls for these and other potential correlates of sex-type of occupation.

Another factor that could be considered a subcategory of discrimination theories is sexual harassment. As mentioned above, women are far more likely than are men to report that they have been the victims of sexual harassment. Harassment victimization is associated with the gender composition of the workplace.[24] In other words, gender diversity has implications for the incidence of sexual harassment and, potentially, for the occupational choices that men and women make.

The human capital model and structural explanations of occupational segregation are complementary in that they focus on different factors that would lead women to be concentrated in stereotypically female occupations. They do, however, make appreciably different predictions about the sources of occupational segregation by sex. For the human capital perspective, to the degree that men and women value different job attributes, they will hold different kinds of jobs. Implicit in this prediction, however, is the idea that once men and women come to value the same job attributes (by whatever process and for whatever reasons), they will seek similar kinds of occupations. These effects should be net of other factors that lead to variations in occupational type.

In contrast, to the degree that structural explanations see normative and structural barriers that block women's access to traditionally male occupations, they predict that even when men and women come to value the same job attributes (by whatever process and for whatever reasons), men and women will still end up in different kinds of jobs because of the tendency of gendered institutions to steer women into certain "female jobs" and away from "male jobs." These effects should also be net of other factors that predict variations in occupational type. Below, we briefly review some of the pertinent findings about the claims of these perspectives.

Findings from Previous Studies

Available research provides conflicting findings about why women and men end up in different kinds of jobs and about which kinds of job-related rewards are preferred by whom. For example, studies in the 1970s and 1980s looking at gender differences in which job characteristics are most highly ranked found that men tended to prefer extrinsic characteristics such as wages and fringe benefits. In contrast, women tended to prefer such intrinsic job characteristics as co-worker relations, opportunities to help others, and comfort and convenience.[25] In contrast, a slightly later study by Jack Martin and Sandra Hanson found no sex differences in the importance placed on intrinsic and extrinsic reward characteristics.[26] They found that intrinsic job rewards have a stronger impact than extrinsic ones for both male and female workers. While they did find some sex differences in the relationship between the convenience of jobs and job satisfaction, this relationship held true only for women who participated in the labor force in secondary, "non-breadwinning" roles.

Similarly, when it comes to tests of the claims of the human capital perspective, there are conflicting findings. Randall Filer found support for the human capital explanation of job segregation.[27] He found that men and women used similar measures in reporting preferred job attributes and that differences in wages were a function of different job characteristics. Men's jobs tended to be more demanding and hazardous than the jobs of women. Women's jobs, in contrast, tended to have greater supervision, better co-worker relations, less commuting time, and hours that are more flexible. As a result, Filer concluded that any differences in wages between men and women were due to differences in job characteristics rather than labor market discrimination.[28]

In a test of Polachek's self-selection explanation, Andrea Beller examined the relationship among selected human capital variables, marital status, number of children, and employment in non-traditional occupations for men and women.[29] When male and female comparisons were made, however, there was little support for Polachek's human capital model. Indeed, Beller found that as women's participation rates approached those of men, their participation in male-typical occupations changed very little.

Other studies by Paula England and her colleagues have found little evidence to support human capital theory's explanation of occupational sex segregation.[30] Moreover, many studies, using various methodological approaches, have found evidence of discriminatory practices by employers.[31] Still, it has not been possible to "prove" that gender-structuring and institutional barriers have played larger roles than self-selection in determining the kinds of jobs in which men and women work. Nor has it been possible to "prove" the opposite. Below, we provide evidence that sheds light on the relative accuracy or inaccuracy of claims about what happens when men and women have similar preferences about which job attributes are most important to them.

Gender Structure and Sex-Typing of Jobs

Do men and women differ in the sex-typing of their jobs? Figure 6.1 shows, not surprisingly, that they do. This figure indicates that while 13 percent of men worked in predominantly female jobs, more than six in ten women

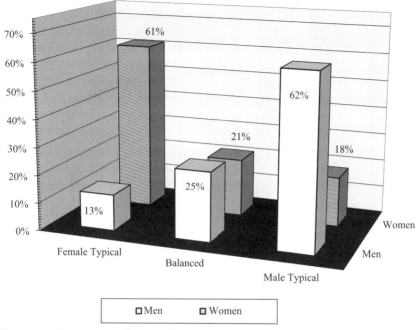

Figure 6.1 Percentage of Men and Women in Sex-Type Jobs

(61 percent) were in such occupations. Similarly, while more than 60 percent of men were in predominantly male jobs, less than 20 percent of women were in such positions. There were, however, smaller differences in the degree to which men and women were employed in sex-balanced occupations, as 21 percent of women compared with 25 percent of men were in such jobs.

According to the human capital perspective, people who value the same job attributes will seek similar kinds of occupations. What about when men and women hold similar beliefs about which job attributes are most important? Figure 6.2 shows that even when men and women held similar outlooks about the most important characteristics of jobs, they worked in vastly different occupations. This figure shows that among those men who ranked income as the most important job attribute, more than 65 percent were employed in predominantly male occupations. In contrast, among women who ranked income as the most important job attribute, less than 25 percent of them worked in predominantly male occupations. The patterns are virtually reversed when we examine the proportions of each sex group employed in predominantly female jobs, as more than 60 percent of women who ranked income as the most important job attribute worked in predominantly female jobs, and less than 20 percent of men who ranked income as most important worked in predominantly female jobs.

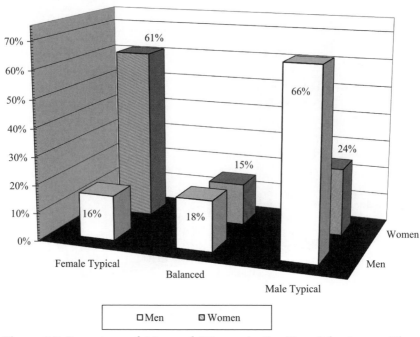

Figure 6.2 Percentage of Men and Women in Sex-Type Jobs Among Those Ranking Income as Most Important Job Attribute

When we examine other job attributes to determine their relationship to job sex type for men and women, we again find dissimilar tendencies among men and women. Even with similar preferences in job attributes, men and women differed substantially in their inclinations to work in predominantly male or predominantly female fields. No matter which of the five attributes men preferred, nearly 60 percent of them tended to work in predominantly male positions. And no matter which of the job features women identified as being most important, nearly 60 percent of them worked in predominantly female positions.

While the relationships among job attributes, occupational segregation, and gender did not support the human capital perspective, some aspects of the results were consistent with the human capital model. In particular, there were substantial differences in the job attributes that were most highly associated with working in predominantly male or predominantly female occupations. For example, while 59 percent of men who ranked the ability to feel a sense of accomplishment on the job as being most important were in predominantly male occupations, 74 percent of those who valued job security most highly were in predominantly male occupations. Similarly, while 58 percent of women who valued job security were in predominantly female occupations, 64 percent of those who valued the opportunity for advancement on the job worked in predominantly female jobs.

Moreover, those job attributes that were associated with increases in the probability of working in predominantly male occupations were generally associated with decreases in the likelihood of working in predominantly female occupations.

The results presented in Figures 6.1 and 6.2 did not take into account other factors that could affect the relationships among occupational sex balance, sex, and preferred job attribute. Nevertheless, these basic patterns were amplified once statistical controls were applied in multivariate (multinomial logistic regression) analysis.

Sexual Harassment and Sex-Typing of Jobs

An additional factor that is related to the gender composition of an organization is sexual harassment.[32] Women in non-traditional jobs experience more sexual harassment than those in traditional jobs.[33] It may be that, as with minority status, "pioneer" status for women results in greater visibility, polarization, and isolation and highlights the incongruity between sex role and work role, leading to harassment.[34] In addition, there is some evidence that women and men working in "sexy climates" report a higher incidence of sexual harassment[35] and the fact that male-dominated workplaces tend to be more sexualized[36] may explain the high incidence of sexual harassment found in male-dominated work environments. Also, women in traditional and non-traditional jobs experience different types of harassment. Harassment in traditional fields is more likely to involve the threat of a woman losing her job for non-compliance, while women in non-traditional fields are more likely to experience sexually demeaning work environments. Similar to the effect of sex segregation at the job level, the sex ratio of the work group also appears to influence the incidence of unwanted sexual behavior. Most studies show that the incidence of harassing behavior increases when the proportion of men in the work group increases.[37] There is, however, evidence that suggests that the incidence of sexual harassment does not differ much in predominantly male and predominantly female departments.[38] We will examine whether (and under what conditions) the gender composition of organizations predicts sexual harassment. In particular, we will test the idea that there will be a higher incidence of sexual harassment in organizations and work groups with higher proportions of men than in gender-balanced or predominantly female organizations and work groups.

Another aspect of the organizational context that may influence the incidence of sexual harassment is the organizational climate with regard to sexual harassment. There is some evidence that organizations that support, allow, or accept sexual harassment are more likely to have a higher incidence of unwanted sexual behaviors.[39] In addition, women and men working in "sexy climates" or organizations in which the management is non-responsive to sexual harassment concerns also report higher frequencies of sexual harassment.[40] The presence and accessibility of internal complaint processes may also have an impact upon incidence. The lack of such procedures may produce feelings of immunity among potential harassers. In turn, this may lead to higher rates of sexual harassment.[41] The existence of such formal procedures may be associated with other factors that reflect the organizational climate.

Environments that do not discourage unwanted sexual behaviors tolerate sexual harassment by not taking sexual harassment reports seriously. Such settings may inhibit filing of formal complaints, as members of such organizations are likely to have negative expectations about the reporting process and general organizational support.[42] Whistle-blowing research also indicates that observers of unethical behavior are less likely to report such behavior if they believe top management is unlikely to correct the wrongdoing.[43] The perceived responsiveness of an organizational policy may also affect whether a target reports behavior internally or seeks advocacy outside the organization.[44] In their study, Donald Maypole and Rosemarie Skaine found a general expectation among their respondents that sexual harassment policies are not effective; as a result, those respondents rarely filed complaints.[45] Normative beliefs an individual holds about the organizational reporting policy will influence reporting. Thus, failure by an organization to resolve a number of sexual harassment complaints will effectively inhibit future reporting behavior.[46]

The influence of different aspects of reporting processes on the likelihood of filing complaints has not been adequately explored.[47] It is likely that reporting policies that are not well communicated or understood will inhibit reporting.[48] Ironically, therefore, we can expect organizations that have instituted formal complaint processes and sexual harassment training for their staff to receive more sexual harassment complaints than organizations that lack such policies.

According to power theories, formal organizational power and social power account for sexually harassing behavior. Thus, it is logical to expect that decentralized organizations that disperse power will result in a lower incidence of sexual harassment. Barbara Schneider found that departments with decentralized decision-making reported lower incidences of sexual harassment.[49] Based on power theory, we can expect job design arrangements characterized by decentralization, participatory management, worker autonomy, and self-directed work teams to create work environments unfavorable to sexually harassing behavior. It can also be argued that confidence in one's job security will have an impact upon one's willingness to file formal complaints by sexual harassment victims. Employees in organizations that offer little job security or stability are less likely to use the internal grievance process.

In recent decades, there has been an increased tendency on the part of businesses to depend on contingent labor due to competitive pressures and a desire to cut costs. Among contingent labor, there is a relative lack of power and an absence of labor rights and benefits often guaranteed to permanent employees. Additionally, the interactions of contingent labor lack the social control aspects of tight social networks. Thus, we can expect organizations that employ a high proportion of contingent labor to experience more sexual harassment.

Movement toward contingent labor will erode organizational commitment to anti-discriminatory policies, as contingent labor has weak co-worker social networks and little bargaining power. Additionally, movement toward contingent labor may represent a general erosion of commitment to the rights of workers, which is likely to be accompanied by a lack of attention to due process concerns. Thus, we can expect the organizational hierarchy in gender balanced and predominantly female firms to be more responsive to concerns of female employees, in general, and, therefore, to sexual harassment concerns.

Changes in anti-discrimination and anti-harassment structures, variations in levels of job security, the changing nature of work from rigid jobs based on "control" to flexible and self-directed work teams, and the increasing use of contingent labor are elements of organizational climate that create the structural conditions or provide the backdrop in which workers and managers discriminate and respond to discrimination. Arguably, these factors influence discriminatory behavior and organizational and victim responses to sexual harassment and should be incorporated in theoretical models designed to explain these processes.

Are gender composition and organizational climate related to sexual harassment? Is there any tangible evidence that there is a relationship between the gender composition of the organization and the incidence of sexual harassment, the likelihood that it will have sexual harassment training available, and that it will have formal procedures for processing claims of sexual harassment?

Figure 6.3 illustrates the percentage of organizations experiencing sexual harassment, having formal procedures for reporting harassment, and having sexual harassment training for managers by the gender composition of the organization. It shows that 15.9 percent of predominantly male organizations in the sample had episodes of sexual harassment. It also shows that 14.4 percent of predominantly female organizations reported incidents of sexual harassment. In contrast, 31.9 percent of gender-balanced organizations (i.e., between 40 and 66 percent female) had reports of sexual harassment within the last year. This pattern is consistent with the idea that the

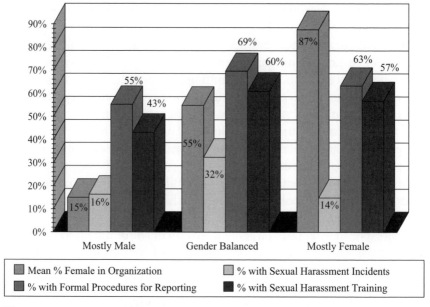

Figure 6.3 Percentage of Organizations Experiencing Sexual Harassment, Having Formal Procedures for Reporting Harassment, and Having Sexual Harassment Training for Managers by Gender Composition of the Organization

incidence of sexual harassment increases as the proportion of women in the organization increases up until the point of equity. After women are a majority of those in the organization, the incidence of sexual harassment apparently decreases as the proportion of workers who are women increases.

One explanation for these findings could be that of thresholds. When women constitute a very small fraction of the organization (i.e., when they are "tokens"), they may be less likely to report incidents of sexual harassment.[50] These women do not expect that they will be supported by others in their efforts at reporting, and they will quit their jobs before reaching the stage of considering filing a formal complaint. But as the proportion of women in the organization approaches parity or balance, men may come to view women as threats to their entrenched social power and formal organizational power, and they may respond by engaging in discriminatory and exclusionary behavior. Nevertheless, in such settings, if women are empowered, they may be more inclined to report occurrences of harassment, and gender-balanced organizations may be more likely to acknowledge such harassment. When organizations become overwhelmingly female, while there may be more inclination to report any occurrences of sexual harassment, it is also likely that such incidents occur less frequently. The results suggest that reports of sexual harassment are most likely when women comprise between 40 and 66 percent of an organization.

Another explanation for the findings could be that gender-balanced organizations provide the most conducive opportunity contexts—based on numbers of men and women—for sexual harassment to occur. Sexual harassment victims are usually women. Perpetrators are usually men. Based only on numbers, organizations with equal numbers of men and women should report the highest incidence of sexual harassment, though the percentage of women experiencing sexual harassment in these organizations could very well be lower than in predominantly male organizations. This type of explanation is buttressed by the finding that organizations with 67 percent or more female employees reported the lowest incidence of sexual harassment.

The flattening of organizational hierarchies and reducing bureaucracy through increasing participation and two-way communication may produce work climates that deter sexual harassment. Organizations using part-time and contract workers who are on another firm's payroll reported higher incidence of sexual harassment than establishments that did not use similar workers. Such contingent labor, in addition to diminished worker rights, appears to create work environments conducive to unwanted sexual behavior. This may occur because its unstable quality is detrimental to close coworker ties and the social control benefits of strong ties.

These results clearly suggest that sexual harassment is related to organizational characteristics such as gender composition or gender diversity. The findings also suggest that such factors may affect discriminatory behaviors and how organizations respond to them.

The human capital perspective argues that concentration of women in low-paying jobs is due to self-selection. Proponents of this view maintain that wage and other sex-based inequalities would be eliminated if greater similarities existed between men and women in their job characteristic preferences. The gender-structuring thesis argues that gendered institutions historically have served to devalue women's work and to steer women toward certain fields and away from others. These mechanisms operate independently of women's aspirations.

The human capital model is correct in its assertion that preferences about job attributes make a difference in the kinds of jobs in which people are employed. Still, the impact of preferred job attributes does not begin to account for the vast differences between men and women in their tendencies to be employed in sex-typed occupations. Thus, the results provided little support for the human capital model's claim that self-selection that matches preferred characteristics of jobs accounts for occupational segregation by sex. These basic patterns were amplified once statistical controls were applied in multivariate analysis.

American society has an entrenched sexual division of labor into which most of us were socialized long before we entered the work world. But with today's women investing more time in the workforce, being more career oriented, less likely to be dependent on a male counterpart for financial security, and having later and smaller families, the assumption that women seek lower paying, less prestigious jobs becomes less tenable.

The increasing number of women in the workforce and their continued integration into the workplace demands that organizations learn what major differences, if any, exist between men and women in the job characteristics they prefer. Even more important is determining the degree to which occupational segregation is due to the fact that women select different jobs from men versus discrimination in the labor market, which places women at a disadvantage in the work world. With respect to understanding the dynamics that undergird occupational segregation by sex, we need to explore more systematically the role of sexual harassment, as well as demand-side factors. To do this, it is necessary to go beyond explanations that focus on self-selection, as there undoubtedly are social, cultural, and social structural factors that play key roles in determining who gets what kind of job.

Notes

1 Simon and Warner, 1992
2 USMSPB, 1995; Fitzgerald et al., 1988; Loy and Stewart, 1984; Adams, Kottke, and Padgitt, 1983; and Schneider, 1987
3 Jacobs, 1989
4 Bielby and Baron, 1984; and Reskin and Roos, 1990
5 Blau and Hendricks, 1979; Beller, 1982; Bridges, 1982; Bielby and Baron, 1986; Treiman and Hartmann, 1981; Cotton, 1988; and Bridges and Nelson, 1989
6 Marini and Brinton, 1984
7 Reskin, 1984; Cohn, 1985; and Bielby and Baron, 1986
8 Herring and Wilson-Sadberry, 1993
9 Edgeworth, 1922
10 Coverman, 1986; Peterson, 1989; Glass, 1990; Wharton and Baron, 1991; and Adler, 1993
11 Cain, 1966; Ashenfelter and Heckman, 1973; Ben-Porath, 1973; Gramm, 1975; Parsons, 1977; Smith-Lovin and Tickamayer, 1978; Smith, 1979; Shapiro and Shaw, 1981; Padavic, 1991; and Herring and Wilson-Sadberry, 1993
12 Mincer, 1962; Becker, 1964; Polachek, 1979, 1981
13 Filer, 1985: 427
14 Polachek, 1979, 1981
15 Mincer, 1962; and Becker, 1964
16 Polachek, 1979, 1981
17 Daymont and Andrisani, 1984
18 Bridges and Nelson, 1989; and Burton, 1991
19 Cotton, 1988
20 Bridges, 1982; and Hodson and England, 1986
21 Bielby and Bielby, 1989; and Herring and Wilson-Sadberry, 1993
22 Powell and Steelman, 1982

23 Herring and Wilson-Sadberry, 1993
24 Vijayasiri, 2008
25 Crowley, Levitin, and Quinn, 1979; Gordon, 1979; Katzell, 1979; Martin and Janson, 1982; and Daymont and Andrisani, 1984
26 Martin and Hanson, 1985
27 Filer, 1985
28 Filer, 1985
29 Beller, 1982
30 England 1979, 1982, 1992; England et al., 1988; Hodson and England, 1986; Reskin, 1984; Reskin and Hartmann, 1986; and Reskin and Roos, 1990
31 Rosen and Jerdee, 1974; Levinson, 1975; Reskin, 1984; Bielby and Baron, 1986; Bridges and Nelson, 1989; and Turner, Fix, and Struyk, 1991
32 Vijayasiri, 2010; Herring and Vijayasiri, 2006; and Vijayasiri, 2008
33 Coles, 1986; Fitzgerald and Shullman, 1993; Lafontain and Tradeau, 1986
34 Knapp et al., 1997
35 Tangri, Burt, and Johnson, 1982
36 Lach and Gwartney-Gibbs, 1993
37 Gutek and Cohen, 1987; Coles, 1986; Ellis, Barak, and Pinto, 1991
38 McKinney, 1990
39 Ellis, Barak, and Pinto, 1991; Fitzgerald and Shullman, 1993
40 Tangri, Burt, and Johnson, 1982; Popovich, 1988
41 Livingston, 1982
42 Gruber, 1989; Gwartney-Gibbs and Lach, 1992; Fitzgerald and Shullman, 1993; Spann, 1990; Popovich, 1988; and Knapp, et al., 1997
43 Miceli and Near, 1988
44 Brandenburg, 1982
45 Maypole and Skaine, 1982
46 Knapp et al., 1997
47 Knapp et al., 1997
48 Livingston, 1982
49 Schneider, 1987
50 Lach and Gwartney-Gibbs, 1993

References

Adams, Jean W., Janet L. Kottke, and Janet S. Padgitt. 1983. "Sexual Harassment of University Students." *Journal of College Student Personnel* 24 (6): 484–490.

Adler, Marina A. 1993. "Gender Differences in Job Autonomy: The Consequences of Occupational Segregation and Authority Position." *Sociological Quarterly* 34: 449–465.

Ashenfelter, Orley and James Heckman. 1973. "Estimating Labor Supply Functions," in G. Cain and H. Watts (Eds). *Income Maintenance and Labor Supply*. Chicago, IL: Rand McNally: 265–278.

Becker, Gary. 1964. *Human Capital*. New York, NY: Columbia University Press.

Beller, Andrea H. 1982. "Occupational Segregation by Sex: Determinants and Changes." *Journal of Human Resources* 17: 371–392.

Ben-Porath, Yoram. 1973. "Labor Force Participation Rates and the Supply of Labor." *Journal of Political Economy* 81: 697–704.

Bielby, William T. and James N. Baron. 1984. "A Women's Place Is with Other Women: Sex Segregation within Organizations," in B. F. Reskin (Ed.). *Sex Segregation in the Workplace: Trends, Explanations, Remedies*. Washington, DC: National Academy Press: 27–55.

Bielby, William T. and James N. Baron. 1986. "Men and Women at Work: Sex Segregation and Statistical Discrimination." *American Journal of Sociology* 91: 759–799.

Bielby, William T. and Denise D. Bielby. 1989. "Family Ties: Balancing Commitments to Work and Family in Dual Earner Households." *American Sociological Review* 54: 776–789.

Blau, Fancine D. and Wallace E. Hendricks. 1979. "Occupational Segregation by Sex: Trends and Prospects." *Journal of Human Resources* 14: 197–210.

Brandenburg, J. B. 1982. "Sexual Harassment in the University: Guidelines for Establishing a Grievance Procedure." *Signs* 8(2): 320–336.

Bridges, William P. 1982. "The Sexual Segregation of Occupations: Theories of Labor Stratification in Industry." *American Journal of Sociology* 88: 270–295.

Bridges, William P. and Robert L. Nelson. 1989. "Markets in Hierarchies: Organizational and Market Influences on Gender Inequality in a State Pay System." *American Journal of Sociology* 95: 616–658.

Burton, Clare. 1991. *The Promise and the Price: The Struggle for Equal Opportunity in Women's Employment.* Sydney: Allen & Unwin.

Cain, Glen. 1966. *Labor Force Participation of Married Women.* Chicago, IL: University of Chicago Press.

Clark, Roger. 1991. "Contrasting Perspectives on Women's Access to Prestigious Occupations: A Cross-National Investigation." *Social Science Quarterly* 72: 20–32.

Cohn, Samuel. 1985. *The Feminization of Clerical Labor in Great Britain.* Philadelphia, PA: Temple University Press.

Coles, F. S. 1986. "Forced to Quit: Sexual Harassment Complaints and Agency Response." *Sex Roles* 14: 81–95.

Cotton, Jeremiah. 1988. "Discrimination and Favoritism in the U.S. Labor Market: The Cost to a Wage Earner of Being Female and Black and the Benefit of Being Male and White." *American Journal of Economics and Sociology* 47: 15–28.

Coverman, Shelley. 1986. "Occupational Segmentation and Sex Differentials in Earnings." *Research in Social Stratification and Mobility* 6: 139–172.

Crowley, Joan E., T. Levitin, and Robert Quinn. 1979. *Facts and Fictions about the American Working Woman.* Ann Arbor, MI: Institute of Social Research.

Davis, James A. and Tom W. Smith. 1990. *General Social Surveys, Cumulative Codebook.* Chicago, IL: National Opinion Research Center.

Daymont, Thomas N. and Paul J. Andrisani. 1984. "Job Preferences, College Major, and the Gender Gap in Earnings." *Journal of Human Resources* 19: 408–428.

Edgeworth, F. Y. 1922. "Equal Pay for Men and Women for Equal Work." *Economic Journal* 32: 431–457.

Ellis, S., A. Barak, and A. Pinto. 1991. "Moderating Effects of Personal Conditions on Experienced and Perceived Sexual Harassment of Women at the Workplace." *Journal of Applied Social Psychology* 21: 1320–1337.

England, Paula. 1979. "Women and Occupational Prestige: A Case of Vacuous Sex Equality." *Signs* 5: 252–265.

England, Paula. 1982. "Failure of Human Capital Theory to Explain Occupational Sex Segregation." *Journal of Human Resources* 17: 358–370.

England, Paula. 1992. *Comparable Worth: Theories and Evidence.* New York, NY: Aldine de Gruyter.

England, Paula and George Farkas. 1986. *Households, Employment and Gender: A Social, Economic, and Demographic View.* New York, NY: Aldine.

England, Paula, George Farkas, Barbara Stanek Kilbourne, and Thomas Dou. 1988. "Explaining Occupational Sex Segregation and Wages: Findings from a Model with Fixed Effects." *American Sociological Review* 53: 544–558.

Filer, Randall K. 1985. "Male–Female Wage Differences: The Importance of Compensating Differentials." *Industrial and Labor Review* 38: 426–437.

Fitzgerald, L. F., S. L. Shullman, N. Bailey, M. Richards, J. Swecker, Y. Gold, M. Ormerod, and L. Weitzman. 1988. "The Incidence and Dimensions of Sexual Harassment in Academia and the Workplace." *Journal of Vocational Behavior* 42: 5–27.

Fuchs, Victor. 1971. "Male–Female Differentials in Hourly Earnings." *Monthly Labor Review* 94: 434–447.

Glass, Jennifer. 1990. "The Impact of Occupational Segregation on Working Conditions." *Social Forces* 68: 779–796.

Gramm, Wendy Lee. 1975. "Household Utility Maximization and the Working Wife." *American Economic Review* 65: 90–100.

Gruber, J. E. 1989. "How Women Handle Sexual Harassment: A Literature Review." *Sociology and Social Research* 74: 3–7.

Gutek, B.A. and A.G. Cohen. 1987. "Sex Ratios, Sex Role Spillover, and Sex at Work: A Comparison of Men's and Women's Experiences." *Human Relations* 40: 97–115.

Gwartney-Gibbs, P.A. and D.H. Lach. 1993. "Sociological Explanations for Failure to Seek Sexual Harassment Remedies." *Mediation Quarterly* 9: 365–374.

Herring, Cedric and Ganga Vijayasiri. 2006. "Employer Reports of Sexual Harassment: Impact of Gendered Organizations and Rights Consciousness." Paper presented at the American Sociological Association Conference, Montreal, Quebec.

Herring, Cedric and Karen Rose Wilson-Sadberry. 1993. "Preference or Necessity? Changing Work Roles of Black and White Women, 1973–1990." *Journal of Marriage and the Family* 55: 314–325.

Hodson, Randy and Paula England. 1986. "Industrial Structure and Sex Differences in Earnings." *Industrial Relations* 25: 16–32.

Jacobs, Jerry. 1989. *Revolving Doors: Sex Segregation and Women's Careers.* Stanford, CA: Stanford University Press.

Janson, P. and Jack K. Martin. 1982. "Job Satisfaction and Age: A Test of Two Views." *Social Forces* 60: 1089–1102.

Katzell, Raymond A. 1979. "Changing Attitudes toward Work," in C. Kerr and J. Roscow (Eds). *Work in America: The Decade Ahead.* New York, NY: Van Nostrand: 35–58.

Knapp, D.E., R.H. Farley, S.E. Ekeberg, and C.L.Z. Dubois. 1997. "Determinants of Target Responses to Sexual Harassment: A Conceptual Framework." *The Academy of Management Review* 22(3): 687–729.

Lach, D.H. and P.A. Gwartney-Gibbs. 1993. "Sociological Perspectives on Sexual Harassment and Workplace Dispute Resolution." *Journal of Vocational Behavior* 42: 102–115.

Lafontain, E. and L. Tradeau. 1986. "The Frequency, Sources, and Correlates of Sexual Harassment among Women in Traditional Male Occupations." *Sex Roles* 15: 433–442.

Levinson, Richard. 1975. "Sex Discrimination and Employment Practices: An Experiment with Unconventional Job Inquiries." *Social Problems* 22: 533–543.

Livingston, J.A. 1982. "Responses to Sexual Harassment on the Job: Legal, Organizational, and Individual Actions." *Journal of Social Issues* 38: 5–22.

Loscocco, Karyn A. and Glenna Spitze. 1991. "The Organizational Context of Women's and Men's Pay Satisfaction." *Social Science Quarterly* 72: 3–19.

Loy, Pamela Hewitt and Lea P. Stewart. 1984. "The Extent and Effects of the Sexual Harassment of Working Women." *Sociological Focus* 17 (1): 31–43.

Madden, Janice. 1973. *The Economics of Sex Discrimination.* Lexington, MA: D.C. Heath.

Marini, Margaret Mooney and Mary Brinton. 1984. "Sex Typing in Occupational Socialization," in B.F. Reskin (Ed.). *Sex Segregation in the Workplace: Trends, Explanations, Remedies.* Washington, DC: National Academy Press: 192–232.

Martin, Jack K. and Sandra L. Hanson. 1985. "Sex, Family Wage-Earning Status, and Satisfaction with Work." *Work and Occupations* 12: 91–109.

Maypole, D.E. and R. Skaine. 1982. "Sexual Harassment of Blue Collar Workers." *Journal of Sociology and Social Welfare* 9: 682–695.

McKinney, K. 1990. "Sexual Harassment of University Faculty by Colleagues and Students." *Sex Roles* 23: 421–438.

Miceli, M.P. and J.P. Near. 1988. "Individual and Situational Correlates of Whistle-Blowing." *Personnel Psychology* 41: 267–281.

Mincer, Jacob. 1962. "Labor Force Participation of Married Women: A Study of Labor Supply," in H.G. Lewis (Ed.). *Aspects of Labor Economics: A Report of the NBER.* Princeton, NJ: Princeton University Press: 63–105.

Newell, C.E., P. Rosenfeld, and A.L. Culbertson. 1995. "Sexual Harassment Experiences and Equal Opportunity Perceptions of Navy Women." *Sex Roles* 32: 159–168.

Padavic, Irene. 1991. "Attractions of Male Blue-Collar Jobs for Black and White Women: Economic Need, Exposure, and Attitudes." *Social Science Quarterly* 72: 33–49.

Parsons, Donald O. 1977. "Health, Family Structure and Labor Supply." *American Economic Review* 67: 703–712.

Peterson, Richard. 1989. "Firm Size, Occupational Segregation, and the Effects of Family Status on Women's Wages." *Social Forces* 68: 397–414.

Polachek, Solomon William. 1979. "Occupational Segregation among Women: Theory, Evidence, and Prognosis," in C.B. Lloyd, E.S. Andrews, and C.L. Gilroy (Eds). *Women in the Labour Market.* New York, NY: Columbia University Press: 137–157.

Polachek, Solomon William. 1981. "Occupational Self-Selection: A Human Capital Approach to Sex Differences in Occupational Structure." *Review of Economics and Statistics* 63: 60–69.

Popovich, P.M. 1988. "Sexual Harassment in Organizations." *Employee Responsibilities and Rights Journal* 1: 273–282.

Reskin, Barbara. 1984. *Sex Segregation in the Workplace: Trends, Explanations, Remedies.* Washington, DC: National Academy Press.

Reskin, Barbara and Heidi Hartmann. 1986. *Women's Work, Men's Work: Segregation on the Job.* Washington, DC: National Academy Press.

Reskin, Barbara and Patricia Roos. 1990. *Job Queues, Gender Queues: Explaining Women's Inroads into Male Occupations.* Philadelphia, PA: Temple University Press.

Rosen, Benson and T.H. Jerdee. 1974. "Effects of Applicant's Sex and Difficulty of Job on Evaluations of Candidates for Managerial Positions." *Journal of Applied Psychology* 59: 511–512.

Schneider, B.E. 1987. "Graduate Women, Sexual Harassment, and University Policy." *The Journal of Higher Education* 58(1): 46–65.

Shapiro, David and Lois B. Shaw. 1982. "Labor Force Attachment of Married Women Age 30 to 34: An Inter-cohort Comparison," in F.L. Mott (Ed.). *The Employment Revolution: Young American Women in the 1970s.* Cambridge, MA: MIT Press: 102–119.

Simon, Curtis J. and John T. Warner. 1992. "Matchmaker, Matchmaker: The Effect of Old Boy Networks on Job Match Quality, Earnings, and Tenure." *Journal of Labor Economics* 10: 306–29.

Smith, James P. (Ed.). 1979. *Female Labor Supply: Theory and Estimation.* Princeton, NJ: Princeton University Press.

Smith-Lovin, Lynn and Ann R. Tickamayer. 1978. "Labor Force Participation, Fertility, Behavior, and Sex Role Attitudes." *American Sociological Review* 43: 541–557.

Spann, J. 1990. "Dealing Effectively with Sexual Harassment: Some Practical Lessons from One City's Experience." *Public Personnel Management* 19(1): 53–69.

Tangri, S.S., M.R. Burt, and L.B. Johnson. 1982. "Sexual Harassment at Work: Three Explanatory Models." *Journal of Social Issues.* 38(4): 33–54.

Treiman, Donald J. and Heidi I. Hartmann. 1981. *Women, Work and Wages: Equal Pay for Jobs of Equal Value.* Washington, DC: National Academy Press.

Turner, Margery Austin, Michael Fix, and Raymond J. Struyk. 1991. *Opportunities Denied, Opportunities Diminished: Discrimination in Hiring.* Report 91–9. Washington, DC: Urban Institute Press.

Vijayasiri, Ganga. 2008. "Reporting of Sexual Harassment: The Importance of Organizational Culture and Trust in the System." *Gender Issues* 25(1): 43–61.

Vijayasiri, Ganga. 2010. *Organizational Context and Sexual Harassment: A Question of Power, Gender, or Rights Consciousness?* Doctoral thesis. Chicago, IL: University of Illinois at Chicago.

U.S. Bureau of the Census. 1992. *Statistical Abstract of the United States: 1991.* Washington, DC: U.S. Government Printing Office.

U.S. Merit Systems Protection Board (USMSPB). 1995. *Sexual Harassment in the Federal Workplace: Trends, Progress, Continuing Challenges.* Washington, D.C.: U.S. Government Printing Office.

Wharton, Amy S. and James N. Baron. 1991. "The Psychological Impact of Gender Segregation on Women at Work." *Sociological Quarterly* 32: 365–387.

7

Continuing Racial and Ethnic Discrimination

To hear much of the political and legal debate in recent years, one might imagine that the issue is whether discrimination in favor of African Americans is justified. However, it is employment discrimination against African Americans, though illegal, that is still at work in America.

In 1996, Texaco settled a case for US$176 million with African-American employees who charged that the company systematically denied them promotions. Texaco originally vowed to fight the charges. But when irrefutable evidence surfaced, Texaco changed its position. The *New York Times* released a tape recording of several Texaco executives referring to Black employees as "niggers" and "Black jelly beans" who would stay stuck at the bottom of the bag. Texaco also ultimately acknowledged that they used two promotion lists—a public one which included the names of Blacks and a secret one which excluded all Black employee names. The US$176 million settlement was then the largest amount ever awarded in a discrimination suit.

Much has changed in American race relations over the past 50 years. In the old days, job discrimination against African Americans was clear, pervasive, and undeniable. There were "White jobs" for which Blacks need not apply, and there were "Negro jobs" in which no self-respecting White person would be found. No laws forbade racial discrimination in employment; indeed, in several states, laws required separation of Blacks and Whites in virtually every public realm. Not only was racial discrimination the reality of the day; there was also widespread support among Whites that job discrimination against Blacks was appropriate. In 1944, 55 percent of Whites admitted to interviewers that they thought Whites should receive preference over Blacks in access to jobs, compared with only 3 percent who offered such opinions in 1972.

Many blatant forms of racism have disappeared. Civil rights laws make overt and covert acts of discrimination illegal. Also, fewer Americans admit to traditional racist beliefs than ever before. Such changes have inspired many scholars and social commentators to herald the "end of racism," and to declare that we have created a color-blind society. They point to declines in prejudice, growth in the proportion of Blacks who hold positions of responsibility, a closing of the earnings gap between young Blacks and young Whites, and other evidence of "racial progress."

But racial discrimination in employment is still widespread; it has gone underground and become more sophisticated. Many citizens, especially Whites who have never experienced such treatment, find it hard to believe that such discriminatory behavior by employers exists. Indeed, 75 percent of Whites in a survey said that Whites were likely to lose a job to a less qualified Black. Nevertheless, there is clear and convincing evidence of such patterns.

In addition to the landmark Texaco case, other corporate giants have made the dishonor roll in recent years. In 2000, a court ordered Ford Motor Company to pay US$9 million to the victims of sexual and racial harassment. Ford also agreed to pay $3.8 million to settle another suit with the U.S. Labor Department involving discrimination in hiring women and minorities at seven of the company's plants. Similarly, in 1999, Boeing agreed to pay $82 million to end racially based pay disparities at its plants. In 2000, Amtrak agreed to pay $16 million to settle a race discrimination lawsuit that alleged that Amtrak had discriminated against Black employees in hiring, promotion, discipline, and training. In addition, in November of 2000, Coca Cola Company agreed to pay more than $190 million to resolve a federal lawsuit brought by Black employees. These employees accused Coca Cola of erecting a corporate hierarchy in which Black employees were clustered at the bottom of the pay scale, averaging $26,000 a year less than White workers.

The list of companies engaged in discrimination against Black workers is long and disturbing. Yet, when incidents of discrimination come into public view, many of us are still mystified and hard pressed for explanations. This is so, in part, because discrimination has become so illegitimate that companies expend millions of dollars to conceal it. They have managed to discriminate without using the blatant racism of the old days. While still common, job discrimination against Blacks has become more elusive and less apparent.

How Common?

Most Whites think that discriminatory acts are rare and sensationalized by a few high-profile cases, and that the nation is well on its way to becoming a color-blind society. According to a Gallup survey, nearly seven in ten Whites (69 percent) said that Blacks are treated "the same as Whites" in their local communities. But the numbers tell a different tale. Annually, the federal government receives about 80,000 complaints of employment discrimination, and another 60,000 cases are filed with state and local Fair Employment Practices Commissions. A major study found that about 60 percent of Blacks reported racial barriers in their workplace in the last year, and a Gallup survey found that one in five reported workplace discrimination in just the previous month.

The results of "social audits" suggest that the actual frequency of job discrimination against Blacks is even higher than Blacks are aware of. Audit studies test for discrimination by sending White and minority "job-seekers" with comparable résumés and skills to the same hiring firms. These audits consistently find that employers are less likely to interview or offer jobs to minority applicants. For example, studies by the Fair Employment Commission of Washington, DC, found that Blacks faced discrimination in one out of every five job interviews, and that they were denied job offers 20 percent of the time. A similar study by the Urban Institute matched equally qualified White and Black testers who applied for the same jobs in Chicago. About 38 percent of the time, White applicants advanced further in the hiring process than equally qualified Blacks. Similarly, a General Accounting Office audit study uncovered significant discrimination against Black and Latino testers. In comparison to Whites, Black and Latino candidates with equal credentials received 25 percent fewer job interviews and 34 percent fewer job offers.

These audit studies suggest that present-day discrimination is more sophisticated than in the old days. For example, discriminating employers do not explicitly deny jobs to Blacks; rather, they use the different phases of the hiring process to discriminate in ways that are difficult to detect. In particular, when comparable résumés of Black and White testers are sent to firms, discriminatory firms will systematically call Whites first and repeatedly until they exhaust their list of White applicants before they approach their Black prospects. They will offer Whites jobs on the spot but tell Blacks that they will give them a call back in a few weeks. These mechanisms mean that White applicants go through the hiring process before any qualified Blacks are even considered.

Discriminatory employers also offer higher salaries and higher status positions to White applicants. For example, audit studies have documented that discriminatory employment agencies will often note race in the files of Black applicants, and steer them away from desirable and lucrative positions. A Fair Employment Commission study found that these agencies, which control much of the applicant flow into white-collar jobs, discriminate against Black applicants more than 60 percent of the time.

Surprisingly, many employers are willing to detail (in confidentiality to researchers) how they discriminate against Black job seekers. Some admit refusing to consider any Black applicants at all. Many others admit to engaging in recruitment practices that artificially reduce the number of Black applicants who know about and apply for entry-level jobs in their firms. One effective way is to avoid ads in mainstream newspapers. In one study of Chicago, over 40 percent of the employers from firms within the city did not advertise their entry-level job openings in mainstream newspapers. Instead, they advertised job vacancies in neighborhood or ethnic newspapers that targeted particular groups, mainly Hispanics or White East European immigrants. For the employer who wants to avoid Blacks, this strategy can be quite effective when employment ads are written in languages other than English, or when the circulation of such newspapers is through channels that usually do not include many Blacks.

Employers described recruiting young workers largely from Catholic schools or schools in White areas. Besides avoiding the public schools, these employers also avoided recruiting from job training, welfare, and state employment programs. Consequently, some job training programs have had perverse, unanticipated effects on the incomes and employment prospects of their African-American enrollees. For instance, research on the impact of such training programs upon the earnings and employability of Black inner-city residents found that those who participated in various job training programs earned less per month and had higher unemployment rates than their counterparts who had not participated in such programs.

Who Suffers?

Generally, no Black person is immune from discriminatory treatment. But there are some factors that apparently make some more vulnerable to discrimination than others. In particular, research has shown that African Americans with dark complexions are likelier to report discrimination—half do—than those with lighter complexions. Job discrimination is also associated with education in a peculiar fashion: Those Blacks with more education report more discrimination. For example, in a Los Angeles study, more than 80 percent of Black workers with college degrees and more than 90 percent of those with graduate-level educations reported facing workplace discrimination. Black immigrants are more likely than are non-immigrants to report discrimination experiences. Residents of smaller communities are more likely than are those of larger ones. And younger African Americans are more likely than are older ones. Rates of job discrimination are lower among those who are married than they are among those who are not wed. Research also shows that some employment characteristics also appear to make a difference: African Americans who are hired through personal contacts less often report discrimination, as do those who work in the manufacturing sector and those who work for larger firms.

Discrimination exacts a financial cost. African Americans interviewed in the General Social Survey who reported discrimination in the prior year earned US$6,200 less than those who reported none. (This penalty is in addition to $3,800 less than Whites that Blacks earned because of differences in educational attainment, occupation, age, and other factors.) A one-time survey cannot determine whether experiences of discrimination lead to low income or whether low income leads to feeling discriminated against. But multivariate research based on data from the Census Bureau that controls for education and other wage-related factors shows that the White–Black wage gap (i.e., "the cost of being Black") has continued to be more than 10 percent—about the same as in the mid-1970s. Moreover, research looking at the effects of discrimination over the life course suggests that there is a cumulative effect of discrimination on wages such that the earnings gap between young Blacks and Whites becomes greater as both groups become older.

How Can There Be Discrimination?

Many economists who study employment suggest that job discrimination against Blacks cannot (long) exist in a rational market economy because jobs are allocated based on ability and earnings maximization. Discrimination, they argue, cannot play a major role in the rational employer's efforts to hire the most productive worker at the lowest price. If employers bypass productive workers to satisfy their racism, competitors will hire these workers at lower-than-market wages and offer their goods and services at lower prices, undercutting discriminatory employers. When presented with evidence that discrimination does occur, many economists will point to discriminators' market monopoly. Some firms, they argue, are shielded from competition that allows them to act on their "taste for discrimination." These economists, however, do not explain why employers would prefer to discriminate in the first place. Other economists suggest that employers may rationally rely on "statistical discrimination." Lacking sufficient information about would-be employees, employers use "average" productivity characteristics of the groups to which the potential employees belong to predict who will make the best workers. In other words, stereotypes about Black workers (on average) being worse than Whites make it "justifiable" for employers to bypass qualified Black individuals. In these ways, those economists who acknowledge racial discrimination explain it as a "rational" response to imperfect information and imperfect markets.

In contrast, most social scientists point to prejudice and group conflict over scarce resources as reasons for job discrimination. For example, racial groups create and preserve their identities and advantages by reserving opportunities for their own members. Racially based labor queues and differential terms of employment allow members to allocate work according to criteria that have nothing to do with productivity or earnings maximization. Those who discriminate against Blacks will often use negative stereotypes to rationalize their behavior after the fact, which, in turn, reinforces racism, negative stereotypes, and caricatures of Blacks.

In particular, labor market segregation theory suggests that the U.S. labor market is divided into two fundamentally different sectors: the primary and the secondary sector. The primary sector is composed of jobs that offer job security, work rules that define job responsibilities and duties, upward mobility, and higher incomes and earnings. These jobs allow their incumbents to accumulate skills that lead to progressively more responsibility and higher pay. In contrast, secondary sector jobs tend to be low-paying, dead-end jobs with few benefits, arbitrary work rules, and pay structures that are not related to job tenure. Workers in such jobs have less motivation to develop attachments to their firms or to perform their jobs well. Thus, it is mostly workers who cannot gain employment in the primary sector who work in the secondary sector. Because race discrimination—not necessarily by employers but at times by restrictive unions and professional associations that fear that the inclusion of Blacks may drive down their overall wages or prestige—plays a role in determining who gets access to jobs in the primary sector. Employers may feel compelled to discriminate. As a consequence, African Americans are locked out of jobs in the primary labor market where they would receive higher pay and better treatment, and they tend to be crowded into the secondary sector.

An alternative explanation of African-American disadvantage in the U.S. labor market is what can be referred to as "structural discrimination." In this view, African Americans are denied access to good jobs through practices that appear to be race-neutral but work to the detriment of African Americans. Examples of such seemingly race-neutral practices would include seniority rules, employers' plant location decisions, policy-makers' public transit decisions, funding of public education, economic recessions, and immigration and trade policies.

Take the seniority rules example. If Blacks are hired later than Whites because they are later in the employers' employment queue (for whatever reason), operating strictly by traditional seniority rules will ensure greater job security and higher pay to Whites than to African Americans. Such rules will virtually guarantee that Blacks, who were the last hired, will be the "first fired" and the worst paid. The more general point is that employers themselves do not have to be prejudiced in implementing their seniority rules for the rules to have the effects of structural discrimination on African Americans. Unequal outcomes are built into the ability to make the rules.

These same dynamics apply when companies decide to locate away from urban areas that have high concentrations of Black residents. They are also in play when policy-makers decide to build public transit that provides easy access from the suburbs to central city job sites but not from the inner city to central city job sites nor from the inner city to suburban job sites. They also occur when public education is funded through local property tax revenues that may be lower in inner city communities where property values are depressed and higher in suburban areas where property values are higher and where tax revenues are supplemented by corporations that have fled the inner city. These dynamics also happen when policy-makers attempt to blunt the effects of inflation and high interest rates by allowing unemployment rates to climb, especially when they climb more rapidly in African-American communities. And they take place when policy-makers negotiate immigration and trade agreements that may lead to lower producer costs but may result in a reduction in the number of jobs available to African Americans in the industries affected by such agreements. Again, in none of these cases do decision-makers need to be racially prejudiced for their decisions to have disproportionately negative effects on the job prospects or life chances of African Americans.

Subordinate racial and ethnic minorities are usually segregated in low-status and low-paying jobs. At the same time, members of the superordinate population are concentrated in high-status, lucrative occupations. Unfortunately, these patterns occur even in organizations that are putatively diverse. Rather than having critical diversity, such organizations have segregated diversity. Social scientists have pointed out that segregation is one of the most often used mechanisms for denying access to economic rewards. Such segregation in organizations serves as a major source of racial and ethnic inequality in organizations.

It is clear that segregation in the labor market has detrimental effects on the socioeconomic positions of racial and ethnic minorities. Still, there are debates about whether concentration of racial and ethnic minorities affects their earnings and those of Whites. In other words, does diversity benefit workers of color? How does it affect White workers? Are there conditions under which racial and ethnic minority groups actually benefit from segregation? For example, when ethnic minorities constitute a numerical majority in an occupational niche, an industry, or a local labor market, can they assume control over the market? Do ethnic enclaves shelter minority groups from the detrimental consequences of discrimination? Are they able to benefit relatively from employment in "segregated ethnic labor markets?" To what degree can earnings inequalities among Whites, Blacks, and Hispanics be attributed to segregation across jobs?

Under conditions of perfect economic competition, minority workers can avoid the detrimental consequences of labor market segregation by changing jobs or by moving from one segment of the labor market to another. In reality, however, such mobility is highly constrained. According to "queuing theory," employers are likely to rank workers according to their desirability on "job queues."[1] Since minority workers are placed at the end of the job queue, employers are reluctant to hire them for high status and lucrative jobs; rather, they tend to hire them into already low-paying jobs.[2] Job segregation, then, is a major source of racial and ethnic inequality in modern societies.

According to the "competition hypothesis," because minority workers find the conditions of work less negotiable than do other workers, they have to render themselves more attractive to employers by "offering" their labor at lower wage rates.[3] That is, in order to get access to lucrative jobs, minority workers are "willing" to supply their labor at a lower cost. When they do so, they trigger a competitive process that results in depressed wages and worse working conditions for all other workers employed in the same labor market. In other words, the presence of minority workers as a source of cheap labor enables employers to reduce wage rates and to suppress the economic benefits of all workers. The mechanisms underlying the process of competition are consistent, indeed, with the theoretical reasoning embodied in the "devaluation" or "degradation" theories.[4] These theoretical models suggest that employers set lower wages in work settings that are predominantly composed of minority workers. This logic is also consistent with economists' propositions that an oversupply of workers belonging to subordinate ethnic minorities depresses wage rates of all workers employed in the labor market, regardless of their ethnic origin.[5] It is also consistent with the idea that a large supply of minority workers provides discriminatory employers with greater opportunities to practice discrimination.[6]

Recent studies have revealed that earnings are suppressed in jobs and occupations in which minority workers are heavily concentrated, and that workers employed in such jobs and occupations suffer from substantial wage penalties.[7] Indeed, the negative association between minority concentration and earnings implies that minority populations earn less and pay penalties due to labor market segregation.

But according to the "minority power hypothesis," when the minority population becomes large enough and reaches a critical mass, it may be able to mobilize resources, develop internal strengths, and gain power to combat discrimination. This hypothesis predicts that a substantial increase in the relative size of the minority population in a workplace is likely to enhance minority workers' negotiating power and, thus, their relative position in the organization. That is, when subordinate groups reach large proportions in a work setting, they are able to accumulate power. They are, thus, in a better position to capture lucrative and prestigious jobs and positions from which they are usually excluded. In other words, the minority power thesis suggests that mono-ethnic labor markets or niche employment can shelter minorities from various forms of ethnic and economic discrimination. While segregation in the labor market excludes subordinate minorities from opportunities and rewards, it can also provide them with temporary protection from discrimination prompted by direct competition with members of the superordinate ethnic group. That is, since members of the dominant ethnic groups are less likely to seek employment in the ethnic economy, competition is minimized. In the absence of competition, minority workers can attain positions that are usually denied them in the outside mainstream economy.[8]

Within the ethnic economy, ethnic solidarity and sentiments replace discriminatory practices against minority workers that prevail elsewhere in the main economy. Although segregation across jobs can shelter minorities from competition and discrimination, this does not mean that ethnic and racial minorities benefit from segregation. Nor are minority populations advantaged in jobs where they are predominant. Nor do they reap higher economic outcomes and greater rewards in such jobs. Rather, segregation is an effective structural mechanism that excludes minorities from equal access to opportunities and rewards. Diversity is a conducive, if not a necessary, condition for competition.

Moshe Semyonov and Cedric Herring distinguished among four types of jobs: predominantly Whites, multi-ethnic (or mixed), predominantly Blacks, and predominantly Hispanics.[9] As Figure 7.1 shows, they found considerable differences among the four types of jobs. Jobs dominated

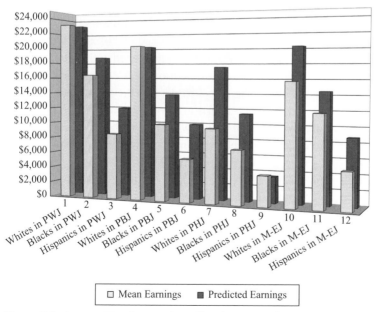

Figure 7.1 Average Earnings and Predicted Earnings by Race/Ethnicity and Racial Composition of Jobs

by White workers are characterized by the highest salaries, by the highest occupational status, and by employees with the highest levels of formal schooling. In contrast, jobs that predominantly employ Hispanics pay the least, have the lowest occupational statuses, and employ workers with the lowest levels of education. Jobs with predominantly Black workers and jobs with multi-ethnic composition are in-between. They also found that within each type of job composition, for the most part, Whites earn the highest wages and have the highest levels of education, while Hispanics earn the least and have the lowest levels of formal education. The data analysis provides only partial support for the hypothesis that ethnic segregation across jobs is responsible for the economic disparities between Whites and minority populations. The findings revealed that workers employed in ethnically segregated jobs are penalized in terms of their earnings when compared with workers employed in jobs dominated by Whites.

The analysis presented by this research underscores significant and meaningful effects of labor market segregation on economic inequality. Had most workers in American society been rewarded like Whites employed in jobs dominated by White workers, their earnings would have increased considerably. This finding holds for all Whites employed in minority-dominated jobs as well as for most Blacks whether employed in or outside White-dominated jobs. That is, relative to Whites, most Blacks are disadvantaged in the attainment of economic outcomes regardless of the ethnic composition of their jobs. The earnings disadvantages for Blacks, however, are considerably more pronounced in ethnically segregated jobs than in jobs dominated by White workers. In contrast, Hispanics employed in ethnic labor markets "benefit" from segregation. The positive effect of job segregation on the economic attainment of Hispanic workers is evident in jobs that are mostly composed of Hispanic workers. In these Hispanic-type jobs, Hispanic workers are advantaged in the attainment of economic outcomes. In the absence of competition with Whites, their earnings in Hispanic-type jobs are higher than the earnings that they would attain in jobs dominated by Whites. That is, in comparison to Whites employed in the White labor market, they are able to attain earnings that are higher than expected on the basis of their lower education, relative youth, and weaker English.

The concept of sheltered (or protected) labor market appears to have some validity in the case of Hispanic workers employed in Hispanic-type jobs. These socioeconomic advantages can be attributed, in large part, to the unique position of Hispanics within the larger economy. Most Hispanic-type jobs operate in an enclave economy providing relative advantages through networks of exchange and support among firms similar to the Cuban economy in Miami.[10] Hispanic job segregation in enclaves becomes a significant resource to Hispanic workers, and the rules according to which these workers are recruited and rewarded differ considerably from mainstream jobs that are predominantly composed of White employees.

The rules by which ethnic and racial minorities achieve socioeconomic status vary substantially from one type of job to another, as well as from one ethnic group to another. Thus, the ethnic composition of jobs and job segregation should be viewed not only as a consequence of the sorting mechanisms of individuals into positions in the labor market, but also as a major cause of socioeconomic and ethnic inequality and of social stratification. Based on these findings, we suggest that more attention should be devoted to studying the underlying mechanisms that dominate the distribution of outcomes and rewards across jobs and ethnic labor markets.

What Can Be Done?

Employment discrimination, overt or covert, is against the law; yet, it clearly happens. Discrimination still damages the lives of African Americans. Therefore, we should strengthen and expand policies designed to reduce discrimination rather than reduce or eliminate them as has recently been occurring. We must shed light on and apply heat to those who engage in discrimination. We can take some modest steps to reduce the incidence and costs of racial discrimination. We must conduct more social audits of employers in various industries of various sizes and locations. In 2000, the courts upheld the right of testers (working with the Legal Assistance Foundation of Chicago) to sue discriminatory employers. We should expand the use of evidence from social audits in lawsuits against discriminatory employers. This provides more information about discriminatory processes, better arms Black applicants, and provides greater deterrence to would-be discriminators who do not want to be exposed. Even when prevention is not successful, the documentation from social audits makes it easier to prosecute illegal discrimination. As in the Texaco case, it has often been through exposure and successful litigation that discriminatory employers mended their ways.

Restrict government funding and public contracts to firms with repeated records of discrimination against Black applicants and Black employees. The government needs to ensure that discriminatory employers cannot use taxpayers' money to carry out their unfair treatment of African Americans. Firms that continue discriminating against Blacks should have their funding and their reputations linked to their performance. Also, as the lawsuits over this issue continue to mount, defense of such practices becomes an expensive proposition. Again, those found guilty of such contemptuous activities should have to rely on their own resources and not receive additional allocations from the state. Such monetary deterrence may act as a reminder that racial discrimination is costly.

We need to redouble affirmative action efforts. Affirmative action consists of activities undertaken specifically to identify, recruit, promote, or retain qualified members of disadvantaged minority groups in order to overcome the results of past discrimination and to deter discriminatory practices in the present. It argues that simply removing existing impediments is not sufficient for changing the relative positions of various groups. And it is based on the premise that to be truly effective in altering the unequal distribution of life chances, it is essential that employers take specific steps to remedy the consequences of discrimination.

We must speak out when episodes of discrimination occur. It is clear that much of the discrimination against African Americans goes unreported because it occurs behind closed doors and in surreptitious ways. Often, it is only when some White insider provides irrefutable evidence that such incidents come to light. It is incumbent upon White Americans to do their part to help stamp out this malignancy.

Now that there are laws forbidding racial discrimination in employment, stamping it out should be eminently easier to accomplish. The irony is that because job discrimination against Blacks has been driven underground, many people are willing to declare victory and, thereby, let this scourge continue to flourish in its camouflaged state. But if we truly want to move toward a color-blind society, we must punish such hurtful discriminatory behaviors when they occur, and we should reward efforts by employers who seek to diversify their workforce by eliminating racial discrimination. This is precisely what happened in the landmark Texaco case, as well as the Coca Cola settlement. In both cases, job discrimination against African Americans was driven above ground, made costly to those who practiced it, and offset by policies that attempted to level the playing field.

Notes

1 Thurow, 1975; Lieberson, 1980
2 Tomaskovic-Devey, 1993; Kaufman, 2002
3 Hodge and Hodge, 1965
4 Kmec, 2003; Catanzarite, 2003; Tomaskovic-Devey, 1993; Huffman and Cohen, 2003
5 Bergmann, 1971
6 Becker, 1971
7 Kmec, 2003; Catanzarite, 2003; Browne et al., 2001; Huffman, 2004
8 Aldrich et al., 1985; Waldinger et al., 1996; Semyonov, 1988; Lewin-Epstein and Semyonov, 1994
9 Semyonov and Herring, 2007
10 Wilson and Martin, 1982; Portes and Jensen, 1987

References

Aldrich, Howard, J. Cater, T. Jones, D. McEvoy and P. Velleman. 1985. "Ethnic Residential Concentration and the Protected Market Hypothesis." *Social Forces* 63: 996–1009.
Becker, Gary. 1971. *The Economics of Discrimination*. Chicago, IL: University of Chicago Press.

Bergmann, Barbara. 1971. "The Effect on White-Income of Discrimination in Employment." *Journal of Political Economy* 79: 294–313.

Browne, Irene., Cynthia Hewitt, Leann Tigges, and Gary Green. 2001. "Why Does Job Segregation Lead to Wage-Inequality among African-Americans? Person, Place, Sector or Skill." *Social Science Research* 30: 473–495.

Catanzarite, Lisa. 2003. "Race-Gender Composition and Occupational Pay Degregation." *Social Problems* 50: 14–17.

Dickinson, Katherine P., Terry R. Johnson, and Richard W. West. 1986. "An Analysis of the Impact of CETA Programs on Participants' Earnings." *Journal of Human Resources* 21: 64–91.

Herring, Cedric (Ed.). 1997. *African Americans and the Public Agenda: The Paradoxes of Public Policy.* Thousand Oaks, CA: Sage Publications.

Hodge, Robert W. and Patricia Hodge. 1965. "Occupational Assimilation as a Competitive Process." *American Journal of Sociology* 71: 249–264.

Huffman, Matt L. and Philip N. Cohen. 2003. "Individuals, Jobs, and Labor Markets: The Devaluation of Women's Work." *American Sociological Review* 68 (3): 443–463.

Huffman, Matt L. 2004. "More Pay, More Inequality? The Influence of Average Wage Levels and the Racial Composition of Jobs on the Black-White Wage Gap". *Social Science Research* 33:498–520.

Kaufman, Robert L. 2002. "Assessing Alternative Perspectives on race and sex employment Segregation." *American Sociological Review* 67: 547–572.

Kirschenman, Joleen and Kathryn Neckerman. 1991. "'We'd Love to Hire Them, But . . .': The Meaning of Race for Employers," in C. Jencks and P. Peterson (Eds). *The Urban Underclass.* Washington, DC: Brookings Institution: 203–232.

Kmec, Julie A. 2003. "Minority Job Concentration and Wages." *Social Problems* 50: 38–59.

Lewin-Epstein, Noah and Moshe Semyonov. 1994. "Sheltered Labor Markets, Public Sector Employment and Socioeconomic Returns of Arabs in Israel." *American Journal of Sociology* 100: 622–651.

Lieberson, Stanley. 1980. *A Piece of The Pie.* Berkeley, CA: University of California Press.

O'Connor, Alice, Chris Tilly, and Lawrence Bobo (Eds). 2001. *Urban Inequality: Evidence from Four Cities.* New York, NY: Russell Sage Foundation.

Portes, Alejandro and Robert L. Bach. 1985. *Latin Journey: Cuban and Mexican Immigrants in the United States.* Berkeley and Los Angeles, CA: University of California Press.

Portes, Alejandro and Leif Jensen. 1987. "What's an Ethnic Enclave?: The Case for Conceptual Clarity." *American Sociological Review* 52: 768–771.

Semyonov, Moshe. 1988. "Bi-Ethnic Labor Markets, Mono-Ethnic Labor Markets, and Socioeconomic Inequality." *American Sociological Review* 53: 255–266.

Semyonov, Moshe and Cedric Herring. 2007. "Segregated Jobs or Ethnic Niches? The Impact of Racialized Employment on Earnings Inequality." *Research in Social Stratification and Mobility* 25: 245–257.

Thomas, Melvin, Cedric Herring, and Hayward Derrick Horton. 1994. "Discrimination over the Life Course: A Synthetic Cohort Analysis of Earnings Differences Between Black and White Males, 1940–1990." *Social Problems* 41: 608–628.

Thurow, Lester C. 1975. *Generating Inequality.* New York, NY: Basic Books.

Tomaskovic-Devey, Donald. 1993. *Gender and Racial Inequality at Work: The Sources and Consequences of Job Segregation.* Ithaca, NY: ILR Press.

Waldinger, Roger. 1996. *Still the Promised City?: African-Americans and New Immigrants in Postindustrial New York.* Cambridge, MA: Harvard University Press.

Wilson, Kenneth and William A. Martin. 1982. "Ethnic Enclaves: A Comparison of the Cuban and Black Economies in Miami." *American Journal of Sociology* 88: 135–160.

Wilson, William Julius. 1996. *When Work Disappears: The World of the New Urban Poor.* New York, NY: Vintage Books.

8

Is Affirmative Action Still Needed?

Policies aimed at improving the employment opportunities for people of color and providing greater representation of minorities in America's mainstream have been the focus of much controversy and research.[1] As mentioned in Chapter 7, affirmative action consists of activities undertaken specifically to identify, recruit, promote, or retain qualified members of disadvantaged minority groups in order to overcome the results of past discrimination and to deter discriminatory practices in the present. It argues that simply removing existing impediments is not sufficient for changing the relative positions of women and people of color.[2] And it is based on the premise that to be truly effective in altering the unequal distribution of life chances, it is essential that employers take specific steps to remedy the consequences of discrimination.

Despite a trend toward lower levels of prejudice in America,[3] Americans are deeply divided by race on the issue of affirmative action. There is also a gap by gender. In particular, according to a 2010 NBC/*Wall Street Journal* poll, 81 percent of African Americans support the view that "affirmative action programs are still needed to counteract the effects of discrimination against minorities, and are a good idea as long as there are no rigid quotas." More than two-thirds of Hispanic respondents (69 percent) support this view. But only 39 percent of Whites are supportive of such policies. Women (56 percent) are also more likely than are men to support affirmative action to redress past discrimination (49 percent).

Affirmative action has come under siege not only for being politically unpopular, but also for being ineffective as a policy for reducing levels of inequality for targeted groups.[4] Some have challenged affirmative action because it purportedly helps those members of minority groups who need assistance least at the same time that it does little for those who are among the "truly disadvantaged."[5] Others have criticized such programs for unfairly stigmatizing qualified minority candidates who must endure the perception that they were selected or promoted only because of their institutions' needs for minority representation.[6] And still others have derided affirmative action policies as "reverse discrimination" which benefits minority groups at the expense of equally or more qualified White males.[7] Yet, little research has been offered to support these assertions.

This chapter addresses some of the factual questions surrounding affirmative action policies. It examines the relationship between affirmative action programs and income, professional status, work-relevant interracial perceptions and attitudes, and mobility patterns of minority and non-minority workers.

Previous Research on the Effects of Affirmative Action

Previous studies of affirmative action have attempted to show the effects of such policies on changes in the employment opportunities and representation of women and people of color in the work setting,[8] the distribution of earnings and incomes,[9] unemployment rates,[10] occupational status,[11] and worker productivity.[12] Generally, these studies have demonstrated that the standing of women and people of color was enhanced during the affirmative action era. Much of the research suggests that affirmative action led to increases in female and minority employment, higher relative incomes for minorities and women, and greater access to skilled white-collar occupations for women and minorities over time.[13] The volume and quality of evidence is compelling.

Yet, there is some question about whether observed changes in the relative positions of women and people of color are due to the existence of affirmative action *per se*. The occurrence of other changes in society might have produced improvements in the positions of minorities even without the existence of affirmative action.[14] For example, women and people of color may have improved their levels or quality of education relatively more than White males. It is possible that many observed improvements in their statuses would have occurred because of improvements in education or the removal of legal barriers to inclusion rather than affirmative action. Alternatively, employers may have reduced their "tastes for discrimination" independently of their concerns about affirmative action policies. Such changes might have led to improvements in the relative statuses of groups who had been subject to discriminatory practices. Or, there may have been differential changes in the age, sex, regional, etc. compositions of groups such that relatively greater proportions of minority groups became members of those demographic categories with favorable stratification outcomes. Such demographic changes might have led to relative improvements for minority groups even without affirmative action. All of these factors are competing explanations for the purported improved status of women and people of color over time, and as Paul Burstein points out, "it proves impossible to assess separately the effects of different interesting variables."[15]

But as James Smith and Finis Welch suggest, the timing of some of the improvements in the status of minorities is surprising—"prior to the establishment of an effective monitoring structure for affirmative action."[16] Some analysts have attempted to determine the effects of affirmative action indirectly by examining aggregate or firm-level differences in the relative standings of racial minorities or women in affirmative action firms and those not in affirmative action firms. As Smith and Welch suggest, there are serious questions about the use of aggregate and firm-level data (especially EEO-1 reports) to disentangle the effects of affirmative action.[17] Demographic differences in the composition of affirmative action and non-affirmative action firms could mask affirmative action effects. Thus, analysts who have compared demographically dissimilar firms or those who have inappropriately lumped together racial minorities and women working for affirmative action employers and those not working for such employers may have severely underestimated the effects of affirmative action. Moreover, these strategies have not always allowed analysts to examine the differences in incomes and occupations between those minorities and women who work for affirmative action firms and those minorities and women who do not.

So, despite the preponderant evidence showing the improving conditions of women and people of color in the affirmative action era, there are lingering doubts about whether it was affirmative action, declining levels of prejudice and discrimination, improvements in female and minority education, or something else that led to minority gains. The use of individual-level data, as is used in this analysis, overcomes some of these limitations and provides a more direct means of assessing the impact of affirmative action.

Objections to Affirmative Action

As mentioned previously, affirmative action programs are the subject of a great deal of contention and discord. The objections are numerous, and the explanations of such opposition are plentiful. William Julius Wilson, for example, explicitly argues that "race-specific" policies such as affirmative action cannot succeed in helping the "underclass" or in reducing inequality.[18] Such policies, he argues, while beneficial to more advantaged minorities, do little for those who are "truly disadvantaged" because the cumulative effects of race and class subordination passed from generation to generation are disproportionately present among the poor. These people lack the resources and skills to compete effectively in the labor market. Thus, policies based on preferential treatment of minorities linked to group outcomes are insufficient precisely because the relatively advantaged members of racial minority communities will be selected and will reap the benefits to the detriment of poor minorities. Moreover, those Whites who are rejected due to preferential programs might be the most disadvantaged Whites whose qualifications are marginal precisely because of their disadvantages.

A second kind of objection raised by opponents of affirmative action is that because Whites often believe women and people of color are less qualified than White males (or even that no qualified candidates from those groups exist), it will stigmatize all minority workers. Those people of color and women who are qualified and can make it in society will be looked down on as having been favorites of the law who did not really make it on their own. In addition, this could have the effect of a self-fulfilling prophecy: Because employers believe that minority workers are less likely than are White male workers to be qualified for employment, they set lower standards in order to satisfy affirmative action requirements. In turn, minority workers have less incentive to perform at higher levels, as better performance will do little to enhance their chances of meeting company standards that have been lowered. Performances by minority workers that do not exceed the employers' lowered expectations serve to confirm the employers' initial beliefs about minority workers' lower levels of preparation and qualification. In other words, legally preferred groups realize that less is expected of them and, therefore, perform at a lower standard. This lower accomplishment, in turn, substantiates the stereotypes that reluctant employers and co-workers held initially.[19]

Another kind of objection to affirmative action is that it is tantamount to "reverse discrimination."[20] Some critics would argue that affirmative action programs are zero-sum undertakings: Under such plans, to the degree that minorities and women make economic progress, White males will suffer. Moreover, they would argue, some innocent White males who have never discriminated against minorities or women might be punished unfairly while some chauvinists and bigots might be spared. This objection to affirmative action makes the judgment (as an empirical fact) that Whites lose out to minorities. This empirical fact *per se* should disallow affirmative action according to these critics.

Other objections to affirmative action plans include such assertions as:

- They bring about too much government intrusion into business, academic, and private institutions.
- There are no good ways to verify who is a racial minority or to determine which minority groups should be included as protected members.
- There are no good ways to determine what numerical goals should be set or to determine when they have actually been met.

- Affirmative action programs are not necessary because progress for women and minorities would be made any way.
- Affirmative action programs are too difficult to administer and monitor.

This chapter will not address all of these issues. It does, however, provide assessment of those objections to affirmative action that are based on the notion that such practices are ineffective in redistributing income and life chances, and deleterious to the economic well-being of White male workers. We test these claims below by examining the effects of affirmative action programs on the incomes and professional statuses of diverse groups of workers. To do so, we draw on data from the General Social Survey.

The Effects of Affirmative Action

How valid are the objections to affirmative action programs raised by opponents of such policies? Are such programs related to increased incomes or professional status? Figure 8.1 presents the relationship between affirmative action and the incomes of various groups in 2012 dollars. Generally, this graph shows that affirmative action programs are associated with higher average income levels for all groups. Blacks who work for affirmative action employers earn US$4,400 more on average than those Blacks who do not work for such employers. Latinos who work for affirmative action

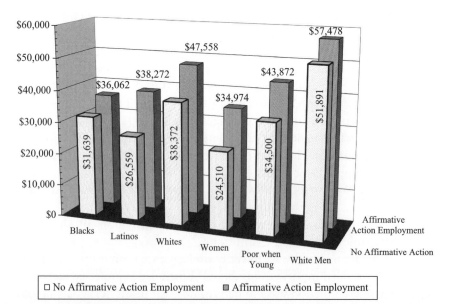

Figure 8.1 Average Incomes for Various Groups by Affirmative Action Employment

employers earn $11,700 more on average than those Latinos who do not work for such employers. Whites in affirmative action firms earn $9,100 more than Whites in non-affirmative action firms. Women employed by affirmative action firms earn more than $10,000 more than those women who work for non-affirmative action firms.

Contrary to William Julius Wilson's arguments,[21] those who were poor when they were young earn about $9,300 more than those who were poor and are not currently employed by affirmative action firms. And contrary to Nathan Glazer's arguments and much popular speculation,[22] the incomes of White males who work for affirmative action establishments are higher than those of White males who do not work for affirmative action companies. Moreover, it should be noted that the incomes of racial minorities under affirmative action do not eclipse those of White males (neither those working for affirmative action firms nor those employed by other companies). The gross difference in income associated with affirmative action employment for all those employed by affirmative action firms versus others is more than $8,400.

Figure 8.2 shows that the presence of affirmative action programs is generally associated with a greater probability of holding a professional, managerial, or technical job. Racial minorities, those who were poor as youths, and White men all have better chances of holding such positions by working for affirmative action employers. For women, affirmative action is associated with a slightly reduced tendency to be a professional, managerial, or

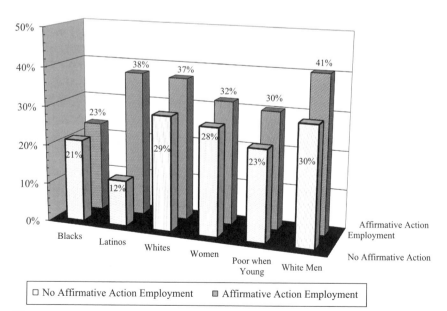

Figure 8.2 Percentage in Professional, Managerial, or Technical Occupations for Various Groups by Affirmative Action Employment

technical worker. This could be due to the tendency for affirmative action employers to have larger clerical components that are filled by women.

The results suggest that affirmative action is associated with higher incomes and occupations for racial minorities and those whose families had low incomes when they were growing up. Moreover, the findings indicate that White men are not penalized by the existence of such programs.

Although these graphs present only the gross relationships between affirmative action and work-related outcomes, these findings persist when we carry out our analysis using multivariate statistical techniques. Affirmative action programs are associated with significant increases in the incomes of racial minorities, women, and those who were poor when they were young; yet, affirmative action is not associated with decreases in the incomes of White males. Such policies are also significantly related to professional status in the same way.

Conclusion

Affirmative action was instituted to improve the employment opportunities for groups that historically had suffered discrimination in the labor market. Initially, there was little resistance to such policies among those who acknowledged the existence of discrimination. However, as affirmative action has become a more familiar term in legal and political debate, it has also become a rallying cry for activists, a slogan for politicians, and a litmus test for both political liberals and conservatives.

Despite the heated debates, not much light has been shed on the effectiveness of affirmative action as a strategy for improving the life chances of those groups that historically have been the victims of employment discrimination. Previous research efforts on the subject were able to show improving conditions for racial minorities and women, but were not really capable of showing that such changes were directly attributable to affirmative action. This chapter put forth a more straightforward strategy for assessing the effects of affirmative action.

One clear-cut result suggests that affirmative action programs in the workplace are associated with higher incomes for those they were intended to help. Indeed, they are correlated with higher incomes for racial minorities, women, and people from low-income backgrounds without appearing to do harm to the economic well-being of White males who work in such settings.

Unfortunately for proponents of affirmative action, the current debate about the merits and demerits of affirmative action is taking place in a context involving two apparent complications that have made the case for affirmative action more difficult to promote. First, there is periodic economic stagnation, which provides real threats to the very existence of good jobs. Second, there are new anti-minority sentiments that couch prejudice in terms of abstract ideological symbols and symbolic behaviors.

As a public policy and strategy for social change, affirmative action faces many peculiar dilemmas: to bring about a "color-blind" and gender-equal society. It must be color and gender conscious; to deliver equality of opportunity for greater efforts to educate, recruit, train, employ, and promote only some citizens. In order to determine whether progress is being made, it must measure present-day employment practices against some standard of what has occurred in the past and what might be achieved in the future. And in order to monitor the progress of women and people of color, it must be subjected to allegations that it is nothing more than "quotas" that promote "reverse discrimination" and the selection of people who are less qualified than their White male counterparts.

Proponents of affirmative action are confronted with a tricky political process that revolves around the obstacles and dilemmas mentioned. As Jennifer Hochschild points out, there are:

> Four rules of thumb [that] can help to shape [a] tricky political process. First, do not expect people to do more than they can—that road leads simply to frustration and rejection of the whole enterprise. Second, do not easily allow people to do much less than they can—that road vitiates the basic principle and demoralizes the full contributors. Third, give people direct, even self-interested, incentives to take action—few people will participate for long in a program that asks them to sacrifice themselves or their resources to an unknown other. Fourth, give people reasons beyond direct incentives for taking action—Americans have a long history of acting to help others if they believe that their actions will be efficacious, are morally right, and are not evidence of being a sucker.[23]

In other words, selling affirmative action will require demonstrating to White males that it does not cost them much. It will also mean convincing America that it can and should do much better by women and people of color. Moreover it requires showing employers that it is in their best interests to pursue equal opportunity policies. Finally, for the nation, it involves establishing that affirmative action is a policy that will strengthen rather than weaken its international competitiveness and general welfare. Still, proponents of affirmative action will also need the help of public leaders who are concerned about helping disadvantaged groups realize equal opportunity and not just interested in using affirmative action as a political symbol. If these public leaders are sincere in their concerns about assisting minorities in realizing equal access, they will need the courage to push for strategies that are effective but not necessarily politically popular.

If affirmative action were ineffective in helping those from disadvantaged backgrounds, there should be little opposition to dismantling such
plans among those who support it because they believe it enhances the
opportunities of the disadvantaged. Similarly, if, as the analysis presented
here suggests, affirmative action has been successful in providing relief to
those who have historically suffered discrimination, those who ostensibly
oppose affirmative action because of its ineffectiveness should re-examine
their views.

Notes

1 Lipset and Schneider, 1978; Welch, 1981; Sears et al., 1980; Burstein, 1985; Kluegel and Smith, 1986; and Bobo, 1988
2 Burstein, 1985
3 Greeley and Sheatsley, 1971; Taylor, Greeley, and Sheatsley, 1978; and Schuman et al., 1997
4 Ornati and Pisano, 1972; Berry, 1976; Cole, 1981; Wilson, 1987; and Loury, 1991
5 Wilson, 1987
6 Carter, 1991; Loury, 1991
7 Glazer, 1975; Sher, 1975; Gross, 1978; and Cole, 1981
8 Hammerman, 1984; Leonard, 1984a, 1984b; Smith and Welch, 1984; Burstein, 1985; and Leonard, 1985a, 1989, 1990
9 Burstein, 1979; Smith and Welch, 1984; and Leonard, 1985b
10 Loury, 1981
11 Ashenfelter and Heckman, 1976; Goldstein and Smith, 1976; Heckman and Wolpin, 1976; and Leonard, 1984b
12 Leonard, 1984c
13 Burstein, 1979, 1985; and Leonard, 1984a, 1984b, 1985a, 1985b
14 Burstein, 1979
15 Burstein, 1979: 381–382
16 Smith and Welch, 1984: 269
17 Smith and Welch, 1984
18 Wilson, 1987
19 Loury, 1991
20 Glazer, 1975
21 Wilson, 1987
22 Glazer, 1975
23 Hochschild, 1989: 29

References

Ashenfelter, Orley and James Heckman. 1976. "Measuring the Effect of an Antidiscrimination Program," in O. Ashenfelter and J. Blum (Eds). *Evaluating the Labor Market Effects of Social Programs*. Princeton, NJ: Princeton University Press: 46–84.
Berry, Margaret C. 1976. "Affirmative Action?," *Journal of the National Association for Women Deans, Administrators, and Counselors* 39: 1–60.
Bobo, Lawrence. 1988. "Group Conflict, Prejudice, and the Paradox of Contemporary Racial Attitudes," in P.A. Katz and D.A. Taylor (Eds). *Eliminating Racism: Means and Controversies*. New York, NY: Plenum: 85–114.

Burstein, Paul. 1979. "Equal Employment Opportunity Legislation and the Income of Women and Non-Whites." *American Sociological Review* 44: 367–391.

Burstein, Paul. 1985. *Discrimination, Jobs, and Politics: The Struggle for Equal Employment Opportunity in the United States Since the New Deal.* Chicago, IL: University of Chicago Press.

Burstein, Paul. 1991. "'Reverse Discrimination' Cases in the Federal Courts: Legal Mobilization by a Countermovement." *The Sociological Quarterly* 32: 511–528.

Carter, Stephen L. 1991. *Reflections of an Affirmative Action Baby.* New York, NY: Basic Books.

Cole, Craig W. 1981. "Affirmative Action: Change It or Lose It." *EEO Today* 8: 262–271.

Davis, James A. and Tom W. Smith. 1990. *General Social Surveys, 1972–1990 Cumulative Codebook.* Chicago, IL: National Opinion Research Center.

Glazer, Nathan. 1975. *Affirmative Discrimination: Ethnic Inequality and Public Policy.* New York, NY: Basic Books.

Goldstein, Morris and Robert S. Smith. 1976. "The Estimated Impact of the Antidiscrimination Program Aimed at Federal Contractors." *Industrial and Labor Relations Review* 29: 523–543.

Greeley, Andrew M. and Paul B. Sheatsley. 1971. "Attitudes toward Racial Integration." *Scientific American* 225: 13–19.

Gross, Barry R. 1978. *Discrimination in Reverse: Is Turnabout Fair Play?* New York: New York University Press.

Hammerman, Herbert. 1984. *A Decade of New Opportunity: Affirmative Action in the 1970s.* Washington, DC: Potomac Institute.

Heckman, James J. and Kenneth I. Wolpin. 1976. "Does the Contract Compliance Program Work?: An Analysis of Chicago Data." *Industrial and Labor Relations Review* 29: 544–564.

Herring, Cedric. 1991. "Splits and Chasms on Affirmative Action." *Illinois Issues* 17: 36–37.

Hochschild, Jennifer L. 1989. "The Politics of the Estranged Poor." Paper presented at the annual meeting of the American Political Science Association in Atlanta, GA.

Kellermann, Donald S., Andrew Kohut, and Carol Bowman. 1991. *The People, The Press & Politics on the Eve of '92: Fault Lines in the Electorate.* Washington, DC: Times Mirror Center for The People & The Press.

Kluegel, James R. and Eliot R. Smith. 1986. *Beliefs about Inequality.* New York, NY: Aldine de Gruyter.

Leonard, Jonathan S. 1984a. "The Impact of Affirmative Action on Employment." *Journal of Labor Economics* 2: 439–463.

Leonard, Jonathan S. 1984b. "Employment and Occupational Advance under Affirmative Action." *The Review of Economics and Statistics:* 377–386.

Leonard, Jonathan S. 1984c. "Antidiscrimination or Reverse Discrimination: The Impact of Changing Demographics, Title VII, and Affirmative Action on Productivity." *The Journal of Human Resources* 19: 145–173.

Leonard, Jonathan S. 1985a. "What Promises Are Worth: The Impact of Affirmative Action Goals." *The Journal of Human Resources* 20: 3–20.

Leonard, Jonathan S. 1985b. "Affirmative Action as Earnings Redistribution: The Targeting of Compliance Reviews." *Journal of Labor Economics* 3: 363–384.

Leonard, Jonathan S. 1989. "Women and Affirmative Action." *Journal of Economic Perspectives* 3: 61–75.

Leonard, Jonathan S. 1990. "The Impact of Affirmative Action Regulation and Equal Employment Law on Black Employment." *Journal of Economic Perspectives* 4: 47–63.

Lipset, Seymour M. and William Schneider. 1978. "The Bakke Case: How Would It Be Decided at the Bar of Public Opinion?," *Public Opinion* 1: 38–44.

Loury, Glenn C. 1981. "Is Equal Opportunity Enough?," *American Economics Review* 71: 122–126.

Loury, Glenn C. 1991. "Affirmative Action as a Remedy for Statistical Discrimination." Paper presented at a colloquium at the University of Illinois at Chicago, IL.

McQueen, Michel. 1991. "Voters' Responses to Poll Disclose Huge Chasm Between Social Attitudes of Blacks and Whites." *Wall Street Journal* (May 17): A16, Politics & Policy Section.

New York Times. 1992. Results from a September 1991 *New York Times/CBS News Poll* reported in *New York Times* Pollwatcher Letter, (May 15): 12.

Ornati, Oscar A. and Anthony Pisano. 1972. "Affirmative Action: Why It Isn't Working." *Personnel Administration* (September): 50–52.

Rose, Stephen. 1977 "Reverse Discrimination Developments under Title VII." *Houston Law Review* 15: 136–156.

Schuman, Howard, Charlotte Steeh, Lawrence D. Bobo, and Maria Krysan. 1997. *Racial Attitudes in America: Trends and Interpretations, Revised Edition.* Cambridge, MA: Harvard University Press.

Sears, David O., Richard R. Lau, Tom R. Tyler, and Harris M. Allen. 1980. "Self-Interest or Symbolic Politics in Policy Attitudes and Presidential Voting." *American Political Science Review* 74: 670–684.

Sher, George. 1975. "Justifying Reverse Discrimination in Employment." *Philosophy and Public Affairs* 4: 1159–1170.

Smith, James P. and Finis Welch. 1984. "Affirmative Action and Labor Markets." *Journal of Labor Economics* 2: 269–299.

Stolzenberg, Ross M. 1978. "Bringing the Boss Back In: Employer Size, Employee Schooling, and Socioeconomic Achievement." *American Sociological Review* 43: 813–828.

Taylor, D. Garth, Andrew M. Greeley, and Paul B. Sheatsley. 1978. "Attitudes toward Racial Integration." *Scientific American* 238: 42–49.

Villemez, Wayne J. and William P. Bridges. 1988. "When Bigger is Better: Differences in the Individual-Level Effect of Firm and Establishment Size." *American Sociological Review* 53: 237–255.

Welch, Finis. 1981. "Affirmative Action and Its Enforcement." *American Economic Review* 71: 127–133.

Wilson, Cynthia A., James H. Lewis, and Cedric Herring. 1991. *The 1991 Civil Rights Act: Restoring Basic Protections.* Chicago, IL: Urban League.

Wilson, William Julius. 1987. *The Truly Disadvantaged: The Inner City, the Underclass, and Public Policy.* Chicago, IL: University of Chicago Press.

9
Wealth and Class Diversity

In America, racial minorities, women, and the poor are typically the targets of stereotyping. Consequently, they have been more likely to be the victims of exploitation and discrimination throughout the nation's history. These groups continue to face discrimination in labor markets, in housing, and when trying to acquire credit. In Chapters 6 and 7, we discussed some of the advances that women and racial minorities have made in recent decades. Many of these advances in the labor market, however, have been concentrated among the affluent and well educated. Many low-skilled women and workers of color have been relegated to occupations that offer few chances for earnings mobility. At the same time, the real earnings of low-income White men have also fallen. Several states have passed anti-union legislation, made taxes less progressive, allowed the minimum wage to decline in real dollars, and drastically reduced spending on social programs. This has resulted in a dramatic widening of the income gap between the rich and poor. Among the advanced industrialized nations, the United States has the dubious distinction of having the most unequal economic distribution.[1] Usually, such inequalities are assessed with indicators such as wages, earnings, and income differences.[2]

But such inequalities pale in comparison to those of wealth. Even more, wealth differences continue to grow.[3] The control of wealth has become the key determinant of advantage and privilege in America.[4] Until the Occupy Movement exposed it, class and wealth inequality was America's dirty little secret for as long as we pretended that it did not really exist or matter. Unfortunately, ignoring these issues is also common among those who are concerned about diversity. Indeed, the thought of adding the issues of class and wealth to the inventory of diversity concerns may be a bit surprising. However, if one is using a critical diversity framework, the inclusion of class and wealth should not be a surprise.

Workplaces are among the few locations where people come into close contact with people from other classes. Most Americans live in class-segregated neighborhoods. Because of housing patterns, neighborhoods are usually quite homogenous. So, too, are the schools that children attend because of where they live. This is also true of most social circles. Even those people who regularly socialize with others from different races, ethnicities, religions, and sexual orientations do not usually spend much social time with people from social classes that are very different from their own.

This chapter provides an overview of wealth and class diversity in the United States by examining the distribution of wealth in America. It also shows how these patterns differ by race, gender, and occupational type. It shows why such disparities in wealth exist, how they are related to critical diversity, and what can be done to reduce unfair disparities in wealth and opportunity.

Wealth and Class in America

We can think of wealth as the total sum of what people own.[5] According to Lisa Keister:

> Wealth is prosperity; it is the value of things people own. Wealth is measured as net worth, defined as total assets (such as stocks, bonds, checking and savings accounts, the value of the family home, vacation homes, and other real estate) minus total liabilities (such as mortgage debt, the balance on credit cards, student loans, and car loans). Income is a flow of financial resources, such as wages or a salary received for work, interest and dividends from investments such as pensions, or transfer payments from the government. In contrast, wealth refers to the stock of resources owned at a particular point in time.

As Melvin Oliver and Thomas Shapiro suggest, the most typical way of measuring wealth is to use "net worth," which is the "value of all assets less any debts . . . [or] net financial assets, [which] excludes equity accrued in a home or vehicle from the calculations of a households available resources."[6] Seymour Spilerman provides yet another common definition of wealth when he says that it includes things such as "family's liquid financial assets (stocks, bonds, saving accounts) and its real property such as a house."[7]

As Keister's definition points out, wealth should be distinguished from income. Oliver and Shapiro suggest that wealth acts as an "invisible faultline in the American stratification system."[8] Wealth also acts differently than income, given that it provides opportunities even when income streams fail, and is more closely related to an individual's "economic well-being and access to life chances."[9] Spilerman asserts that wealth has several features that distinguish it from income. Wealth is earned without the owner giving up leisure time. It does not decline simply because the owner is sick or can no longer work. Wealth can be enjoyed without consuming it (e.g., viewing a painting). Tax laws treat wealth differently than earned income. Finally, during times of crisis, wealth can be used to protect a family or a business when income earning is muted or delayed.[10]

Social inequality may emerge from social differentiation because roles and social positions poise different kinds of people to acquire greater shares of valued goods and services. Social stratification occurs when three conditions exist: inequality is institutionalized; inequality is systemic and usually group based; and there are norms in place to support such group-based inequality. This means that there is a system of layered hierarchy that is well established. Moreover, there is a system of social relationships that determines who gets what and why. Finally, there are norms in place so that people have come to expect that individuals and groups with certain positions will be able to demand more influence and respect and accumulate greater shares of goods and services. Although such inequality need not be accepted to the same degree by various groups in the society, it is generally recognized as the way things are.

We can think of social classes in at least two different ways. We can think of them as groups of people who share roughly similar incomes and wealth, occupations, and levels of education. For most people income, occupation, and education are highly related. Social scientists refer to the combination of these characteristics as socio-economic status, or SES. While these characteristics are usually related, it is important to remember that exceptions do exists—for example, truck drivers who typically have high school diplomas and can earn up to US$100,000. Conversely, college professors with PhDs can earn less than unskilled workers.

According to this view, a second dimension of class deals with lifestyles. Classes of people tend to share not only similar incomes and education levels, but also similar lifestyles. By lifestyle, we mean taste in music, fashion, and cuisine, and cultural knowledge. We can all recognize that if you wish to sustain a certain lifestyle you need an income that is able to support it; thus, these two dimensions are intertwined. Patterns of behavior between classes are measurable. For example, while we all know that people from any income group can like classical music or country music, on average the income of those who typically listen to these genres is different.

Many Americans generally have a low level of class consciousness. They have difficulty understanding how social class has an impact upon their lives and how the political, economic, and social interests of different classes often conflict with each other. Essentially, they believe that anyone can achieve the American Dream if they work hard enough, no matter where they start. Their notion is that America is basically a "classless" or "middle-class" society.

There is, however, a different view of class. In that framework, class refers to one's ownership or non-ownership of production forces. The capitalist (or owning) class owns the means of production. Members of the working class sell their labor power for wages. Here, there is much more emphasis on ownership of wealth and the great disparities in who owns what.

If there were true equality in the distribution of income, the top 20 percent of income earners would get 20 percent of the income, and the bottom 20 percent would receive 20 percent of the income. However, the reality is that the top 20 percent of the income earners get 50 percent of all income, and the bottom 20 percent of earners receive 3 percent.

Inequality in America became a hot-button political issue in 2011 as poverty and inequality continued to climb. The Occupy Movement, which began near Wall Street in New York City, rapidly spread across the United States. That movement's slogan, "We are the 99 percent," refers specifically to the huge income disparity in the United States between those in the top 1 percent and the other 99 percent of Americans. Other issues included resentment over government efforts to bail out multinational corporations and financial institutions, corporate greed, and the corrupting influence of money and the rich on the government.

The real (inflation-adjusted), after-tax, average family income of the top 1 percent of earners in the United States almost tripled between 1979 and 2007.[11] Others in the top 20 percent of income earners also did well with an increase of 65 percent in income. At the lower end of the income spectrum, the income of those in the bottom fifth increased by only 18 percent. The bottom 20 percent had only 5 percent of all income (down from 7 percent in 1979). These figures suggest that the top 20 percent of the population had over 50 percent of all income. They also received more money than the other 80 percent of the population combined.

The relative share of income of the top 1 percent of Americans increased dramatically between 1979 and 2007. This contributed a great deal to America's already large income inequality. In fact, during that time, the share of income received by the top 1 percent doubled. Even more striking was the fact that the top 0.1 percent of the American population received more than 12 percent of all income. This concentration of income among the super-rich is a great indicator of the inequality that fueled the rage of those involved in the Occupy Movement.

As mentioned above, wealth, more than income, contributes to class hierarchy because the concentration of wealth is even greater than the concentration of income. The largest differences between the haves and have-nots can be linked not to disparities in income, but rather to the vast differences in wealth.

Those with great wealth live lifestyles beyond the wildest dreams of those who live on the lowest rungs of the wealth ladder. Wealth brings with it the ability to invest in stocks, bonds, real estate, and assets that can yield greater income and to generate even greater wealth. It can also be used to purchase material comforts such as large homes, luxury cars, lavish vacations, custom-made clothes, and the services of maids, butlers, personal trainers, and others. Wealth can provide high levels of material security that allow early retirement but with the ability to live well for the rest of one's life. It can also grant freedom and great amounts of autonomy to its possessor. These are just some of the ways in which wealth benefits individuals and families.

Substantial wealth often brings with it income, power, and independence. Wealth in significant quantities releases wealth holders from dependence on others for an income. When wealth is used to purchase significant ownership of the means of production, it often generates income. It can buy things like stock in major corporations. It can bring authority to the holder of such wealth. Substantial wealth is also important because it can be transferred from generation to generation more easily than income. This makes it more possible to produce inheritance of positions and opportunities.

Figure 9.1 presents the results from a survey asking Americans to estimate the distribution of wealth in the United States versus what they would like for it to be ideally, plotted against the reality of the wealth distribution. Respondents estimated that the top 20 percent of Americans own about 60 percent of the wealth. The reality is that the top 20 percent own 85 percent of the nation's wealth. More strikingly, Americans said ideally that the bottom 40 percent should own 25 percent. However, the reality is that the bottom 40 percent own less than 0.5 percent. Most people

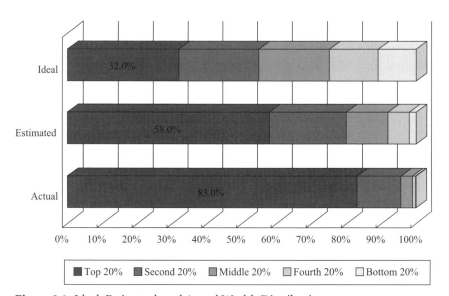

Figure 9.1 Ideal, Estimated, and Actual Wealth Distribution

have little or no wealth. The wealthiest 10 percent of families in 2007, for example, had a median net worth of US$1,119,000—more than 138 times as much as the poorest 20 percent of families. For the poorest 20 percent, the median net worth was only $8,100. Whatever they have attained in the form of wages and salaries cannot be accumulated because it must be used for immediate necessities.

Racial Differences in Wealth and Poverty

In addition to being unequally distributed in the general American population, the distribution of wealth is racialized and gendered. It is also very unequally distributed by occupation type. In particular, according to data from the 2009 Panel Study of Income Dynamics, the median amount of wealth for adults in America is US$27,500. But these amounts vary greatly by race and ethnicity. As Figure 9.2 shows, during the height of the Great Recession, Whites had a median wealth of more than $79,000. In contrast, African Americans had a median net worth that was almost 20 times less than that of Whites at $4,000. Latinos had a median wealth of $12,100. And Asian Americans had wealth of $84,500. Figure 9.2 also shows that there were extreme differences by gender, as households headed by men had a median wealth of $51,500 and those headed by women had a median wealth of $5,000.

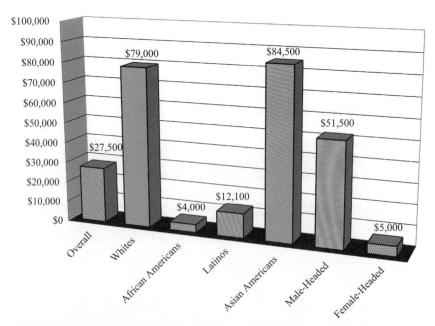

Figure 9.2 Median Wealth by Race and Gender of Head of Household

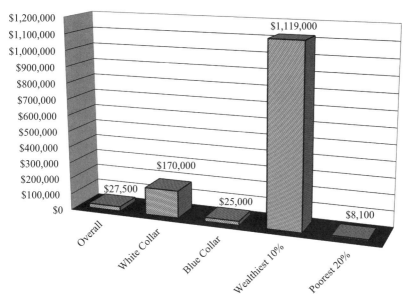

Figure 9.3 Median Wealth by Occupation and for the Top 10 Percent and Bottom 20 Percent of Families

Figure 9.3 presents wealth differences by occupation type and for the wealthiest 10 percent of the population and the poorest 20 percent of the population. White-collar occupations had a net worth of US$170,000 and blue-collar occupations had a median net worth of $25,000. As mentioned above, the wealthiest 10 percent of families had a median net worth of $1,119,000 compared with $8,100 for the poorest 20 percent.

What are some of the reasons for the racial disparity in wealth? Melvin Oliver and Thomas Shapiro argue that it is easier for Whites to obtain assets, even when they have fewer resources than Blacks, because discrimination affects the racial gap in homeownership.[12] Blacks are rejected for mortgages 60 percent more often than Whites, even with the same qualifications and creditworthiness. When Blacks do receive mortgages, they are more likely to take "subprime" mortgage loans that charge more in interest. In 2006, 30.3 percent of Blacks took out subprime home loans, compared to 24 percent of Hispanics and 17.7 percent of Whites.

Of course, the flip side of wealth is poverty. Millions of impoverished people find themselves at the bottom of the American class system. During the 1960s when President Lyndon B. Johnson declared a War on Poverty, the poverty rate in America declined dramatically. But in the 1970s until the early 1990s, it began a steady climb upward. Since then, the number of poor people declined again, but it has been on the rise since 2007. In 2008, the number of people living in poverty stood at 37 million, or roughly

13 percent of the population.[13] This poverty rate greatly exceeds that of most other advanced industrial nations.

Oliver and Shapiro asserted that African Americans have been histori- cally disadvantaged from accumulating wealth by state-sanctioned racial policies such as slavery and Jim Crow segregation and through institu- tional discrimination.[14] These policies not only affected those who lived during these eras, but also created generational consequences that continue to affect African Americans today (e.g., inherited poverty). They argued that, historically, Whites through governmental policies have been able to secure wealth in the form of businesses, homes, and stocks. Thus, Oliver and Shapiro suggested that African Americans were denied the opportu- nity to acquire and pass down accumulated wealth until the 1960s.

Dalton Conley argued that historical factors such as sustained low wages may also be related to the wealth gap between Whites and African Ameri- cans.[15] Scholars have also argued that discrimination in financing may be related to this disparity. For example, Andrew Brimmer argued that:

> to a considerable extent [not having wealth] can be traced to a long history of
> deprivation in this country . . . This means that Blacks have had much less oppor-
> tunity than Whites to earn, save, or to inherit wealth. Because of this historical
> legacy, Black families have had few opportunities to accumulate wealth and to
> pass it on to their descendants.[16]

Doug Massey and Nancy Denton also argued that housing and finance discrimination are major historical factors contributing to wealth inequal- ity.[17] They claimed that African Americans were often denied housing loans in geographic locations that would allow them to acquire housing that would appreciate at a considerable rate. This resulted in current and future gaps in wealth holdings between African Americans and Whites.

Given that African Americans under slavery were typically not allowed to hold property legally,[18] the ability for wealth accumulation and wealth transfer from generation to generation was nearly impossible. This inabil- ity to amass wealth is a historical factor that plays a role in the disparity in wealth. Oliver and Shapiro challenge the assertions made by some analysts that cultural factors such as saving and spending patterns are simply the result of learned behavior under slavery.[19] They suggest that conservative claims in essence blame the victim because they use individual and collec- tive psychology as the underlying explanation for behavior that results in lack of wealth.[20]

Dalton Conley asserts that past governmental policies also contributed to the racial wealth gap.[21] The United States government had put in place the Federal Land Grant Program to provide freed slaves the opportunity to establish farms and become self-sufficient. However, through discrimi- nation, selfish actions, and illegal practices by those in power, this policy was never fully implemented. This denial of promised land supported the development of the tenant farming system that dominated the southern economy after slavery. This system consisted of tenants (i.e., farmers who worked for the landowners) being provided minimal living standards, farming tools, and seeds on credit.[22] Conley asserts that these tenants were to cultivate the land, repay debt incurred from the housing and farming supplies, and earn a portion of the profit. While this system was not slavery *per se*, legal policies, discrimination, and outright theft kept African Americans in a perpetual state of credit bondage. During this time, African Americans were also denied access to loans for business development by banks and could not deposit their earnings in banks in order to save and earn interest on the money. Whites, on the other hand, were provided low interest loans and access to wealth-generating banking options.[23] This was one of many practices that contributed to racial disparity in farm ownership (i.e., wealth accumulation). African Americans also faced institutional racism such as laws that prevented them from owning businesses. One such example included requiring that African Americans have the support of a White person and pay exorbitant amounts for licensure fees. These practices were coupled with threats and incidents of physical violence when African Americans created businesses that competed with White-owned businesses. The exclusion of agricultural and domestic workers also disadvantaged African Americans disproportionately. This most likely resulted in the reduced ability of African Americans to pass down accumulated savings to the next generation because they had to rely on these savings during retirement.[24]

According to Conley, one of the most significant historical factors contributing to the racial wealth gap was the practice of "redlining."[25] "Redlining is a process by which goods or services are made unavailable, or are available only on less than favorable terms, to people because of where they live regardless of their relevant objective characteristic."[26] Prior to the Civil Rights Act of 1964, "fewer than one percent of all mortgages in the nations were issued to African Americans."[27] This was a direct result of redlining practices supported by the United States government.

These examples highlight the historical barriers that African Americans faced with respect to wealth accumulation. Scholars have and continue to argue over the historical reasons for the racial wealth gap. These scholars have debated the relative importance of cultural, structural, and institutional factors which contribute to the gap. These arguments over cultural, structural, and institutional factors continue to inform debates about the contemporary causes of the racial wealth gap today.

Currently, African Americans generally have lower levels of socioeconomic status than do Whites or other racial and ethnic groups. This results in lower earnings. This makes it more difficult for African Americans to purchase homes, which are leading vehicles for wealth accumulation for the majority of Americans. African Americans also have larger families, are more likely to be divorced, and are more likely to have households headed by single women. These factors are a reflection of discrimination in the labor market, housing market, and educational system.

One factor that is not typically related to the racial wealth gap debate directly is age. There is, however, literature that focuses on life-cycle issues that might be linked to theories that help to explain racial differences in wealth. The life-cycle model argues that once a person reaches retirement, the individual will deplete assets and lower overall wealth.[28] This theory does not fully account for findings that show differential patterns of accumulation and depletion of wealth over the life course for different groups.[29] Not only does this framework fail to fully account for differential accumulation patterns, it also fails to deal with differential racial patterns of accumulation and spending by race. There are, however, other theories that attempt to explain consumption patterns that have implications for the racial wealth gap.

Under the conspicuous consumption thesis, individuals will purchase goods and services that are not needed and this will result in a lack of financial assets. This argument is used to help explain the wealth gap between African Americans and Whites by asserting that African Americans spend their money frivolously and fail to invest in income-generating assets.[30] However, Oliver and Shapiro debunk this claim by demonstrating that while the assets owned by African Americans and Whites differ, these differences can be attributed to structural factors rather than cultural ones.[31] For example, they show that at lower incomes African Americans place more of their money into homes and cars rather than into income-producing assets. However, they argue that this is a function of housing mortgage discrimination and the need for many African Americans to purchase reliable vehicles due to labor market segmentation. This forces many African Americans to work long distances from their homes. They also show that, at higher incomes, African Americans save more while Whites invest in more income-generating instruments.[32] Although there are differences in investment strategies between African Americans and Whites, these strategies reflect structural barriers for some groups and privileges for others rather than cultural patterns that demonstrate pathology or cultural competence.

Andrew Brimmer argues that the investment patterns of African Americans reflect risk aversion and unfamiliarity with the stock market.[33] These deficiencies are related to the lack of social connections in the African American community that would allow them to share information about the inner workings of the stock market. He argues that the lack of productive investment strategies and household family structure are related to differential asset holdings between African Americans and Whites. Brimmer does highlight that African American women are more likely to invest in the stock market. While he does not offer scientific evidence of why this pattern has emerged, he suggests that Whites may have higher savings; thus, they are more likely to use these savings to invest in the market. Overall, Brimmer argues that as African Americans invest in the stock market and develop the cultural capital to share with others in their communities, their participation will increase along with their share of the market. Although Brimmer does consider some historical factors, his arguments about individual skill, risk-taking, and household structure are based on cultural arguments that suggest personal responsibility and choice are the major factors related to the Black–White wealth gap.[34]

Contemporary analysts have also focused on the role of inheritance and wealth transfer in producing and reinforcing the racial wealth gap.[35] The theory of the "simple life-cycle model implies that the bulk of wealth might be acquired not by intergenerational transfers, but instead be accumulated from scratch by each generation to be consumed eventually by the end of life."[36] Other scholars argue that any examination of wealth accumulation or the racial wealth gap must include a discussion of inheritance and wealth transfers because these mechanisms lead to a large portion of household accumulated wealth.[37] Marc Szydlik argued that examining inheritance is crucial for several reasons.[38] First, anticipated inheritance leads to certain behaviors and emotions. For example, anticipating inheriting wealth often causes individuals to feel connected to those who have left them something, and it signals the value of the recipient to the grantor. Second, bequests of businesses have financial implications for society through jobs and taxes. And, third, inheritance maintains and creates social inequality.[39] James Smith also found that African Americans have lower wealth due, in part, to lower intergenerational transfers of wealth.[40]

Szydlik puts foward a theory of inheritance that he terms "intergenerational solidarity."[41] He argues that there are three dimensions of interconnectedness: individual, structural, and societal. Individuals are nested in families that are embedded within society, and they are intertwined by solidarity. He further argues that there are four bases of this model: opportunity, family, need, and cultural-contextual that make intergenerational solidarity work.[42] He asserts that there must be an opportunity to give and receive. There must also be a relationship based on a family tie. Often, the heir will be seen as needing or deserving of the gift. Finally, there must be a cultural component in place to sustain the act of giving.

William Gale and John Karl Scholz identify the difference between inheritance and wealth transfer—"*inter vivos* wealth transfer (that is, a transfer between living people) or a bequest [inheritance] (a transfer that occurs at the death of the donor.)"[43] There remains uncertainty about the accurate definitions of inheritance and wealth transfer. For example, one may receive an inheritance and choose to leave it in an account where it earns interest. This interest is then counted as money earned by the receiving party because of their decision to save the money. This makes measuring the process of wealth accumulation difficult.[44] Szydlik also notes the difficulty in accounting for inheritance given that respondents are less willing to answer questions about it because it is often received during times of grief and mourning.[45] Therefore, future research is needed to accurately assess wealth transfers and inheritance and the role they play in the racial wealth gap.

Oliver and Shapiro argued that, via inheritance, children of Whites and Blacks charter very different economic courses.[46] Through inheritance and wealth transfers, families pass on more than money. They also transfer class and racial privileges, as well as disadvantages from one generation to another.[47] Understanding the impact of wealth transfers and inheritance remains crucial to the discussion of the racial wealth gap because many individuals fail to consider the role that wealth transfers play in their own portfolios or the lack of such transfers on others portfolios. According to Shapiro, "Blacks received 8 cents of inheritance for every dollar inherited by Whites."[48] Yet, it remains more important to analyze wealth transfers between living parties because as much as 43 percent of all wealth may be transferred while both parties are living.[49] He also documented that "twenty-eight percent of Whites received bequests, compared to just 7.7 percent of Black families."[50] This can be explained partly by the lower wealth holdings of African Americans that lead to lower intergenerational wealth transfers; however, this does not fully explain the racial wealth gap or why African Americans provide lower amounts of inheritance to their children.[51]

Shapiro also noted that many of his interviewees acknowledged that they had received substantial wealth transfers from their parents and other family members in the form of low or no interest loans, cash, and college tuition.[52] Yet, they continued to proclaim that they had earned their wealth through their own hard work and smart investment strategies. They denied the connection between their unearned wealth, social class, and how this related to the social class of others in the social hierarchy.[53] Beyond the difficulty of discussing inheritance gained after the death of a loved one, inheritance and wealth transfers also create a paradox for the American value system. Obtaining unearned wealth runs counter to the notion of meritocracy. However, not providing an inheritance for your children or securing as many assets as possible and then bequeathing them to one's relatives also appears to be antithetical to American values with respect to achieving the American Dream. This paradox makes the discussion of wealth accumulation uncomfortable for those who have acquired their wealth through such means. More importantly, it makes it extremely difficult to create public policy changes that would limit such transfers or equalize wealth accumulation for those who do not have such advantages.

Maury Gittleman and Edward Wolff argue that there is a need for public policies to address wealth accumulation disparities.[54] They find that African Americans would have benefited significantly if they had received similar inheritance as Whites. Thomas Shapiro argues that having college payments covered versus finishing college with student loans should have an impact upon potential savings and wealth accumulation.[55] Although this claim appears to be indisputable, researchers need to examine whether it is accurate. They need to determine whether it varies by occupation, type of school attended, and other factors. Scholars need to examine the effect of student loans on wealth and the racial wealth gap. Researchers could examine these issues by conducting research that looks at racial differences in wealth outcomes for those who do take loans to get through school compared with those who do not in order to determine whether such factors have implications for different saving and spending patterns.

Gender, Wealth, and Asset Poverty

In terms of gender and inequality, those who have attempted to incorporate gender as an issue in understanding wealth have usually examined gender-related issues such as divorce, family structure, and parenthood.[56] Lisa Keister takes us beyond the macro-structures within society that impact wealth inequality.[57] In her article "Race, Family Structure, and Wealth: The Effect of Childhood Family on Adult Asset Ownership," Keister suggests that racial differences in family structure are central to understanding the gap in wealth holdings between Whites and Blacks. Her central argument is that family structure differs by race in the United States; therefore, racial differences in adult wealth are a function of differences in family structure and resources. She uses data from the National Longitudinal Survey of Youth 1979 cohort to examine these issues. Keister argues that those who experience family disruptions (i.e., divorce or separation), increased numbers of siblings, and extended family in the home have lower levels of wealth.[58] Given the increased number of minority families that tend to experience such family structures, this helps to explain the wealth gap between Whites and Blacks. Keister further argues that female-headed households are disadvantaged compared to two parent (i.e., husband–wife coupled) households because women continue to work in segregated labor markets, earn less than men, and have more difficulty securing resources that translate into income-generating assets.[59]

Keister argues that married couples who live in the same household have, on average, greater wealth than do other households.[60] Similarly, Wilson argues that the female-headed household is one factor related to poverty.[61] Other scholars also support the claim that married couples are more likely to own homes, have higher housing values, and have greater wealth compared with other family types.[62] Married couples have a distinct advantage in wealth accumulation over other family types because they have the potential for dual earners. However, there is also a distinct gender dynamic that occurs. Even when there is only one earner in the married family, these households earn more than female-headed households. Yet, when married couples send the wife into the workforce, their wealth lags behind those families that send only the husband into the workforce. This is directly related to gender inequality in the labor market.[63]

Although enlightening, these factors do not provide a clear picture of wealth inequality in terms of gender differences *per se*. Particularly problematic is the idea that wealth has been treated conceptually as a family-unit phenomenon. The assumption that wealth is shared equally by all family members or that all family members have equal say over the allocation of resources has not been substantiated in the literature.[64] Furthermore, when the family unit dissolves, family assets are not typically divided equally, nor equitably, and women often bear the brunt of the financial burden.[65] Thus, wealth, arguably, is gendered. Amelia Batso and her colleagues, for example, argue that people inaccurately believe that the family unit becomes a sort of "black box" where resources enter and then are distributed equally.[66] Moreover, the literature on the feminization of poverty suggests that when families face divorce, women and children tend to have far fewer resources and wealth than do their male counterparts. But as long as wealth is measured as a family concept, it will be difficult to demonstrate how its distribution affects men and women differently.[67] This major methodological flaw within most household-level data makes it nearly impossible to disentangle who actually owns what assets or debts within the household.

Research that continues to rely on household-level data fails to account for women's decision-making power, access to credit, or disproportionate rates of violence in the home, and it definitely fails to examine the intersection of race and class on these issues. Until researchers change this method of data collection, they will continue to compare apples to oranges when it comes to comparing married households to female-headed households. However, one possible solution may be to examine who gets what assets after a divorce and compare these data to household information prior to the divorce, evaluating how the legal system identifies who owns what and who is responsible for what debts. Researchers may also want to develop panel data that ask information about individual household members and then aggregate up rather than starting from this point.

Analysts have continued to grapple with the role gender plays in the racial wealth gap. There is a dearth of research on gender and wealth *per se*. There is, however, a vast literature focusing on asset poverty among women, especially women of color. This discussion of asset poverty can be found in aspects of the "feminization of poverty" literature. Asset poverty can be understood as not having enough resources to sustain a household or individual during times of illness or unemployment for longer than three months.[68] Asset poverty, then, becomes the flip side of wealth. Caner and Wolff find that asset poverty is more concentrated among Blacks than Whites.[69] Understanding those factors that lead to asset poverty reveals mechanisms that hinder wealth accumulation.

Wealth and Class Diversity: Some Policy Solutions

The income gap between top corporate executives and typical work-ing Americans skyrocketed between 1990 and 2007. According to *Forbes* magazine, the average compensation for the 25 best-paid CEOs in the United States was more than US$125 million per year. In 2007, the total compensation of the CEOs of the largest 500 American corporations was more than $7.5 billion. This was an increase of 38 percent over the amount they received the year before. In contrast, the typical blue-collar worker in America received less than $17 per hour in 2006.[70] Between 1990 and 2004, the pay of production workers increased by less than 5 percent. In real (inflation-adjusted) dollars, the purchasing power of workers who received the minimum wage actually declined by 6 percent between 1990 and 2004. Meanwhile, the pay for CEOs increased by more than 300 percent.

Why have levels of inequality in America grown so much over the past few decades? There are several reasons. The political climate helps to explain widening inequality.[71] There is, for example, political resistance to raising the minimum wage in the United States. As a consequence, in real dollars, the minimum wage has actually declined in recent years. Workers who hold minimum wage jobs have lost ground relative to those in higher-paying occupations. Powerful conservative political forces work hard to maintain the current system of inequality that benefits those on top and, thereby, increase inequality.

This is reflected in the series of tax policies instituted during the presi-dency of George W. Bush and extended during the Obama administration. Many people believe that such tax policies favored the rich and disadvan-taged most others. The Congressional Budget Office contended that federal taxes were less progressive in 2007 than they had been in 1979. During the last three decades, tax policies have been shifted to favor long-term capital gains. This involves income derived from investments in capital such as real estate, stocks, and bonds that are held for more than a year. Today, long-term capital gains are taxed at a rate that is less than half the rate for ordinary income. This provides a great advantage for the after-tax income of the mega-rich who own a disproportionate share of the capital and, therefore, reap almost all the benefits of the low capital gains tax.

At the same time, social welfare benefits during this timeframe were doing less to address inequality. For example, social security payments went to the increasing number of older Americans, irrespective of their economic statuses.

We can also look at patterns of income growth and decline. At the same time that there were real declines in the earnings of most workers, the incomes for executives skyrocketed. This is part of what has been called "the winner-take-all society."[72] In such an economy, the wealthy use their clout and material advantages to succeed, and the poor, with few if any advantages, grow increasingly worse off.[73]

Wealth and class diversity have great implications for the functioning of organizations. Control of employees is often considered a fact of life for wealthy people who own businesses or run other organizations. Their demand for financial, household, and personal services gives them fiscal power. In addition, they have the ability to influence the activities of, and set the agendas for, many charities and civic groups. In addition, the wealthy can wield more clout by making large campaign contributions to their favorite political organizations or politicians. Such generous contributions often give these contributors great access and power. In many cases, the wealthy may choose to use their money to finance their own campaigns for public office.

An additional advantage of wealth is the ability to pass it across generations. Financial mechanisms such as "generation-skipping" trusts allow the wealthy not only to pass their wealth on to the next generation but to ensure wealth in their families for generations to come. Thus, wealth tends to be self-perpetuating over the long term. The wealthy are able to carry forward their wealth because they are able to use their money to influence and resist taxation systems that are designed to redistribute wealth in society. In particular, the wealthy have fought consistently against estate taxes that place higher taxes on assets exceeding US$5 million that are bequeathed to relatives upon death.

Critical diversity seeks both to understand unjust inequality and to redress it. If we want to eradicate unfair wealth disparities, we need to put forward solutions that attempt to alter structural rather than cultural factors to reduce the racial and gender wealth gap. Oliver and Shapiro argue that a family's ability to accumulate and access assets before and during times of hardship is essential to their economic well-being.[74] Therefore, they support assets-based public policies that promote wealth accumulation among families. Their policy recommendations are different from income-based policies that only provide supplements and often hinder asset accumulation because income-based policies such as welfare often require that recipients have little to no assets in order to qualify. While they do argue for changing the parameters of welfare programs, they are not arguing in favor of denying individuals income supplements during times of economic hardship. They are suggesting that individuals be provided with assistance-based programs that do not require them to be at the poverty level in order to receive any type of welfare assistance. They are also arguing that programs support asset building for those who are very poor as well as for those who are middle income. One of their policy recommendations revolves around homebuyers' accounts. These accounts would be established at age 18, and the individual would need to be a first-time home buyer or a homeowner for no more than three years. This program would be open to all individuals so that anyone could set up an interest-free account. Those who fall below specific income and asset levels would be matched at some dollar amount by the government based on individual contribution. After ten years, the accounts could be used for education, a down payment for a home, or toward current home principle.[75] Other policy solutions involve self-employment and business accounts that would help individuals to obtain the needed start-up capital to invest in a business through matching grants.

Some of the most controversial policy recommendations revolve around taxation and inheritance. Many scholars argue that the tax code needs significant reform.[76] For example, homeowners typically receive a tax deduction for their interest and property tax. On average, this subsidy benefits affluent and middle-class families, and it leaves renters and the very poor excluded. One solution suggested by Oliver and Shapiro would be to create a simple housing credit that would be tied to income.[77] This credit would reach more families who really need it. Conley also suggests that a national wealth tax be instituted.[78] This tax would require individuals to pay tax on certain portions of their assets if their assets exceed the allowed deduction.

In terms of inheritance, tax shelters and loopholes are the driving forces that help inheritance sustain the racial wealth gap.[79] Scholars typically agree that getting rid of inheritance altogether would be viewed negatively. Moreover, eliminating it is not realistic for American society since Americans tend to want to pass down their assets to their families. However, alternatives to the abolishment of inheritance are policies such as increasing the inheritance tax, creating matching programs for poorer families to send their children to college, and to help them purchase first homes. Some wealthy Americans are also pledging to give at least 50 percent of their wealth away to charity once they die. These and other policies may help to reduce the wealth gap; however, none of these policies alone or in combination will work to fully eliminate the wealth gap because the gap is also a function of other forms of social inequality.[80]

In Chapter 8, we identified affirmative action as a policy that could help to ameliorate some of the racial and gender inequity that occurs in American society. Dalton Conley suggests that class-based (in addition to race- and/or gender-based) affirmative action could "maintain set-asides for certain government contractors, demonstrate preferential hiring practices, and facilitate quotas for college admissions—but these decisions would be based on socioeconomic background rather than on race."[81] To be successful in achieving its goal of fostering racial and class equality, Conley suggests, such policies "must not rely solely on traditional measures of socioeconomic status (income, occupation, and education) but must take assets into account."[82] In addition, he discusses the role of welfare and asset accumulation. He argues that allowing welfare recipients to maintain their assets by relaxing the strict asset tests that welfare policy currently enforces would help to reduce wealth disparities at the lower end of the wealth distribution. If welfare recipients were given the ability to earn and save without being penalized for accumulating assets, those on public assistance would have a greater ability to draw on their own reserves, they would be more capable of riding out rough financial times, and they would have greater incentive to acquire and maintain assets. Relatedly, if public housing residents were allowed to accumulate equity in their publicly subsidized housing, the government could create a whole new class of urban homeowners who could eventually own property and gain a share in the American Dream.

In addition, Conley identifies Child Development Savings Accounts (similar to Social Security accounts for workers) as a strategy that could help to decrease disparities in wealth. When children are born, each year at tax time funds could be placed in an account for the child's future use (like a deduction for a dependent or a child care credit). The money would then be released only for educational or occupational expenses such as tuition, licenses, fees, or capital investments. Policies that encourage savings and thrift might be able to garner support from the political right as well as the left. The benefit would be that children from disadvantaged backgrounds (again, disproportionately minorities) would have funds available for college educations or other career-relevant expenses, regardless of their parents' earnings or savings habits. Funds not used for education or job training would be returned to the government. This would level the wealth playing field for each generation, and it would have the added benefit of encouraging additional education. Although Conley does not really endorse any of these proposals, something like this could begin to close the wealth gap and combat the harmful effects of class inequalities if Americans have the desire to do so.

Although there is some truth in the idea that America's class structure has some fluidity and that people's class positions can and do change over their lives, the greater reality is that wealth and class are far less malleable than most people believe. Especially during periods of economic uncertainty, without a framework for understanding social inequality, people will often view others as scapegoats. They will fail to see underlying, systemic causes of inequality. Inequitable policies that tilt opportunities in favor of the haves will remain invisible. Frustrated members of the middle class will blame poor people for causing fiscal crises as the government seeks to cut more social support programs. The unemployed will come to see immigrants as the reason for their plight. Gays and lesbians will come to be seen as the reason for moral decay in society and the breakdown of the nuclear family. Needless to say, such a situation is not good for critical diversity.

Issues of wealth and class diversity intersect with other forms of oppression in society. Class-based inequalities, if not properly managed, may be manifested through intolerance toward the poor and working classes in the form of disrespect, violence, and even hate crimes. It is obvious that working-class people are cheated of opportunities when they are isolated from professional people. But also, professional people are deprived of meaningful experiences when they are cut off from working-class people or if they are led to believe that they are somehow superior to them. They are misled by inaccurate information about how American society works.

As we stated earlier, critical diversity seeks both to understand unjust inequality and to redress it. At times, silence on an issue maintains its power. Part of the challenge of redressing unfair wealth disparities is bringing it to the fore of the diversity discussion. We do not believe that we can be successful in combating racism, sexism, heterosexism, and religious bigotry until we also take on the issues of unfair wealth disparities and class-based inequalities.

Notes

1 Neckerman and Torche, 2007; and Massey, 2007
2 Keister and Moller, 2000; Neckerman and Torche, 2007
3 Neckerman and Torche, 2007
4 Winnick, 1989
5 Keister, 2000: 6
6 Oliver and Shapiro, 1995: 58
7 Spilerman, 2000: 500
8 Oliver and Shapiro, 1995: 89
9 Oliver and Shapiro, 1995: 2
10 Spilerman, 2000: 500
11 Congressional Budget Office, 2011
12 Oliver and Shapiro, 1995

13 U.S. Bureau of the Census, 2010
14 Oliver and Shapiro, 1995
15 Conley, 1999
16 Brimmer, 1988: 153
17 Massey and Denton, 1993
18 Oliver and Shapiro, 1995
19 Oliver and Shapiro, 1995
20 Oliver and Shapiro, 1995
21 Conley, 1999
22 Conley, 1999
23 Conley, 1999
24 Conley, 1999
25 Conley, 1999
26 Squires, 1992: 2
27 Kirp et al., 1995: 7
28 Ando and Modigiliani, 1963
29 Keister and Moller, 2001
30 Brimmer, 1988
31 Oliver and Shapiro, 1995
32 Oliver and Shapiro, 1995
33 Brimmer, 1988
34 Brimmer, 1988
35 Conley, 1999; Semyonov and Lewin-Epstein, 2001; Gittleman and Wolff, 2004; Oliver and Shapiro,
    1995; Shapiro, 2005; Collins, 1998
36 Gale and Scholz 1994: 156
37 Semyonov, and Lewin-Epstein, 2001; Gittleman and Wolff, 2004
38 Szydlik, 2004
39 Szydlik, 2004: 31
40 Smith, 1995
41 Szydlik, 2004
42 Szydlik, 2004: 33
43 Gale and Scholz, 1994: 145
44 Gale and Scholz, 1994
45 Szydlik, 2004
46 Oliver and Shapiro, 1995
47 Shapiro, 2005: 61
48 Shapiro, 2005: 69
49 Shapiro, 2005
50 Shapiro, 2005: 69
51 Smith, 1995
52 Shapiro, 2005
53 Shapiro, 2005
54 Gittleman and Wolff, 2004
55 Shapiro, 2005
56 Keister, 2004
57 Keister, 2004
58 Keister, 2004
59 Keister, 2004
60 Keister, 2005: 210
61 Wilson, 1987
62 Sykes, 2003; Rosenbaum, 1994; and Oliver and Shapiro, 1995
63 Oliver and Shapiro, 1995; and Rosenbaum, 1994
64 Oliver and Shapiro, 1995
65 Holden and Smock, 1991
66 Batso et al., 2009
67 Klasen, 2004

68 Sykes, 2003
69 Caner and Wolff, 2004
70 Bureau of Labor Statistics, 2007
71 Levy, 1999
72 Frank and Cook, 1996
73 Frank, 1999
74 Oliver and Shapiro, 1995
75 Oliver and Shapiro, 1995
76 Wilson, 1987; Shapiro, 2005; and Gittleman and Wolff, 2004
77 Oliver and Shapiro, 1995
78 Conley, 1999
79 Conley, 1999
80 Keister, 2005
81 Conley, 1999: 137
82 Conley, 1999: 137

References

Ando, Albert and Franco Modigliani. 1963. "The 'Life Cycle' Hypothesis of Saving: Aggregate Implications and Tests." *American Economics Review* 53 (1): 55–84.

Batso, Amelia, Sara F. Casaca, Fransico Nunes, and Jose Pereirinha. 2009. "Women and Poverty a Gender-Sensitive Approach." *The Journal of Socioeconomics* 38: 764–778.

Bureau of Labor Statistics. 2007. *U.S. Trade Deficits Worth 26 Million Jobs, Credit.* Washington, DC: Bureau of Labor Statistics.

Brimmer, Andrew F. 1988. "Income, Wealth, and Investment Behavior in the Black Community." *American Economic Review* 78: 151–155.

Caner, Asena and Edward N. Wolff. 2004. "Asset Poverty in the United States, 1984–99: Evidence from the Panel Study of Income Dynamics." *Review of Income and Wealth* 50 (4): 493–518.

Collins, Patricia Hill. 1998. "It's all in the Family: Intersections of Gender, Race, and the Nation." *Hypatia* 13 (3): 62–82.

Congressional Budget Office. 2011. *Trends in the Distribution of Household Income Between 1979 and 2007.* Washington, DC: Congressional Budget Office.

Conley, Dalton. 1999. *Being Black, Living in the Red: Race, Wealth, and Social Policy in America.* Berkeley, CA: University of California Press.

Conley, Dalton. 2001. *Wealth and Poverty in America: A Reader.* Oxford, UK: Blackwell.

DeNavas-Walt, Carmen, Bernadette D. Proctor, and Jessica C. Smith. 2011. *U.S. Census Bureau. Current Population Reports, Income, Poverty, and Health Insurance Coverage in the United States: 2010.* Washington, DC: U.S. Government Printing Office.

Frazier, E. Franklin. 1947. *The Negro Family in the United States.* Chicago, IL: University of Chicago Press.

Frazier, E. Franklin. [1957] 1997. *Black Bourgeoisie.* New York, NY: Free Press Paperbacks.

Gale, William and John Karl Scholz. 1994. "IRAs and Household Saving." *American Economic Review* 84(5): 1233–1260.

Gittleman, Maury and Edward N. Wolff. 2004. "Racial Difference in Patterns of Wealth Accumulation." *Journal of Human Resources* 39 (1): 193–227.

Holden, Karen C. and Pamela J. Smock. 1991. "The Economic Costs of Marital Dissolution: Why Do Women Bear the Disproportionate Cost?" *Annual Review of Sociology* 17 (1): 51–78.

Keister, Lisa. 2000. *Wealth in America.* New York, NY: Cambridge University Press.

Keister, Lisa. 2004. "Race, Family Structure, and Wealth: The Effect of Childhood Family on Adult Asset Ownership." *Sociological Perspectives* 47: 161–187.

Keister, Lisa. 2005. *Getting Rich: America's New Rich and How They Got That Way.* New York: Cambridge University Press.

Keister, Lisa, and Stephanie Moller. 2000. "Wealth Inequality in the United States." *Annual Review of Sociology* 26: 63–81.

Kirp, David L., John P. Dwyer, and Larry A. Rosenthal. 1995. *Our Town: Race, Housing, and the Soul of Suburbia*. New Brunswick, NJ: Rutgers University Press.

Klasen, Stefan. 2004. "In Search of the Holy Grail: How to Achieve Pro-Poor Growth." *Toward Pro Poor Policies-Aid, Institutions, and Globalization*. New York: Oxford University Press.

Levy, Frank. 1999. *The New Dollars and Dreams: American Incomes and Economic Change*. New York: Russel Sage.

Massey, Douglas S. 2007. *Categorically Unequal: The American Stratification System*. New York: Russel Sage Foundation.

Massey, Douglas S. and Nancy Denton. 1993. *American Apartheid: Segregation and the Making of the Underclass*. Cambridge, MA: Harvard University Press.

Mendenhall, Ruby, Greg J. Duncan, and S.A. DeLuca. 2006. "Neighborhood Resources, Racial Segregation, and Economic Mobility: Results from the Gautreaux Program." *Social Science Research* 35: 892–923.

Neckerman, Kathryn and Florencia M. Torche. 2007. *Inequality: Causes and Consequences: Annual Review of Sociology* 33: 335–357.

Oliver, Melvin L. and Thomas M. Shapiro. 1995. *Black Wealth–White Wealth: New Perspectives on Racial Inequality*. New York, NY: Routledge.

Rosenbaum, Emily. 1994. "The Constraints on Minority Housing Choices, New York City 1978–1987." *Social Forces* 72 (3): 725–747.

Ryan, William. 1971. *Blaming the Victim*. New York, NY: Pantheon.

Semyonov, Moshe and Noah Lewin-Epstein. 2001. "The Impact of Parental Transfers on Living Standards of Married Children." *Social Indicators Research* 54: 115–137.

Shapiro, Thomas. 2005. *The Hidden Cost of Being African American: How Wealth Perpetuates Inequality*. New York: Oxford University Press.

Shapiro, Thomas. 2006. "Race, Homeownership and Wealth." *Poverty, Justice, and Community Lawyering: Interdisciplinary and Clinical Perspectives* 20: 53–74.

Smith, James. 1995. "Racial and Ethnic Differences in Wealth in the Health and Retirement Study". *The Journal of Human Resources* 30: S158–S183.

Spilerman, Seymour. 2000. "Wealth and Stratification Processes". *Annual Review of Sociology* 26(1): 497.

Squires, Gregory. 1992. "Community Reinvestment: An Emerging Social Movement," in *From Redlining to Re-Investment: Community Responses to Disinvestment*. Philadelphia, PA: Temple University Press: 1–37.

Steckel, Richard and Jayanthi Krishnan. 2006. "The Wealth Mobility of Men and Women during the 1960s and 1970s." *Journal of Income and Wealth* 52(2): 189–212.

Sykes, Lori Latrice. 2003. "Income Rich and Asset Poor: A Multilevel Analysis of Racial and Ethnic Differences in Housing Values among Baby Boomers." *Population Research and Policy Review* 22 (1): 1–20.

Szydlik, Marc. 2004. "Inheritance and inequality: Theoretical reasoning and empirical evidence." *European Sociological Review* 20(1): 31–45.

Taylor, Paul, Rakesh Kochhar, Richard Fry, Gabriel Velasco, and Seth Motel. 2011. *Wealth Gaps Rise to Record Highs between Whites, Blacks and Hispanics*. Washington, DC: Pew Research Center.

Terrell, Henry. 1971. "Wealth Accumulation of Black and White Families: The Empirical Evidence: Discussion". *Journal of Finance* 26: 363–377.

Wilson, William J. 1979. *The Declining Significance of Race: Blacks and Changing American Institutions*. Chicago, IL: University of Chicago Press.

Wilson, William J. 1987. *The Truly Disadvantaged*. Chicago, IL: Chicago University Press.

Winnick, Andrew J. 1989. *Toward Two Societies: The Changing Distributions of Income and Wealth in the US Since 1960*. New York: Praeger.

Yamokoski, Alexis and Lisa Keister. 2008. "The Wealth of Single Women: Marital Status and Parenthood in the Asset Accumulation of Young Baby Boomers in the United States." *Feminist Economics* 12: 1–2, 167–194.

10

Addressing Homophobia and Heterosexism

Popular images of lesbian, gay, bisexual, and transgendered (LGBT) people suggest that they are better off economically and occupationally than their heterosexual counterparts. Media representations of LGBT affluence often conceal the possibility of workplace discrimination against these groups. At the same time, scholarly research suggests that LGBT people suffer a discrimination penalty in terms of wages and occupational prestige. This is due to the fact that American society is stratified based on sexuality.

Although sexuality is usually a less obvious characteristic of individuals than their race or gender, it does become salient within institutional settings, especially when those holding power within the workplace categorize employees' sexuality or rely on perceptions of employee sexuality to make discriminatory distinctions. So, even when gay, lesbian, or bisexual employees choose not to disclose their identities to coworkers or employers, others still may speculate about their identities "given military discharge records, arrests and/or convictions, marital status, residential neighborhood, or silences in conversations and gossip."[1]

Over the past two decades, the number of companies addressing sexual orientation as part of their valuing diversity initiatives has increased fairly rapidly. As of 2010, 87 percent of the *Fortune* 500 companies had implemented non-discrimination policies that include sexual orientation, and 46 percent had policies that include gender identity.[2] But as of 2012, there is no federal law that consistently protects LGBT individuals from employment discrimination. It remains legal in 29 states to discriminate based on sexual orientation, and in 35 states to do so based on transgender identity or expression. As a result, LGBT people face discrimination in employment, including being fired, being denied promotions, and experiencing harassment on the job. Hard-working lesbian, gay, bisexual, and transgender Americans have lost their livelihoods simply because of who they are. And millions more go to work every day facing that threat. The purpose of this chapter is to investigate stratification patterns in the economic sphere that are based on sexual orientation and to identify organizational best practices designed to create more inclusive, equitable, and productive workplaces for LGBT employees.

Sexual Orientation and Identity

How large is the LGBT population in the United States? Understanding the size of the LGBT population is an important step in attempting to inform diversity research, public policy, and research topics. But knowing the answer to this question is not as easy or straightforward as we would like. For example, according to Gary Gates, an estimated 19 million Americans (8.2 percent) report that they have engaged in same-sex sexual behavior.[3] More than 25 million Americans acknowledge at least some same-sex sexual attraction. Still, less than 4 percent of adults in the United States identify as lesbian, gay, or bisexual. An estimated 0.3 percent of adults are transgender. This implies that there are approximately 9 million LGBT Americans.

Why are there such disparities in these numbers? A debate continues as to the true nature of sexual orientation and identity.[4] On one side of the debate are those essentialists who view sexual orientation and identity as "real," an essence that is universal that can be seen throughout history and across cultures. Such views often assume that sexual identity is both biologically based and static. In addition, most of the essentialist literature on sexual identity upholds a binary scheme of sexuality that suggests that individuals classify themselves as either heterosexual or homosexual. And homosexuals are "gay" if they are male, and "lesbian" if they are female. On the other side of the debate are social constructionists who hold that sexual orientation and identity are not fixed, but rather are historically contingent and culturally specific. Proponents of such views often suggest that sexual identities are shaped by social, political, economic, and cultural forces, and these identities can challenge or reinforce heterosexist notions of sexuality.[5]

Theorizing on this topic is varied and reflects the social location (e.g., race, class, and sexual orientation) of participants in the discourse. Although an increased awareness of LGBT sexual identities exists, contemporary analyses are often conducted by those who are located within several dominant societal groups (e.g., White, middle class, formally educated academics, etc.). As a consequence, there remains a shortage of systematic research focusing on the sexual identities of those who are not part of dominant social groups.[6] In order to promote a more complex understanding of those within subjugated groups, it is crucial to examine the experiences of those facing multiple oppressions.

Early scholarship and theorizing about sexual identity began with the juxtaposition of homosexuality and heterosexuality. In his article "The

Invention of Heterosexuality," Jonathan Katz argues that contrary to what most believe or are taught, the idea of heterosexuality is a modern invention, dating to the late nineteenth century.[7] Katz supports his argument by tracing back the evolution of the acts and terms of heterosexuality and homosexuality. Heterosexuality and homosexuality should not be labeled as binary forms of sexual identity; rather, it is the act of sex that is hetero or homosexual, not the person. People were committing these acts of hetero and homosexuality before these terms were even invented. And back before medicine, psychology, and society wanted to label these acts, sex with people of different sex and the same sex was quite common. Dr. James G. Kiernan is known for first using the term heterosexuality in 1892. However, how he used the term in 1892 is different from today. Kiernan claimed heterosexuality to be "inclinations to both sexes." He did not have a name for those who demonstrated an inclination for only the opposite sex. However, Dr. Krafft-Ebing did not agree with Kiernan's ideas, and later that year he defined heterosexuality as it is currently understood: an erotic feeling toward the opposite sex. Krafft-Ebing defined homosexuality as an erotic feeling toward the same sex, and psychosexual hermaphroditism as an erotic impulse towards both sexes. Doctors normalized heterosexuality. However, Kinsey explains that there is no normal and abnormal in science. Kinsey claims that homosexuality and heterosexuality are nature's doing. He suggests that humans do not choose whether to be homosexual or heterosexual.

Along with the social construction of the categorization of these sexual identities came a hierarchal relationship between the two categories. Heterosexuality became the dominant, normal identity. Homosexuality came to be viewed as the abnormal, deviant identity. This could be due to the fact that intercourse with different sexes, between a man and a woman, produces procreation whereas sex between two men or two women does not. Early works viewed homosexuality as deviant and, at worst, pathological.[8] The essentialist perspective framed sexual identity within a binary system that is biologically based. It suggested that homosexuality is an abnormal condition which needs to be studied and cured. However, during the 1970s, research on sexual identity increased. This was due, in large part, to the gay and lesbian liberation movement, which focused on eradicating the stigma of homosexuality.[9]

Homophobia—negative feelings toward homosexuality and people who are identified or perceived as being homosexual—rather than the stigma of homosexuality *per se* is the true culprit that contributes to the silencing, abuse, and psychological and physical trauma faced by hundreds of thousands of members of the LGBT community.[10] The stigma of homosexuality is a reflection and product of homophobia rather than a separate social dynamic.

The symbolic interactionist framework provides some of the core concepts that inform contemporary social constructionists. For example, one might view LGBT status as a stigma—a "spoiled identity" in Erving Goffman's terms—that needs to be managed. Homophobia and the stigma of bisexuality may contribute to the "closet"-type behaviors exhibited among some LGBT people.[11] One way members of the LGBT community may manage their impressions is by controlling the naming process. In part, this is accomplished by choosing their own labels and encouraging others to make use of these names. "Bisexuals," for example, by identifying themselves as bisexuals rather than straight or gay, determine the degree to which their behaviors and ideas fit a heterosexual identity or a homosexual identity. They form the meanings that one attaches to one's self as an object, and they carry expectations for particular kinds of behaviors.[12]

As Paula Rust points out, however, scientists have attempted to elaborate developmental models of coming out that suggest that it is a linear process of self-discovery.[13] She argues that such depictions of a linear process are inaccurate. They usually replace a socially imposed notion of heterosexual identity with a lesbian or gay identity as the accurate reflection of the essence of the individual. But as Rust notes, these models rarely account for bisexual identity as an authentic identity. When they acknowledge bisexual identity at all, they usually cast it as a phase one might pass through on the way to adopting a lesbian or gay identity. Researchers operating within these linear developmental models of coming out usually ask people about the ages at which they experienced particular sexual milestones, and then, reporting the average ages, describe coming out as an ordered sequence of events. Such research suggests that lesbians first experience sexual attraction to other women at an average age of 12 or 13, but do not become aware of these sexual feelings until late adolescence. Rust argues that the portrait of sexual identity formation that is painted by these average ages is not only grossly simplified but factually inaccurate. Based on research with lesbian-identified and bisexual-identified women, she shows that average ages conceal a great deal of variation in the coming out process, both among and between lesbian and bisexual women. In contrast to the linear portrait painted by average ages, she suggests that lesbian and bisexual women experience each milestone event at a wide range of ages; many women do not experience all of the so-called milestone events; women who do experience these events experience them in various orders, and some women experience some events repeatedly.

Postmodern and queer theorists have problematized the notions of sexual identities as real categories. They argue that labeling one's self replicates the binary boundaries of sexuality and continues to establish hegemonic ideals of heterosexuality. Postmodern and queer theorists attempt to move beyond the labels and challenge the limits that sexual identities create.[14]

They argue that people should abandon identities altogether and search to understand the social and political oppressions that labels recreate. Queer theory becomes a frontal assault on the notions of homosexuality as "deviant." Overall, these theorists analyze the underlying meanings of sex and sexual identity as socially constructed. A critique of queer theory is that postmodernists fail to "acknowledge the very real structures and physical bodies . . . in which individuals live."[15] This line of scholarship once again silences the voices of marginalized groups such as African American women who identify as gay, lesbian, and bisexual at a point in history when their voices have the greatest opportunity to be heard. It does so without creating space to acknowledge that these women continue to experience the world as if their identities are real and fixed within society. It is ironic that just as African-American women who sleep with women are gaining a toehold in the corridors of power, the authority of their voices as African-American gay, lesbian, or bisexual women is challenged through destabilizing these identities.

Revealing one's sexual identity places him or her in a position to be labeled as "lesbian," "gay," "bisexual," etc. These terms take on personal and political meanings that may or may not reflect the internalized views that individuals hold for themselves.[16] For example, Jeffery Weeks points out that homosexually inclined individuals may participate in the LGBT community and take on a homosexual identity while not engaging in homosexual behavior.[17] Others, however, may have sex with someone of the same gender and reject homosexual identity entirely. Weeks continues to remind us that homosexual identity depends on the meanings that the actors attribute to homosexuality, and that sexual identities are historically and culturally specific. Weeks also demonstrates that sexuality has become a potent political issue that creates the bases for political mobilizations among LGBT people. He asserts that lesbian identity, in particular, is constructed within Western society as a political choice that women make in order to demonstrate solidarity, sisterhood, and affection with other women and feminism, as well as an expression of sexual preference.

According to Shane Phelan, mainstream notions of lesbianism are often framed by essentialist ideals that construct lesbians as politically active, middle-class, anti-male feminists who have sex only with women.[18] Lesbianism, however, may not be simply a part of someone's essence. Nor does it necessarily exist outside of a specific historical period. Rather, it may be a critical space located within social structures that are more about challenging patriarchy and heteronormativity than sexual behavior.[19] Phelan asserts that identifying as lesbian involves a creation of the self in a community that guides the process of becoming lesbian.[20] Moreover, it involves enacting and inventing the meanings of lesbianism in a specific historical period which is both personal and political. Taking on a lesbian identity, then, reflects both individuals' internal beliefs about who they are as well as their politics.

Dwight McBride also discusses the role that politics play in the sexual identification of women who sleep with women, specifically when identifying as gay versus lesbian.[21] He reveals that even the mainstream media presents women such as Ellen DeGeneres as a non-threatening, all-American girl-next-door with whom Americans can be comfortable. In addition, referring to them as "gay" instead of "lesbian" creates the idea that homosexuals are just like heterosexuals. They want the same entrenched American dream of the house with a picket fence and someone to love them (e.g., someone who shares similar values and politics).

Steve Valocchi claims that the construction of labels such as homosexual, gay, and lesbian is a class-inflected process that is the product of the class dynamics associated with the making of a capitalist state.[22] He states that the lesbian and gay movement of the 1970s worked from the premise of shattering the invisibility of gays and lesbians in order to support an essentialized identity through social institutions, practices, and cultural traditions. Advertisers within the consumer culture then monopolized these niche markets by constructing lesbian and gay identities around consumption. They conflated income with gay identity. The use of advertisement, then, enables individuals to claim their identities by the products they consume and the activities in which they partake. Individuals then associate gay/lesbian identity with middle-class status, ultimately moving these identities away from the political arena to a consumer category about style and fashion.

Revealing one's sexual identity is as much personal as it is political. Such identities are socially constructed. This ability to manage what some might view as a spoiled identity allows LGBT people to manage the impressions others have of them. But sexual identities are not binary or fixed; rather, they are historically contingent, culturally specific, and shaped by social, political, economic, and cultural forces.

Sexual Orientation and Stratification Outcomes

There are several theories that may help us to frame and understand the question of whether income and prestige are stratified according to sexual orientation. "Human capital" theory, for example, holds that education is a key to obtaining higher levels of income and occupational prestige. In this view, there is a direct relationship between educational attainment and increased income and status on the job. However, there is debate as to exactly how education matters for gains in income and status. Human capital theory argues that inequality occurs because some people make the choice to invest in themselves and their futures by gaining additional education and job-related skills while others do not. According to this theory, individuals invest in their stock of skills by paying or foregoing something in the present for the sake of some future gain. For example, people invest in education in order to increase their future wages. School involves the direct cost of tuition, and the opportunity-cost of foregone wages and foregone opportunities to use one's time for leisure. Human capital investments include such things as education, job training, seeking out information, willingness to relocate, making sure that one is healthy, etc. or any other factor that will make a person potentially more productive to his or her employer. Human capital theory suggests that some people earn more simply because they have invested more in themselves in terms of human capital. There is also the tendency for those who are "abler" to invest in themselves more than those who are not as capable. Talented people invest more in themselves than less talented people.

According to human capital theory, employers also act rationally. They seek to hire employees who will be the most productive so that their efforts will lead to greater profitability. If two workers show up for a job, the employer will select the worker who offers the greatest marginal productivity for a given wage. If the employer fails to do this, his competitor will do so and will be able to sell his widgets for less and ultimately drive the other employer out of business. Human capital theory, then, argues that higher education increases skills and makes people more productive on the job; thus, highly educated people will receive greater financial rewards and pay than those with less education and experience.[23]

But sometimes, even if groups are equally talented and have made equal investments in themselves, some employers still express tastes for discrimination. That is, they will prefer certain types of workers over others for non-rational reasons. While the employer may go out of business in the long run, in the short run, the discriminated-against worker will earn less. To the degree that this happens systematically against certain groups, there will be inequality (stratification).

In 2007, more than 12 percent of Americans were officially below the poverty line.[24] These statistics include people from every race, gender, age group, and region. As mentioned above, a popular stereotype suggests that lesbians and gay men are more affluent, more highly educated, and have higher incomes than do their heterosexual counterparts.

Research consistently shows, however, that LGBT people, especially lesbians and transgender people, endure vast income inequality compared to their heterosexual peers.[25] Lesbians, gays, and bisexuals are as likely to live in poverty as are heterosexual people and their families.[26] Lesbian couples, for example, tend to have much higher poverty rates than either heterosexual or male couples. They are twice as likely as straight married couples to live in poverty. Lesbian couples are especially hard-hit, as women continue to make 78 cents to every dollar that men make. Still, bisexual women are more than twice as likely as lesbians to live in poverty (17.7 versus 7.8 percent), and bisexual men are over 50 percent more likely to live in poverty than gay men (9.7 versus 6.2 percent). And nearly two in three (66 percent) transgender people make less than US$25,000 a year. The children of gay couples are twice as likely to be poor as are the offspring of straight, married couples. Randy Albelda and his colleagues suggest that "vulnerability to employment discrimination, lack of access to marriage, higher rates of being uninsured, less family support, or family conflict over coming out" all contribute to higher poverty rates among lesbians, gays, and bisexuals.

One of the solutions to such disparities is marriage equality and equalization of tax laws. Marriage equality is part of the solution, but there are other more basic measures, like passing the Employment Non-Discrimination Act (ENDA), eliminating LGBT discrimination in housing, making higher education and vocational training less expensive and more accessible, and improving education overall for everyone.

Albelda and his colleagues also suggest that "labor market reforms that help boost the wages of low-income workers will also benefit LGBT earners as well, such as higher minimum wages or larger earned income tax credits (EITC). Policies promoting equal pay for women would help raise the incomes of . . . lesbian couples, and might reduce the poverty gap for lesbian couples."[27]

LGBT Initiatives within Corporate America

Over the years, the federal government has enacted legislation to ensure that the rights of women, people of color, pregnant women, and employees with disabilities are protected in the workplace. Progressive companies then use these data to assess progress toward internal hiring and other diversity benchmarks. We believe that identifying work teams that need additional support, more education, and new policies and processes to improve employee engagement are important to organizations that are attempting to move from good to great in the diversity efforts. Unfortunately, many of these organizations lag behind when it comes to similar efforts with respect to sexuality. But the good news is that some best practices and factors have emerged as more companies implement LGBT Self-Identification programs. Many organizations have implemented nondiscrimination policies and provided benefits to LGBT employees. Frequently companies attend local LGBT Pride celebrations. Some sponsor programs that reach out to the emerging LGBT market. All of these programs are based on diversity, market share, and social responsibility goals.

How successful are companies in these efforts? How can you begin to evaluate LGBT initiatives within your company? It is important to have senior leaders within the organization acknowledge the significance of issues of equity and fairness, as well as the business case for inclusion as they relate to sexuality. A first step is the awareness that the data need to be collected. If an LGBT member or Employee Resource Group (ERG) exists within your organization, enlist their help to promote LGBT employees' willingness to self-identify. Be aware that many employees may not respond during the first year of a survey because they are unsure if their responses are anonymous or what the company will do with the information. Indeed, low return rates may occur in the first few years, but once a company shows a commitment to LGBT diversity, higher return rates will usually follow. A second step is for companies to realize what kind of data they need to collect and what they will do with the data in order to measure sexual orientation and gender so that they can take steps to make necessary improvements in the workplace. Allowing employees to opt in or opt out should be a goal of the program to develop a workplace where LGBT employees feel safe to "come out" and self-identify. A third step may include conducting an anonymous survey in order to assess the climate for LGBT employees. Anonymous climate surveys can include optional demographic questions on gender identity and sexual orientation that can then be reported through aggregated data broken down by business unit or function. Such surveys allow organizations to assess the climate of the workplace for LGBT employees. Results from such surveys can help guide changes that may lead to improved recruiting goals, higher promotion rates, and increased proportions of LGBT employees in management positions. As with any type of survey that involves demographic data (e.g., race, ethnicity, gender), organizational leaders should be prepared to take necessary corrective actions if and when the data reveal that discrimination is occurring.

The efforts of LGBT employee resource groups have been instrumental in initiating many of the changes that occur in organizations with respect to sexual orientation. We believe that developing leader-sanctioned resource groups is fundamental to building organizational culture-change processes. It is critically important to such resource groups to gain early support and endorsement of top organizational leaders. Often, a powerful strategy is for members of the LGBT resource groups to present the organizations' leaders with a clear "business case" for why sexual orientation matters in the workplace and in the larger community. It is also helpful for members of the LGBT resource group to meet with the organizations' leaders to discuss the impact of homophobia and heterosexism upon employees' lives. To gain the support of top leaders, some groups have collected and shared personal examples of how employees in their organization have been hurt by the current policies, business practices, or workplace dynamics. It is also instructive for LGBT members of the organization to explain how they and others have been passed over for promotions or how they have experienced harassing behaviors and homophobic comments so that they can help the organizations' leaders better understand and realize the depth and scope of the problems.

We believe there are several things organizations can do to improve the climate for LGBT members. In particular, as stated above, we believe that developing leader-sanctioned resource groups is important to generating organizational culture-change processes. We also believe that it is important that "leaders . . . use opportunities to re-emphasize their commitment to a policy of zero tolerance for homophobic harassment, discrimination and prejudice in the workplace, and state their expectation that all [members] strive to create a safe and productive . . . environment."[28]

We also believe that organizations can improve the climate for LGBT members by creating and then publicizing the existence of resource groups so that they can increase their membership. Usually, organizations can accomplish this by publishing articles in their newsletters or other outlets. They can also do so by advertising at Pride events or in the gay press. It is also possible to hold informal educational sessions for members. It may also be possible to conduct team-building sessions for group members. It is important to emphasize that such activities are open to all members.

Organizations should also offer awareness training programs to increase their members' knowledge about sexual orientation as an issue in the organization. Often, members of the LGBT resource group will take the lead in identifying potential speakers, educational topics, and group activities. These efforts should be partnered with the organization's diversity officers in order to include sexual orientation as a critical component of the organization's diversity training efforts. The goal of these efforts should be to help participants of various sexual orientations realize the similarities they share with each other. But consistent with the idea of critical diversity, such sessions should also shed light on the negative impact of prejudice and discrimination, especially on those who are LGBT. A challenge of such sessions is to show that the organization has no agenda in changing people's personal values or beliefs, but at the same time that it wants to create a safe and productive space for all organization members. Such sessions need to be geared toward providing members—especially senior leaders—with tools that will help them deepen their understanding and commitment to such issues.

Organizations should also consider developing LGBT Safe Zones. Such safe spaces are designed both to raise awareness about LGBT issues and to create space for people to voluntarily show their support for a LGBT-friendly environment. This should also be where members can openly hold conversations about issues related to sexual orientation. These LGBT Safe

Zones may also be locations where rank-and-file members discuss LGBT issues of common concern.

Organizations also need to create policies that may help to manage homophobic behavior. Such policies need to include all relevant organizational policies that do not specifically include sexual orientation. Of course, these must include policies related to nondiscrimination and harassment. In keeping with critical diversity, they should also include policies related to fair business practices (recruiting, compensation, job assignments, promotions, and terminations), standards of conduct, and performance reviews. It is also important that organizations include benefit packages that ensure equitable benefits for LGBT members for themselves, their domestic partners, and their families. Such benefits may include things such as health, life, and disability insurance; family leave options; pensions, retirement plans, and stock options; emergency and bereavement options; flex time; and adoption assistance. Several organizations have come to realize that by offering equitable benefits they will increase their success at attracting and retaining talented members.

Finally, it is important that organizations communicate consistent messages. Leaders of LGBT resource groups often emphasize the need to communicate with managers and employees about the goals, activities, and purpose of their diversity efforts. It is important to raise issues about sexual orientation and to advertise educational events in newsletters, on webpages, on posters, and on list serves. As we mentioned previously, it is also important that members from the LGBT resource group meet personally with top leaders of the organization and diversity officers on a regular basis to keep the dialogue progressing on these issues. Even more, in order to sustain progress and organizational changes, it is critical that organizations create an infrastructure that ensures continued attention to and action on these issues.

Notes

1 Badgett, 2001: 49
2 Day and Greene, 2006
3 Gates, 2011
4 Kohm and Yarhouse, 2002
5 Simon, 1996
6 Moore, 2008
7 Katz, 1990
8 Eliason, 2001; Esterberg, 1997; Lemelle and Battle, 2004; Newman, 2007; Bradford, 2004; and Collins, 2004
9 Stockdill, 2002
10 Battle and Bennett, 2000
11 Lemelle and Battle, 2004
12 Esterberg, 1997

13 Rust, 1996
14 Simon, 1996
15 Esterberg, 1997: 24
16 Lorde, 1982; and Takagi, 1996
17 Weeks, 1985
18 Phelan, 1993
19 Rich, 1980; and Phelan, 1993
20 Phelan, 1993
21 McBride, 2005
22 Valocchi, 1999
23 England, 1992
24 Albelda et al., 2009
25 Badgett, 2001; Badgett, Sears, and Ho, 2006; and Albelda et al., 2009
26 Albelda et al., 2009
27 Albelda et al., 2009: 15
28 Obear, 2000: 27

References

Albelda, Randy, M.V. Lee Badgett, Alyssa Schneebaum, and Gary J. Gates, 2009. *Poverty in the Lesbian, Gay, and Bisexual Community.* Los Angeles, CA: The Williams Institute, UCLA School of Law.

Badgett, M.V. Lee. 2001. *Money, Myths, and Change: The Economic Lives of Lesbians and Gay Men.* Chicago, IL: University of Chicago Press.

Badgett, M. V. Lee, R. Bradley Sears, and Deborah Ho. 2006. "Supporting Families, Saving Funds: An Economic Analysis of Equality for Same-Sex Couples in Jersey." *Rutgers Journal of Law & Public Policy* 4 (1): 8–93.

Battle, Juan and Michael Bennett. 2000. "Research on Lesbian and Gay Populations within the African American Community: What Have We Learned?" *African American Research Perspectives* 6(2): 35–47.

Bradford, Mary. 2004. "The Bisexual Experience: Living in a Dichotomous Culture," in R. Fox (Ed.). *Current Research on Bisexuality: The Intersection of Race and Bisexuality: A Critical Overview of the Literature and Past, Present, and Future Directions of the "Borderlands".* Binghamton, NY: Harrington Park Press: 7–24.

Collins, Fuji. 2004. "The Intersection of Race and Bisexuality: A Critical Overview of the Literature and Past, Present, and Future Directions of the "Borderlands," in R. Fox (Ed.). *Current Research on Bisexuality: The Intersection of Race and Bisexuality: A Critical Overview of the Literature and Past, Present, and Future Directions of the "Borderlands".* Binghamton, NY: Harrington Park Press: 101.

Day, Nancy E. and Patricia G. Greene. 2006. "A Case for Sexual Orientation Diversity Management in Small and Large Organizations." *Human Resource Management* 47(3): 637–654.

Eliason, Michele. 2001. "Bi-Negativity: The Stigma Facing Bisexual Men." *Journal of Bisexuality* 1(2/3): 137–154.

England, Paula. 1992. *Comparable Worth: Theories and Evidence.* New York, NY: Aldine de Gruyter.

Esterberg, Kristin G. 1997. *Lesbian and Bisexual Identities: Constructing Communities, Constructing Selves.* Philadelphia, PA: Temple University Press.

Gates, Gary J. 2011. *How Many People Are Lesbian, Gay, Bisexual, and Transgender?* Los Angeles, CA: The Williams Institute, UCLA School of Law.

Katz, Jonathan Ned. 1990. "The Invention of Heterosexuality." *Socialist Review* 20(1): 7–34.

Kohm, Lynne Marie and Mark A. Yarhouse. 2002. "Fairness, Accuracy and Honesty in Discussing Homosexuality and Marriage." *Regent University Law Review* 14: 249–266.

Laumann, Edward, John Gagnon, Robert T. Michael, and Stuart Michaels. 2000. *The Social Organization of Sexuality: Sexual Practices in the United States.* Chicago, IL: University of Chicago Press.

Lemelle, Anthony and Juan Battle. 2004. "Black Masculinity Matters in Attitudes toward Gay Males." *Journal of Homosexuality* 47: 39–51.

Lorde, Audre. 1982. *Zami: A New Spelling of My Name.* Berkeley, CA: The Crossing Press.

McBride, Dwight. A. 2005. *Why I Hate Abercrombie & Fitch: Essays on Race and Sexuality.* New York, NY: New York University.

Moore, Mignon R. 2008. "Gendered Power Relations among Women: A Study of Household Decision Making in Black, Lesbian Stepfamilies." *American Sociological Review* 73 (April): 335–356.

Newman, David. 2007. *Identities and Inequalities: Exploring the Intersections of Race, Class, Gender and Sexuality.* New York, NY: McGraw-Hill.

Obear, Kathy. 2000. "Best Practices that Address Homophobia and Heterosexism in Corporations." *Diversity Factor:* 27.

Phelan, Shane. 1993. "(Be) Coming Out: Lesbian Identity and Politics." *Signs* 18(4):765–790.

Rich, Adrienne. 1980. "Compulsory Heterosexuality and Lesbian Experience." *Signs* 5: 631–660.

Rust, Paula C. 1996. "Sexual Identity and Bisexual Identities: The Struggle for Self-Description in a Changing Sexual Landscape," in B. Beeyman and M. Eliason (Eds). *Queer Studies: A Lesbian, Gay, Bisexual, and Transgender Anthology.* New York, NY: New York University Press: 64–86.

Simon, William. 1996. *Postmodern Sexualities.* London and New York: Routledge.

Stockdill, Brett. 2002. *Activism against AIDS: At the Intersection of Sexuality, Race, Gender, and Class.* Boulder, CO: Lynne Rienner.

Takagi, Dana Y. 1996. "Maiden Voyage: Excursion into Sexuality and Identity Politics in Asian America," in R. Leong (Ed.). *Asian American Sexualities.* New York and London: Routledge: 21–35.

Valocchi, Steve. 1999. "The Class-Inflected Nature of Gay Identity." *Social Problems* 46: 207–224.

Weeks, Jeffery. 1985. *Sexuality and Its Discontents: Meanings, Myths, and Modern Sexualities.* New York and London: Routledge.

11

Diversity Success on Campus

Diversity is fundamental to higher education's central goal of enabling students to lead the examined life. Diversity helps prepare students to maintain democracy by getting them ready to participate fully in the national and global economy. Achievement of this goal requires breaking down barriers that isolate students from the world. It also calls for a critical diversity that genuinely exposes students to a range of viewpoints. Critical diversity does not dictate a particular point of view. It does, however, require examining issues of parity, equity, and inequality in all forms. As mentioned previously, it requires confronting issues of oppression and stratification that revolve around issues of diversity. We, therefore, believe that critical diversity is central to the mission of higher education.

We believe that those in institutions of higher learning have a critical burden. Most people are keenly aware that colleges and universities play a major role in picking winners and losers in our society. They are obliged to produce the next generation of leaders who will guide the nation in the professions. They must teach those who will provide ideas that will help meet society's pressing needs. They are required to guide those whose success will be important to the independence, prosperity, and world leadership of the United States. We believe that it is in government's interest to foster rather than impede diversity in higher education. After all, the majority of the world's leading universities are located in the United States. The U.S. leads the world in average years of education for its typical citizen. It invests more resources in higher education per student than any other nation. The American professoriate is typically thought of as being the most accomplished in the world. In short, American higher education sets the world standard, in large part, because the United States has a long tradition of following progressive educators' judgments in carrying out higher education. When universities are granted the freedom to assemble student bodies that feature multiple types of diversity, the result is a highly sought-after learning environment that attracts talented and motivated students.

As the demography of this country has changed, even on college campuses, we are reminded of how difficult it is to eradicate racism, sexism, classism, and heterosexism. In an era of economic uncertainty, many people make the argument that access to colleges and universities should focus on merit, and only when necessary on family income rather than racial diversity. But we must be mindful that prejudices, stereotypes, and resentments shade our notions of merit and, thus, poison the well against certain groups. Not only is it nearly impossible to get rid of prejudices, stereotypes, and resentments that permeate the larger society, it is also very difficult to keep them from poisoning interactions on campuses. Such issues make it difficult for people from different backgrounds to hear or truly see one another. Under such circumstances, it is nearly impossible for them to get to know each other.

This chapter examines differences in educational attainment and explanations of them. It also points to some of the challenges of diversity on campuses. It offers some strategies for redressing racism, sexism, classism, and heterosexism in higher education. It also examines students' views of affirmative action and provides an overview of students' perceptions of the diversity climate on campuses. Finally, it makes the business case for critical diversity in higher education.

Differences in Educational Attainment

The levels of educational attainment of African Americans and Latinos lag behind those of Whites and Asian Americans. As Figure 11.1 shows, according to the U.S. Census in 2010, 84 percent of African Americans over age 25 had completed high school. This compares with 87 percent for Whites, 62 percent of Hispanics, and 88 percent of Asians. Between 1980 and 2010, college graduation rates increased for all races. Among African Americans over age 25, 19 percent had completed college. This compares with 29 percent for Whites, 13 percent of Hispanics, and 52 percent of Asians.

What accounts for such differences in educational attainment? There are several explanations. According to "status attainment" theory, education sorts people according to academic or intellectual ability. Although status attainment is affected by achieved factors (such as educational attainment) and ascribed factors (such as family income), a person's status is largely determined by his or her own efforts and abilities. For the status attainment approach, the focus has been on the special role of schooling in the attainment process because education is a proxy for merit (i.e., intelligence, motivation, and aspirations).

Those who put forward a *socialization* or *meritocratic* variant of status attainment theory suggest that, while all of these things are true, there are no direct links between a person's socioeconomic origins and destination.

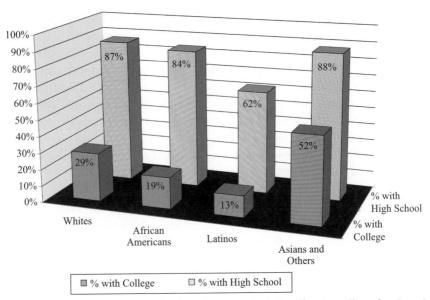

Figure 11.1 Percentage Graduating from High School and College by Race/ Ethnicity

This approach begins with a basic demographic model and then introduces social psychological variables to link origins to educational attainment and educational attainment to occupational prestige. Socialization variants claim that the link between socioeconomic status (SES) of origin and educational attainment can be explained by differential socialization processes that occur along class lines. Because significant others (such as parents, teachers, and friends) influence the goals of the young, and because goals and aspirations are consequential for actual attainment, different levels of encouragement will lead to different levels of education.

Proponents of a *credentialing* variant of status attainment theory emphasize a very different status attainment view of education. According to the credentialing perspective, schooling has effects on socioeconomic status mostly because it certifies winners and losers for reasons that go well beyond merit. Employers prefer highly educated workers because their credentials help to rationalize picking them over comparable workers. Cognitive skills matter less to socioeconomic outcomes than does educational attainment *per se*. The type of friends students are likely to make, the values they are exposed to, and satisfaction or dissatisfaction with the school are all dependent upon the character of the student body. For example, parochial schools show status advantage for their graduates, but this is really due to the fact that the parents of such graduates are more mobility conscious than are the parents of public school graduates.

Christopher Jencks and his colleagues concluded that the achievement of students was related to the socioeconomic level of their classmates, as long as impoverished students were in a significant minority of the school student body.[1] This usually meant that a student's achievement was also related to the race or, more accurately, the class of his classmates, since Black classmates tended to be poorer. Jencks also concluded that when the socioeconomic level of a student's classmates was held constant, however, their race had no relationship to achievement. This conclusion is consistent with the idea that school social class has an effect on academic achievement independent of the individual student's family background.

Jencks treats attainment as a function of family background and school factors. Still, these factors can explain no more than 25 percent of the person-to-person variability in what people earn. Schooling itself explains no more that 10 percent. Perhaps surprised by the lack of explanatory power of these factors, Jencks and his colleagues attributed the remaining variability in income to unmeasured factors such as personality and luck. The authors were left with the conclusion that schooling makes only a modest contribution to adult income. In other words, schools may do fine things such as teach people to read, write, solve math problems, and speak foreign languages, but they do not bridge the income gap between the advantaged and the disadvantaged.

In contrast to status attainment theory, structural discrimination theories locate the source of disadvantage, especially for people of color, in the social structure of society as a whole. Institutional discrimination exists when the criteria for selection are applied uniformly but are not relevant to the task to be performed and systematically have a more negative effect on some groups. Acts of individual discrimination are often both conscious and obvious. Thus, they can be dealt with by either removing the person who discriminates from any position where such actions are meaningful or by inducing the person to halt the behavior in question. In contrast, institutional discrimination is built into the structure itself. Thus, it is usually more covert and tenacious. It can occur regardless of the desires or intentions of the people perpetuating it.

As institutional discrimination is built into the normal working relationships of institutions, its perpetuation requires only that people continue "business as usual." Its eradication requires much more than good will. It requires active review of the assumptions and practices by which the institution operates and revision of those practices found to have discriminatory results. Such an operation cannot be approached casually.

Institutional discrimination usually begins with the recruitment process. Positions, especially the most desirable ones, often are not openly advertised. Since such patterns of association tend to be homogenous, knowledge of opportunities rarely gets to members of groups that are not

routinely included in certain circles. Many opportunities depend on recommendations. Those in exclusive circles rarely know about those outside of their circle, and when they do, they are often reluctant to take the
chance of recommending someone who might be thought "unacceptable"
for whatever reason. To break these patterns, it is necessary not only to
open up the recruitment process, but also to actively seek members of previously excluded groups and work with their organizations to find capable
applicants.

In positions requiring interviews, problems of "style" often interfere
with accurate perceptions of ability. Unless they have special training or
sensitivity, it is difficult for most interviewers to escape their own social
conditioning that members of many social groups are assumed to be inferior. The fact that members of such groups may have a style of life, speech,
dress, action, and even thought that differs from that of White middle-class
men often creates "noise" which obscures real ability. Too often merit is
confused with conformity to the personal standards of those already in
positions of power.

According to this perspective, much institutional discrimination results
from judgments made on secondary rather than primary characteristics.
Race and sex may be consciously eliminated as concerns, but criteria such
as educational background, employment history, supervisory experience,
age, income, etc., which are consequences of group membership, often act
as legal substitutes that lead to the same outcomes. We must realize that
people who have not had the same life chances will not have the same lifestyles or life results.

It often happens that there are perceived deficits between the qualifications of some applicants and those that the institution would like such
applicants to possess. Sometimes these perceived deficits are spurious
because there is a gut-level distrust of backgrounds of those who are different from the interviewer. Or, when judgments are subjective, the interviewer will fail to see some abilities because they are not expected to be
there. Often the unfortunate fact is that members of many groups have not
had the opportunities to gain the experience or training felt to be desirable to perform in a particular setting. Thus, more flexible standards may
be necessary. Otherwise, institutional discrimination may have a multi-
plier effect. In particular, opportunities denied on one level may become
resource deficiencies on another. As a result, the candidate is prevented
from gaining additional opportunities.

Institutions have great power to reward and penalize. They provide
material goods, opportunities, resources, services, and psychological sat-
isfactions. While these benefits are never distributed perfectly equitably, it
is now illegal for them to be allocated on the basis of race, sex, religion, or
national origin. Nevertheless, since many institutions were structured to

discriminate in the past, without self-conscious changes in their policies they will not have changes in their results.

Institutional discrimination is systemic, self-perpetuating, and often invisible to those who have become accustomed to its operation. Changing it requires intentional efforts.

The Challenges of Diversity on Campuses

Most people on college campuses agree that diversity is not just a good policy. Most well-intentioned people in academic settings also believe that diversity is better for learning, doing business, and competing in the global economy. Many, however, become concerned about how their efforts to improve diversity will be injured if the Supreme Court decides to once again re-examine affirmative action. They are concerned that recent gains will be lost.

According to projections from the National Center for Educational Statistics, enrollment in postsecondary degree-granting institutions is expected to increase by 13 percent between 2009 and 2020. During this same time, enrollments are expected to increase by 1 percent for students who are White; 25 percent for students who are Black, 46 percent for students who are Hispanic, and 25 percent for students who are Asian or Pacific Islander. Enrollments are also expected to increase by 6 percent for men and 15 percent for women. There has also been an increase in the minority share of degrees conferred. In 2000, Black students made up 8.4 percent of all graduate students, compared with 12 percent in 2009. In 2008, Black students earned 10.4 percent of Master's degrees awarded and 6.5 percent of PhDs. This was an increase from 4.9 percent of Master's degrees and 3.2 percent of PhDs in 1990.

Statistics like these illustrate the potential for changing the face of the college student body and future pools of its faculty and staff. But with the continued legal assault on affirmative action in higher education, cuts in financial assistance for students, and increases in educational costs, these relative increases in female students and students of color may be unsustainable. They also raise the questions of how more diverse student bodies can be nurtured, and how institutions will respond to the needs of a more diverse population. They also speak to the growing social and academic imperative for diversity initiatives on college campuses. Ensuring an environment in which people from diverse backgrounds can interact may also speak to issues of social justice.

Today's colleges serve various constituencies from diverse racial, ethnic, and socioeconomic backgrounds and viewpoints. Students, for example, bring great vitality to campus, but they also place significant new demands on faculty knowledge and skill. Many students and their parents see college primarily as the springboard to good jobs. Consequently, they want job-related courses. At the same time, policy-makers view college as a tool to generate regional economic growth. They urge highly targeted workforce development. Business leaders want college graduates who can think analytically, communicate effectively, and solve problems in collaboration with diverse colleagues and customers. Faculty members want students who will develop sophisticated intellectual skills and learn about science, society, the arts, and human culture. For the higher education community as a whole, college is a time when faculty and students can explore important issues in ways that respect a variety of viewpoints and deepen understanding.

As demonstrated above, there are increasing numbers of people seeking higher education. This provides an extraordinary opportunity for the nation to ensure an education of genuine and lifelong value that can prepare citizens and knowledgeable employees who will offer a great deal in the new knowledge-based society.

Yet, there is a real danger that the United States will squander this opportunity because of short-sightedness. Whether they believe in the benefits of diversity on college and university campuses, many Americans seem unsure of race-sensitive admissions policies and support programs. Some feel that any consideration of race is discriminatory. They suggest that basing admissions decisions even partially on racial background negatively stigmatizes and categorizes students of color. Another popular belief is that considering race in admissions decisions may lead to the rejection of qualified White candidates in favor of less-qualified prospects of color. Still others believe that admitting students with information about their race mostly serves students of color who need it least and who may, by virtue of higher socioeconomic status, have received greater academic preparation. Others propose that admission based on race is preferential treatment that increases racial animosities in larger society. However, as William Bowen and Derek Bok have observed, "if race-sensitive admissions were truly poisoning race relations, one might expect to see some evidence of growing dissatisfaction among the White alumni/ae who were most exposed to these policies and most likely to have experienced them when they applied to graduate school."[2] In fact, according to Bowen and Bok's study of several cohorts passing through several selective colleges and universities, "the very opposite is true."[3]

Debates about the value and challenges of diversity persist in higher education. Central to these debates is the role diversity should play in the academic enterprise. A great deal of literature exists on the benefits that diversity brings to student learning outcomes and social experiences. In order to realize these benefits, however, institutions must actively engage in creating diverse learning environments. Diversity planning needs to remain part of universities' agendas. Universities need to be intentional in bringing about effective diversity. They can do this by including curricular programs that create more socially and racially just environments for learning.

Admittedly, doing so is not easy, especially in a context in which sentiments toward diversity and inclusion are souring. A 2010 NBC News/*Wall Street Journal* Poll showed that 43 percent of Americans agreed that "affirmative action programs have gone too far in favoring minorities, and should be ended because they unfairly discriminate against whites." This was a 15 percent increase in the percentage who held such beliefs in previous years. The changing social, political, and economic context of race in America, spurred on by recent Federal Court decisions and political pronouncements about affirmative action, obviously has affected such views.

Despite these shifting opinions, substantial research shows that racial inequality, prejudice, and discrimination continue to exist on campuses across the country. So, the continued push for affirmative action is still warranted. But how, exactly, can we continue to press for greater representation of previously excluded people in higher education, especially in the current political climate? In the next section, we outline some ideas.

Challenging Racism, Sexism, Classism, and Heterosexism

When asked about their impressions of discrimination, 66 percent of Americans in a 2011 Pew Survey said that "there is not a lot of discrimination against Blacks." Indeed, most Whites believe that "today discrimination against Whites has become as big a problem as discrimination against Blacks and other minorities."[4]

Similar polls show that 41 percent of Americans believe that "discrimination against women is no longer a problem in the United States." More than one third of Americans say that there "is not a lot of discrimination against gays and lesbians." And 37 percent said that "there is not a lot of discrimination against Muslims." It is clear that a substantial proportion of Americans believe that discrimination is not a major problem that needs to be attended to directly. These sentiments spill over into the educational realm, and they make it more difficult to implement equal opportunity educational policies and programs without generating the perception that such efforts unfairly provide advantages to some groups and thereby unfairly punish others.

So, what can we do in the current political climate to continue to press for greater representation of previously excluded people in higher education? Institutions can proactively consider applicants' socioeconomic status, not only as part of consideration for financial assistance, but also as part of the admissions process itself. Based on the premise that those who start at the bottom have farther to go in order to make it to the top, educational institutions should select those from disprivileged backgrounds when choosing among equally or near equally qualified applicants according to conventional indicators. Similarly, they should select first-generation applicants rather than "legacies" or the offspring of alumni. In addition, colleges should include in their admissions criteria special consideration for applicants who have endured residential instability (e.g., homelessness, migratory work patterns, etc.) or other residential hardships. Along the same lines, universities should view high-achieving students who come from low-performing schools in a positive light. Too often, universities do the opposite and instead view average students from elite (prep) schools as being meritorious.

There are other things that can be done to provide more equal opportunity to disprivileged students. Institutions can implement plans that guarantee admission to a top percentile of students graduating from all in-state high schools or even subsets of schools. In many cases, such plans take advantage of the unfortunate existence of residential segregation to provide more racial diversity. For example, after being banned from using racial affirmative action in *Hopwood v. Texas,* the University of Texas at Austin experienced a sharp decline in the percentage of African American and Latino students being admitted. Subsequently, Texas employed a "Top 10 Percent" plan and a system of socioeconomic affirmative action. The Texas Top 10 Percent plan and the socioeconomic affirmative action program increased racial diversity without resorting to race or ethnicity *per se.* Prior to the *Hopwood* decision, when race-based affirmative action was in place, the University of Texas at Austin had a student population that was 4 percent Black and 14 percent Latino. During the "Top 10 Percent" plan, the freshman class at the University of Texas actually became more diverse. The percentage of African Americans grew to 4.5 percent, and Latinos grew to 17 percent. As a bonus, the retention rates of Latino and African American students admitted to the university increased as well. The "10 Percenters" performed better overall as the diversity of the university increased.

As we mentioned, the Texas "Top 10 Percent" plan increased diversity at the University of Texas in part because of racial residential segregation and segregation in high schools. Over time, the plan may have also increased integration at high schools in Texas, as more White students began attending public schools that had mostly students of color. While it is clear that some of these students were simply "gaming" the system in order to be automatically admitted under the "Top 10 Percent" plan, we must not lose sight of the fact that the plan did, indirectly, lead to more diversity at the high school level. It also allowed some students of color who might not have been admitted previously the opportunity to demonstrate their merit.

Fortunately, there are other options that can also lead to greater diversity in higher education. For example, many colleges and universities have extensive outreach programs that concentrate their recruitment efforts on schools and school districts that disproportionately educate students who are traditionally under-represented in college rather than expending these efforts at wealthy, predominantly White suburban schools that are already well represented. This is related to the idea of expending more resources to assess the merit and qualifications of low-income students and students of color.

Other efforts that yield diversity dividends include making special investments in especially promising low-income students or students of color. Not only could these efforts include doing things such as creating special scholarships or in-state tuition rates, but they also might include such benefits as reimbursement for travel and lodging for campus visits during recruitment. Many colleges and universities make such efforts on a routine basis when recruiting student-athletes. In many cases, such visits may mean making minor adjustments to the criteria used for determining eligibility for subsidized visits to campus.

There are also things that colleges and universities can do that would usually result in a leveling of the playing field a bit more for low-income students and students of color. In particular, because most of these students do not have parents who are alumni of these colleges and universities, simply removing special "legacy" consideration for the children of alumni will make the deck less stacked in favor of the wealthy and Whites. Similarly, if colleges and universities were to stop awarding applicants extra admission points for coming from "academically enriched" programs, they would stop penalizing students who graduate from schools without such opportunities.

Colleges and universities could also remove some of the race and class bias from the admissions process if they were to reduce their reliance on race- and class-biased standardize test scores such as the ACT and the SAT. The tests serve to reinforce race and class advantages, especially when expensive test preparation classes and services are readily available and affordable to students from wealthy schools and seldom available or affordable to students from other schools. Such test preparation services and classes offer a cumulative advantage to those who come from backgrounds of relative privilege.

While it is a bit more nuanced, adding additional points for participation in extracurricular activities reproduces some of the same class and race biases. To the degree that students of different class and racial backgrounds attend high schools with different resources and opportunities for participation in extracurricular activities, it can be much less likely for low-income students and students of color to have the opportunity to participate in such activities. Moreover, because low-income students and students of color may have fewer family resources (e.g., transportation, money to pay for participation fees, leisure time to devote to outside activities), additional admission points for participating in these activities could constitute a systematic bias against low-income students and students of color. Yet, such participation is now considered a routine aspect of the college admissions process.

Of course, there are affirmative action-like programs that generally serve to boost the diversity of colleges and universities. But in some cases, this is precisely why such efforts are unpopular. Whites argue that they lead to the selection of less qualified students of color over more qualified Whites.

Policies aimed at improving the educational opportunities for people of color and providing greater representation of minorities in America's mainstream have been the focus of much controversy and research. Despite a general trend toward lower levels of prejudice in America, concrete programs aimed at providing equal opportunity or altering the relative positions of Whites and people of color are not very popular among Whites. Affirmative action, perhaps more than any other contemporary policy, demonstrates the gap between progressive principles and traditional views about what we should do to reduce racial inequality.

The literature has provided several competing explanations of why Whites oppose affirmative action (especially for African Americans and other people of color). The "principles-implementation gap" has generated considerable scholarly attention, and several explanations have been put forward to account for it. We group such explanations into three basic types:

1 those that point to racial symbolism and group-based differences in values and ideologies;
2 those that focus on group interests and real or perceived threats to resources or other material goods; and
3 those that make claims about justice and fairness.

As will become clear below, these explanations are not mutually exclusive of each other.

One explanation of Whites' opposition to policies such as affirmative action is the idea that there has been a shift from "overt" to "symbolic" racism. This type of argument suggests that while most Whites no longer endorse blatantly anti-minority statements of the "old fashioned" racism, they still reveal an underlying prejudice (or tolerance) toward people of color by their views on contemporary issues such as busing, admissions programs, and affirmative action. This perspective contends that Whites' distaste for equal opportunity policies represents a new form of "symbolic racism" that is an attitudinal mix of anti-minority (especially anti-Black) sentiments and traditional moral values closely linked to the Protestant ethic of hard work, individualism, and self-reliance. It is the "expression in terms of abstract ideological symbols and symbolic behaviors of the feeling that Blacks are violating cherished values and making illegitimate demands for changes in the racial status quo."[5]

In this view, Whites' responses to issues such as affirmative action are based not on tangible threats to assets or resources that such programs might pose, but simply to the symbolism that they represent. The opposition stems in part from underlying attitudinal predispositions toward racial minorities instilled during early childhood, and in part from the challenge that group-based policies represent to treasured values such as individualism. This perspective would suggest that Whites oppose affirmative action because they see minorities and programs to aid them as intrusions that violate established traditions that are highly cherished.

A related view of why Whites generally oppose affirmative action while Blacks tend to support it puts more emphasis on racially based differences in values and how Blacks and Whites differ in their explanations of inequality. Proponents of this perspective would explain the racial gap as a consequence of Black–White differences in explanatory modes used in accounting for racial inequalities. Whites, the argument goes, are more likely than are Blacks to explain inequality in individualistic terms, and to attribute it to a lack of effort, motivation, or ability by Blacks themselves. Those who hold such beliefs, moreover, would also be less likely than others to endorse government intervention to assist minority groups. Thus, an individualistic world view has conservative consequences for racial policy attitudes. Such sentiments are not, however, necessarily linked to anti-minority prejudice. Often, they reflect a genuine value commitment rather than a camouflage for racism. Moreover, such value commitments dictate beliefs about how perceived rewards in life should be distributed, irrespective of race or other group characteristics. Such a perspective would suggest that Whites oppose affirmative action while Blacks support it simply because Blacks and Whites differ fundamentally about the legitimacy of group-based policies.

The group conflict perspective argues that Whites' opposition to large-scale change in racial stratification stems from their sense of group position. This perspective does not suggest that resistance to equal opportunity policy requires prejudice *per se*. Rather, such objections result from the fact that Whites feel vulnerable to minority gains. Whites' aversions to racial change are "based on an acceptance of and stake in standards and institutional priorities rather than a rejection of Black people."[6] Individualism, then, is only a culturally approved basis for many Whites to "respond to issues raised by Blacks in ways that continue their position of social advantage and therefore maintain their privileges."[7] Group conflict revolves around the distribution of scarce resources between groups, as well as attempts to influence the process and patterns of their distribution. Groups come into conflict not only over actual distributions of rewards, but also over the values to be used in guiding the stratification process. This perspective focuses on the fact that Whites accept the general principle of racial equality but reject the specific means to implement such principles because the new rules of distribution fundamentally challenge Whites' ability to retain the lion's share of the good things in life. Larry Bobo and his colleagues suggest that the gap between principles and implementation can be viewed as the emergence of a new American racial ideology of "bounded racial change"[8] which holds that "although Blacks are entitled to full citizenship rights, moving beyond equal rights to assuring equal opportunities, or to implementing policies that may impose substantial burdens on Whites, are illegitimate goals."[9] Such a perspective would suggest that affirmative action has become a battleground for contention and racial group conflict precisely because changes in institutional practices have altered the rules of the stratification process such that Whites believe that minorities materially benefit at the expense of Whites.

Simply put, the relative positions of Whites and Blacks in the American stratification system largely determine support or opposition for programs to advance equality. Whites, as the dominant group, are more inclined to justify the distribution of wealth, power, and prestige in a manner that benefits Whites, the dominant group. Blacks and other people of color are less likely to support such views because such views represent efforts of the dominant group to justify and maintain its unequal relations with a subordinate group. In short, the group conflict perspective suggests that affirmative action has become a zone for conflict and racial group dissension because specific attempts to implement programs that materially benefit Blacks to the detriment of Whites unleash latent prejudices that give way to open hostilities and discrimination. According to this framework, we should expect that Whites who feel threatened by minority gains will be the least likely to support affirmative action, and those who report no such threat will be more inclined to support affirmative action efforts.

As we summarized in Chapter 8, other explanations of affirmative action attitudes often point to claims about reverse discrimination and unfairness. Nathan Glazer, for example, explicitly argues that affirmative action is tantamount to "reverse discrimination."[10] This objection to affirmative action makes the judgment (as an empirical fact) that Whites unfairly lose out to minorities. This supposed fact should disallow affirmative action according to these critics.

The Business Case for Critical Diversity in Higher Education

Recall that Chapter 3 showed that diversity in the corporate setting offers a direct return on investment. Diversity is linked to increased sales revenue, more customers, greater market share, and greater relative profits. Racial and gender diversity in a workforce lead to positive business outcomes over a more homogeneous one because growth and innovation depend on people from various backgrounds working together and capitalizing on their differences.

However, the rhetoric about diversity in higher education is different.[11] Rather than putting forth the business case, proponents of inclusion have argued that it is necessary to safeguard diversity in America's institutions of higher education for the sake of their students. Typically, university officials and others have argued for affirmative action because such policies allows students "to live and study with classmates from a diverse range of backgrounds, [which] is essential to students' training for this new world, nurturing in them an instinct to reach out instead of clinging to the comforts of what seems natural or familiar."[12] In other words, the central argument has been that universities have a compelling interest in promoting diversity because their students benefit from their doing so.

The purpose here is not to argue that students do not benefit from diversity. They do.[13] But universities may have a compelling interest in promoting diversity for reasons very similar to businesses. In particular, it is possible that research universities benefit directly from diversity—much like business organizations—because diversity (among their faculty and their students) enhances their reputational bottom lines. As Lee Bollinger puts it:

> Universities understand that to remain competitive, their most important obligation is to determine—and then deliver—what future graduates will need to know about their world and how to gain that knowledge. While the last century witnessed a new demand for specialized research, prizing the expert's vertical mastery of a single field, the emerging global reality calls for new specialists who can synthesize a diversity of fields and draw quick connections among them.[14]

"Critical diversity" is the equal inclusion of people from varied backgrounds on a parity basis throughout all ranks and divisions of an organization. It especially refers to those who are considered to be different from the traditional members because of exclusionary practices. The critical diversity perspective argues that as organizations become more diverse, they benefit relative to their competitors. This is in contrast to other accounts that view diversity as either inconsequential to success or actually detrimental.

Using data from the 2011 National Academy of Sciences (NAS) Rankings of U.S. Research Universities, we examined whether racial and gender diversity "pay" in terms of the rankings of academic programs at research universities. The NAS dataset consists of several indicators relating to research productivity, student support and outcomes, and program diversity from over 5,000 doctoral programs at U.S. research universities. Our analysis examined the relationship between departmental rankings at research universities and diversity, net of factors such as program size, region, publication rates, grants, scholarly awards, and whether the institution is public or private.

How is diversity related to the rankings of programs in research universities? In order to answer this question, programs were divided by their relative levels of diversity. For illustrative purposes, those with diversity rankings in the lowest third of programs are classified as having low diversity (34 percent); those with diversity rankings in the middle third of programs are classified as having medium diversity (33 percent); and those with diversity rankings in the top third of programs are classified as having high diversity (33 percent). Similarly, those with program rankings in the lowest third of programs are classified as having low rankings (34 percent); those with program rankings in the middle third of programs are classified as having medium rankings (33 percent); and those with program rankings in the top third of programs are classified as having high program rankings (33 percent).

Figure 11.2 shows that programs with low diversity, medium diversity, and high diversity differ in their program rankings. In particular, it shows that low-diversity programs are over-represented among low-ranking departments and slightly under-represented among those with medium and high diversity. Nearly four in ten programs with low diversity are low-ranking programs. This compares with less than one in three of those with medium and high levels of diversity that are low-ranking programs. Similarly, those with more racial and gender diversity have higher program

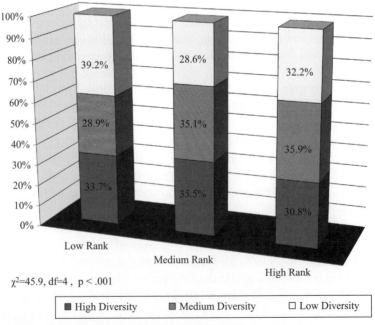

Figure 11.2 Program Rankings by Level of Diversity

rankings. When other things that matter to departmental rankings such as program size, region, publication rates, prominence of faculty publications, grants, and whether the institution is public or private are taken into account, the relationship between diversity and program rankings becomes even stronger. The results suggest that greater diversity is related to higher program rankings. The analysis of data from the National Academy of Sciences Rankings of U.S. Research Universities shows that universities have a compelling business interest in promoting diversity. Diversity among faculty and students enhances the research university's *reputational* bottom line. And this reputation is a university's bottom line.

These findings clearly run counter to the expectations of affirmative action skeptics. They are, rather, consistent with arguments that diversity is related to success because it allows organizations to think outside the box by bringing previously excluded groups into their social and decision-making milieus. This process enhances an organization's creativity, problem-solving, and performance. It is likely that diversity in universities—much like in business settings—produces positive outcomes over homogeneity because growth and innovation depend on people from various backgrounds working together and capitalizing on their differences. In short, diversity is not only good for educational institutions because it allows students to live and study with classmates from a diverse range of backgrounds; it also offers a direct return on investment by promising better reputational rankings.

Higher education is a fiercely competitive market in which organizations compete to recruit diverse individuals. Leading universities strategize about how to gain a competitive edge in the rapidly changing academic marketplace and its new demographic reality. Diversity is an essential ingredient for realizing and keeping a competitive advantage over other educational institutions.

As we have argued throughout this book, we believe that affirmative action is a necessary component to effectively challenging entrenched White privilege. Affirmative action is, in a sense, remedial; however, we need to understand that it compensates for deficiencies in the *system*, not in students.

Intentional change in institutions of higher learning is necessary. Making it happen requires planning and cultivation. Setting goals, engaging various identity groups, locating the necessary resources, and continually assessing progress are all important to ushering in institutional change. Moreover, we need to realize that anti-affirmative action students, faculty, and administrators do not get their racial views in an environmental vacuum. They will not change their views without a substantial push from more socially progressive colleagues, collegiate missions that are more comprehensive, and cultures that are more inclusive. The main element of any effective plan is having a dedicated team designated to lead the effort because such efforts require persistence, patience, and resource mobilization.

Notes

1 Jencks et al., 1972
2 Bowen and Bok, 1998: 269
3 Bowen and Bok, 1998: 269
4 Public Religion Research Institute Pluralism, 2011
5 McConahay and Hough, 1976: 38
6 Wellman, 1977: 234
7 Wellman, 1977: 235
8 Bobo, 1983; Bobo and Gilliam, 1990; and Bobo and Kluegel, 1993
9 Bobo, 1998: 190
10 Glazer, 1975
11 Berrey, 2011
12 Bollinger, 2007: 26
13 Gurin, Nagda, and Lopez, 2004
14 Bollinger, 2007: 27

References

Berrey, Ellen C. 2011. "Why Diversity Became Orthodox in Higher Education, and How It Changed the Meaning of Race on Campus." *Critical Sociology* 37(5): 573–596.

Bobo, Lawrence D. 1983. "Whites' Opposition to Busing: Symbolic Racism or Realistic Group Conflict?" *Journal of Personality and Social Psychology* 45(6): 1196–1210.

Bobo, Lawrence D. 1998. "Race, Interests, and Beliefs about Affirmative Action: Unanswered Questions and New Directions." *American Behavioral Scientist* 41(7): 985–1003.

Bobo, Lawrence D. and Franklin D. Gilliam, Jr. 1990. "Race, Sociopolitical Participation, and Black Empowerment." *The American Political Science Review* 84(2): 377–393.

Bobo, Lawrence D. and James R. Kluegel. 1993. "Opposition to Race-Targeting: Self-Interest, Stratification Ideology, or Racial Attitudes." *American Sociological Review* 58(4): 443–464.

Bollinger, Lee. 2007. "Why Diversity Matters." *Education Digest* 73(2): 26–29.

Bowen, William and Derek Bok. 1998. *The Shape of the River: Long-Term Consequences of Considering Race in College and University Admissions*. Princeton, NJ: Princeton University Press.

Glazer, Nathan. 1975. *Affirmative Discrimination: Ethnic Inequality and Public Policy*. Cambridge, MA: Harvard University Press.

Gurin, Patricia, Biren (Ratnesh) A. Nagda, and Gretchen E. Lopez. 2004. "The Benefits of Diversity in Education for Democratic Citizenship." *Journal of Social Issues* 60(1):17–34.

Jencks, Christopher, Marshall Smith, Henry Acland, Mary Jo Bane, David Cohen, Herbert Gintis, Barbara Heyns, and Stephanie Michelson. 1972. *Inequality: A Reassessment of the Effect of Family and Schooling in America*. New York, NY: Harper Colophon Books.

Kalev, Alexandria, Frank Dobbin, and Erin Kelly. 2006. "Best Practices or Best Guesses? Assessing the Efficacy of Corporate Affirmative Action and Diversity Policies." *American Sociological Review* 71: 589–617.

McConahay, John B. and Joseph C. Hough Jr. 1976. "Symbolic Racism." *Journal of Social Issues* 32(2): 23–45.

Public Religion Research Institute Pluralism, 2011. *Immigration, and Civic Integration Survey*. Washington, DC: Public Religion Research Institute Pluralism.

Wellman, David T. 1977. *Portraits of White Racism*. New York, NY: Cambridge University Press.

12
Building Political Support
for Diversity Programs

In the past, efforts by organizations to broaden the access of women and people of color were driven by corporate goodwill and by the regulatory environment. But as the nation's demography continues to alter consumer profiles and the constituencies that employers draw from, the concept of diversity in business organizations increasingly has become an important topic under discussion. Changing workforce demographics require that people from different backgrounds know how to work effectively in diverse environments. The problem is that often they do not, and workplace conflict is common. Indeed, the fact that bias flourishes both in the culture and structure of companies can be seen in the wave of successful employment discrimination suits filed against major employers.

Although scholars know a great deal about the increasing diversity of the nation and the workforce, relatively little is known about the usefulness of attempts to manage such changing diversity in the work setting. This chapter discusses what we must do to reduce bias in organizational settings through programs meant to improve intergroup relations in diverse work environments. It also addresses related issues. Looking at racial, ethnic, gender, and socioeconomic differences in the workforce, first we examine how well diversity initiatives are understood by various kinds of people within work organizations. Second, we examine how committed to diversity various kinds of people believe their companies to be. We are also concerned about the impact of diversity training, and so we examine how much different categories of workers improve their understanding of their company's diversity initiative and how much people in these categories change their beliefs about their company's level of commitment to diversity.

Chapter 5 of this book was concerned with diversity training and its impact upon productivity, performance, and business success. This chapter has a slightly different focus. It discusses managing diversity to achieve political success in organizations.

Managing Diversity: A Political Necessity

Managing diversity in the workplace is more than just an acquired skill or a set of recruitment and retention programs. It is a way of thinking. To manage diversity means to create an environment that enables all employees to contribute to organizational goals and to experience their full potential. Organizations that are successful in their diversity efforts create the conditions for members to be motivated, productive, and beneficial for the organization. The focus is on how relationships among different people can be improved and understood to better the organization as a whole.[1]

Yet, a diverse workforce can be a double-edged sword. For example, as we pointed out in Chapter 3, on the one hand, research on heterogeneity in groups suggests that diversity properly managed can improve the culture and productivity of organizations. The assumption here is that diversity offers a competitive advantage that will enhance a company's bottom-line performance when managed effectively. Conversely, when mismanaged, diversity can create enormous challenges. Negative interpersonal attitudes connected to diversity can disrupt group cohesion, communication, and performance. With this in mind, we note that well-managed diversity increases the chances of positive results by increasing intergroup tolerance and understanding. Group commitment and individual job satisfaction should also increase. These outcomes, in turn, produce greater productivity and, ultimately, greater corporate profitability.

Managing diversity, while increasingly popular, is not a new phenomenon. During the 1960s and 1970s, with the globalization of multinational corporations and rising racial tensions in America's urban centers, multicultural training emerged as an area of specialization. Global companies realized that sending unprepared managers to locations around the world without the necessary training led to major cultural misunderstandings and problems. Managers who missed cultural nuances could inadvertently cause cultural misunderstandings that led to conflicts. Others found it tricky to assimilate to foreign cultures. Their families often found it difficult to transition culturally. These companies also found that when managers and their families had been abroad for long periods, they often found it difficult to readjust to America and American culture. Consequently, these companies often brought in multicultural specialists to help manage these cultural transitions.

Companies undertook similar efforts during the 1960s and 1970s when several inner city riots and acts of civil disobedience erupted. Not only did these companies engage in more diverse hiring at that time, but they also brought in mediators and joined civic organizations dedicated to ending civil unrest. As a result, several African Americans developed intergroup relations consultancies and diversity management classes to address community relations, boycotts, demands for greater inclusion of African Americans and other people of color, and other intergroup dynamics that threatened business organizations. Today, managing diversity has become a more routine business function in companies themselves. Large business organizations routinely include women, people of color, and members of the lesbian, gay, bisexual, and transgendered (LGBT) community to reconcile intergroup tensions.

As managers scramble to reshape their organizations to better reflect their communities, there are some groups that obviously feel anxious. For example, large numbers of White men believe they have to overcome the handicaps of race and gender that have traditionally worked against women and minorities. Although they acknowledge that past injustices need to be remedied, they feel threatened, frustrated, and, in many cases, angry. But because they often feel that it is not politically correct to question the goals of diversity, most White men are reluctant to say so on the record. Minorities, conversely, deride White male angst and maintain that many business organizations are still not doing enough.

Among Whites—especially White men—there is often the perception of reverse discrimination. At times, it is fueled by rumors. At other times, it is based on the reality that organizations are, in fact, stepping up and aggressively seeking diverse applicant pools. In such cases, these organizations are hiring consulting firms, holding diversity seminars, participating in minority job fairs, announcing special hiring policies, and emphasizing minority figures. We believe these are the kinds of things organizations should be doing in order to bring about genuine, critical diversity. Still, many who feel that they will be left behind by such changes complain that diversity efforts have been handled poorly.

The move to diversify the workplace is happening at corporations across the country. It is creating angst amongst White men. White male professionals are generally uncomfortable with the newfound passion with which managers are trying to promote diversity. These efforts are even more threatening when they take place in the midst of a sluggish economy that has organizations slashing their budgets and trimming their staffs. Often, what White men are now experiencing is the feeling that they are not going to get what they want or deserve when they apply for positions. This is a feeling that women and people of color have had for a long time. Among these women, people of color, and others who have been the targets of anger, there is the temptation to dismiss the feelings that White men have and to say "so what". This, however, is not a very productive or helpful response. Far more helpful would be for people on all sides of the diversity issue to try to understand the perspectives of one another. Far too often, people of color, women, and members of the LGBT community are expected to adapt to existing straight White male culture in order to fit in.

The anxiety and anger that White men are expressing over the push toward diversity in business organizations has also been framed by the national debate over affirmative action and recent Supreme Court rulings restricting it. The affirmative action debate, coupled with slow growth and downsizing, has prompted some White men to act on their anger. However, the angst that White men feel seems disproportionate to the actual changes that are being made. White males may feel threatened, but the diversity-threat is a long way from reality.

How do we get beyond this sense of diversity-threat, especially among White men? We believe that doing so requires:

- demonstrating to White males that it does not cost them much;
- convincing them that they can and should do much better by women and people of color;
- showing employers that it is in their best interests to pursue equal opportunity policies; and
- establishing for the nation that critical diversity is an approach that will strengthen rather than weaken its international competitiveness and general welfare.

Critical Diversity Does Not Cost White Males Too Much

We should acknowledge that it is not easy to get political buy-in on critical diversity. It is similar to convincing people that taxes are necessary. It is difficult to convince some people that taxes serve the common good by making it possible to accomplish tasks collectively that benefit us all. For example, we all benefit from taxes that go toward building and maintaining good and safe roads and bridges. Those who do not drive might say that they should not be expected to contribute tax monies for such things, as there is no direct benefit to them. Yet, it is clear that they benefit because society is better off when goods and services can be delivered more inexpensively with good transportation infrastructure. We ignore the common good, in this case, at the peril of the entire community that benefits from the existence of tax-supported infrastructure. By showing people step by step what we all get from paying taxes, it is possible to convince most reasonable people that collecting taxes is for the common good.

In order to sell critical diversity politically, first we have to convince White men that it does not cost them too much. We have to convince them that it is fair and just for them to give up a piece of the pie and that they will not be asked to give up all of it. For example, recall the controversy when First Lady, Michelle Obama, called on privileged Americans to give up some of their pie in order for there to be pie for everyone. She called for shared sacrifice for the greater good. Conservative commentator Glenn Beck took exception to this call for sharing by saying that he did not want to give up any of his pie. He claimed that the privileged already pay more than their fair share in taxes.

Convincing people about critical diversity is similar. Several people will feel that critical diversity does not benefit them. They will ask why they should make any sacrifice. But if we look at societies in which people are allowed to free ride and not contribute to the common good, we see societies that do not make as much progress as they could. They are societies that do not have transportation systems that are as developed as they might be. They are societies in which the water filtration and sewer systems are not as hygienic as they should be. They are societies in which the educational systems are not fully developed. And in the case of equal opportunity and diversity, they are societies in which the residents are not as educated and skilled as they could be. Such societies suffer from the squandering of human talent and ability. Eventually, the concentration of wealth and opportunity in such societies becomes so concentrated that it is difficult for the masses to get a foothold. The balance of power becomes very skewed, and it is very difficult to make the argument that the quality of life for the typical resident is as good as it could be with more sharing of opportunities and resources. At some point, such societies become unhealthy places for everyone, even the very few who own the lion's share of resources and opportunities.

Critical diversity insists that we must be able to get people to overcome their selfish impulses so that they can realize that it is fair that everyone have opportunity. No one is asking the privileged to give more than they have, and no one is asking them to put themselves behind others in the queue. Indeed, no one is asking them to give more than what would be considered their fair share. The problem, however, is when they consider it to be unfair to have to give up any of what they have so that others can have some. This is the essence of opportunity hoarding that says all opportunities should belong to those who have the ability to prevent others from getting them. Such attitudes suggest that we should have no expectations of those who are fortunate to have attained privilege. We, however, believe that it is both fair and necessary that those with privilege be solicited, indeed required, to share opportunities with the disprivileged.

Again, no one expects for White men to put themselves in positions of disadvantage. No one wants to see White men become a disadvantaged group. We understand that this is, in part, what White men are guarding against. They do not want to become the disadvantaged group. They need to realize that bringing about equity does not put them in danger of becoming the disadvantaged group.

Some White men will argue that sharing opportunities and other resources still puts them at a relative disadvantage. For example, if they currently constitute 30 percent of the people but receive 70 percent of the opportunities and resources, requiring them to reduce their share down to 50 percent would mean a relative loss of opportunities and resources. Although this is true, it would not mean that they would become part of the disprivileged. People who are committed to the principle of fairness and equal opportunity would see that a group that still has a disproportionately high amount of opportunities and resources is not disprivileged, whether they feel they are or not. In America, one of the guiding principles is that everyone should be provided equal opportunity. Perhaps it is more difficult to hold on to such beliefs when one is in a position to hoard opportunities. Nevertheless, believing in opportunity hoarding that serves one's own interests does not negate the validity of equal opportunity as a legitimate value.

We Can Do Much Better by Women and People of Color

A second thing that we must do in order to effectively sell critical diversity politically is to explain that we can and should do much better by women, people of color, and other historically disprivileged groups. In an important study, Alexandria Kalev, Frank Dobbin, and Erin Kelly asked whether diversity management programs work and are worth the money that companies pay for them.[2] They conclude that some diversity management programs work and some do not. The ones that are the most likely to be successful are those that assign clear responsibility for change.

Diversity awareness training is a central tool used by larger employers for resolving employee tensions and for human resource management. The majority of firms involved in diversity consultations offer some form of cultural sensitivity training. Yet, surveys of efforts to evaluate training find that these evaluations typically are confined to distributing questionnaires to trainees at the end of training sessions. Thus, we have almost no systematically collected data to evaluate the impact of diversity training beyond data that aggregate effects. By extension, we know even less about why diversity training and related programs in corporations have been largely ineffective in equalizing opportunities, despite legislative, business, and grassroots efforts.

As mentioned above, diversity training is not a new idea. Diversity trainers use their expertise in conflict resolution, in preparing organizations for increases in racial, ethnic, cultural, and gender diversity, to prepare employees for international work, to safeguard against harassment and unfair employment lawsuits, to take advantage of employee diversity to increase productivity, in order to conduct cultural audits, to manage sexual attraction and romantic relationships in the workplace, and to develop competencies needed to exploit the international marketplace. It is conceivable, however, that diversity training can cause more harm than good to an organization or its individual employees, especially if the diversity training program is ill conceived or if the diversity trainers are ill prepared. Well-intentioned diversity trainers may leave participants with an angry and bitter taste for such training.

We have had the opportunity to work with various organizations, educational institutions, companies, and government agencies. The case of Caterpillar is illustrative of both the importance of diversity and putting initiatives in place to handle the ripple effects that result from the changing gender make-up of a company.

Caterpillar is a U.S.-based maker of agricultural, construction, and mining machinery. It is also a *Fortune* 100 company that is globally engaged in manufacturing, product distribution, and product servicing. Historically, Caterpillar was a laggard in terms of gender diversity. But after the 1980s, when it came close to bankruptcy, it stepped up its recruitment of women. By 2004, the company reported record-breaking profits and sales. However, the company's diversity policies were not universally welcomed by its own employees. Male workers complained that women were getting promoted above men into management. In response, an internal educational program was established with the help of consultants to promote greater understanding of company goals and practices. In 2006, Caterpillar also created the Women's Initiatives Network (WIN) to promote cultural awareness, mentoring, employee recruitment and retention, career development, and community outreach—which increased support for its diversity programs. By 2009, Caterpillar was ranked number 44 in the *Fortune* 500, and since 2010, the company has consistently been named one of the "Top 50 Employers" by *Woman Engineer Magazine.*

How did Caterpillar do it? It worked with consultants to institute diversity training and a diversity initiative aimed at providing its employees with a better understanding of its diversity objectives so that it could more effectively combat sexual harassment, decrease the gender and racial inequalities in managerial jobs, and reduce the likelihood of legal action. In doing so, it addressed how well diversity initiatives were understood by various kinds of people within the company, what the various actors within the company thought constituted "successful diversity," and what impact the interventions had upon the various groups at the company.

Reducing the Appearance of Reverse Discrimination

A profile of the workforce of the company revealed that the modal employee is White, male, 35 to 49 years old, with a high school education, who is also an hourly employee who has worked for the company for more than 25 years and does not have decision-making authority. At the time, the company was experiencing hostilities between managers and labor, between strikers and strikebreakers, and even among family members. This conflict put additional stress on workplace relationships. Added to these stresses were diversity-related problems that occurred when women working on the production line began getting promoted above men into management and the subsequent backlash from men.

Did diversity training affect the understanding that these employees had about their company's diversity objectives? Did it have any effects on how they thought about their company's commitment to diversity? If so, were these changes positive? Were they uniform across subgroups? If not, which groups benefited most from exposure to diversity management efforts? Figure 12.1 summarizes information about changes in the employees' understanding of the company's diversity objectives by selected characteristics. The graphs illustrate the changes between Time 1 and Time 2. The charts show that all groups improved their understanding of the company's diversity objectives after the diversity training sessions. They were not, however, uniform in the amount of improvement. For example, Figure 12.1 shows that those employees who reported working in highly diverse settings (who

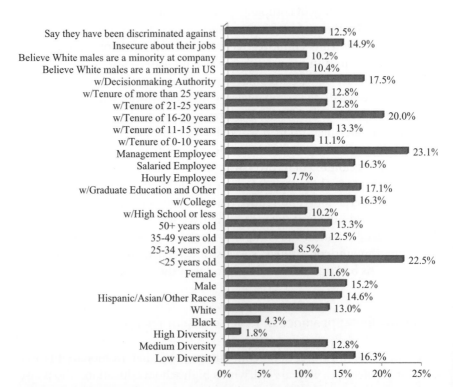

Figure 12.1 Percentage Increase in Understanding of Diversity

already had the best understanding of the company's diversity objectives to begin with) increased their understanding of diversity but not by as much as those employees who worked in low diversity settings (1.8 percent increase compared with 16.3 percent increase).[3]

These relative changes differed by race and ethnicity, however. In particular, prior to the diversity training, Blacks reported a better understanding of the company's diversity objectives than did Whites. Other racial and ethnic groups had higher scores than both Blacks and Whites. After the sessions, however, Whites reported higher scores than Blacks. Yet, Hispanics, Asians, and other racial/ethnic groups outpaced both Blacks and Whites by improving their scores by 14.6 percent. Men initially scored higher than did women on their understanding of diversity. After the diversity training session, this gap grew, as men's scores improved by 15.2 percent versus 11.6 percent for women. In terms of age, the youngest employees started with the lowest scores but showed the greatest percentage improvement (22.5 percent), yet they still lagged behind all other age categories.

The employees with the most education (graduate school) reported the least understanding of diversity but recorded the greatest percentage improvement in their understanding (up 17.1 percent), and yet still lagged behind other educational categories in terms of their understanding of the company's diversity objectives. When making comparisons by job grade, we found that although managerial employees reported the greatest improvements between Time 1 and Time 2, they reported the lowest scores on the understanding index, both before and after the diversity training. No clear pattern emerged out of the relationship between job tenure and understanding of the company's diversity objectives other than the fact that those employees with the longest tenure reported the highest scores on the understanding index, both initially and after the diversity training program. Finally, those with decision-making authority improved their understanding of diversity by 17.5 percent; those who felt insecure about their jobs improved their understanding by 14.9 percent; and those who reported that they had been discriminated against improved their understanding of the company's diversity objectives by 12.5 percent.

Pursuing Equal Opportunity Is in Our Best Interests

Diversity management programs should not be just like orientation programs that only familiarize members with policies and procedures. While familiarization is necessary, it is not sufficient. Critical diversity programs should also have as their aim cultural change, policy change toward more inclusion, and political buy-in of critical diversity as a value. This includes not only those who are new to the organization, but also long-standing members who need to become more aware of shifts that are taking place in the organization. They need to be apprised of why these changes are taking place and why they are in the interest of the organization. Such critical diversity training programs will need to be scrutinized and assessed to ensure that they are meeting organizational expectations and goals.

This is precisely what was done in the case of Caterpillar. We explicitly measured changes in the organization. Figure 12.2 presents information about changes in employees' beliefs about the company's commitment to diversity by selected characteristics. The graphs illustrate the changes between Time 1 and Time 2. The chart shows that all groups increased in their beliefs about the company's commitment to diversity after the diversity training sessions. Again, however, they were not uniform in the amount of change in beliefs. Those employees who reported working in highly diverse settings had the greatest beliefs in the company's commitment to diversity objectives to begin with. Their beliefs in the company's commitment increased but not by as much as those employees working in low diversity units (1.7 percent increase versus 7.4 percent increase).[4]

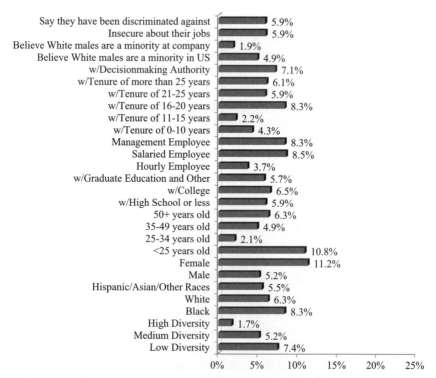

Figure 12.2 Percentage Change in Beliefs about the Company's Commitment to Diversity

Generally, people of color reported stronger beliefs in the company's commitment to diversity than did Whites prior to the diversity training. After the sessions, all racial/ethnic groups reported stronger beliefs in the company's commitment, but the gap between Blacks and Whites grew, as did the one between Whites and other racial/ethnic groups. Before the training sessions, men and women reported similar beliefs about commitment to diversity, but after the sessions they diverged, as women increased their beliefs in the company's commitment to diversity increased by 11.2 percent compared with 5.2 percent for men. In terms of age, the youngest employees started with the lowest commitment index scores but showed the greatest percentage movement (an increase of 10.8 percent). Of those working in various job grades, managerial employees showed the least belief in the company's commitment to diversity in both Time 1 and Time 2. Hourly workers started with the highest scores but changed the least. No clear pattern emerged out of the relationship between job tenure and beliefs about the company's diversity commitment. Employees with decision-making authority increased their beliefs in the company's commitment to diversity by 7.1 percent. Those who felt insecure about their jobs increased their beliefs about the company's commitment to diversity by 5.9 percent. And those who reported that they had been discriminated against also showed increases in their beliefs about the company's commitment to diversity by 5.9 percent.

All groups improved their understanding of the company's diversity objectives after the diversity training sessions. They were not, however, uniform in the amount of improvement. For example, those employees who worked in highly diverse settings had the best understanding of the company's diversity objectives to begin with, but their levels of understanding did not increase by as much as those employees who worked in low diversity settings. These general patterns continued to hold up even with multivariate analysis that controlled for several characteristics of employees.

We also examined changes in employees' beliefs about the company's commitment to diversity. Again, all groups increased in their beliefs about the company's commitment to diversity after the diversity training sessions. Again, however, the results suggest that the greatest change in beliefs about the company's commitment to diversity occurred among those employees who worked in low diversity settings.

Critical Diversity Strengthens International Competitiveness

We believe that efforts with Caterpillar were quite effective in getting political buy-in for critical diversity. There was, however, a rather ominous message in some of our findings. In particular, more than 40 percent of employees reported that they have been the victims of discrimination. Moreover, many apparently believed that White males are a minority both in the U.S. and in the company, despite the fact that more than 85 percent of employees are White and 90 percent of them are male. While it is possible that these employees understand the company's diversity objectives and believe that the company is committed to diversity, it is possible that these workers see such initiatives as direct threats to them and their jobs. Indeed, more than half of the employees report that they are insecure about their jobs.

We believe that a critical diversity framework can help to mitigate against the perceived psychological harm caused by instituting new diversity practices. Let us be clear. We are not arguing that diversity itself is harmful; rather, we are acknowledging the all-too-common perception, especially among White men, that diversity harms them. These reactions include expressions of prejudice that produce hostile environments, engender conflict among members, and stir up suspicion of those outside of people's usual social groups. These situations can lead to toxic environments that are full of distrust and lack of cooperation in the organization.

With the globalization of multinational organizations, a critical diversity framework may be helpful in reminding all members of the organization of the importance of diversity, and it may reduce intergroup conflict and prejudice. Members of the organization need to be made aware that three conditions need to be present in order to derive benefit from diversity. First, the organization must have members with a diversity of backgrounds, perspectives, and social groups.

Second, it is important that diversity also occurs along some dimension relevant to the tasks at hand because different types of diversity may help organizations in different ways. Such diversity potentially helps organizations to avoid insular thinking. It also assists organizations in recruiting and retaining top talent from larger talent pools. As we have suggested throughout this work, properly managed critical diversity leads to better organizational outcomes.

Members should also be reminded that a third component is important to reaping the benefits of diversity: structuring the organization in such a way that members feel comfortable offering their unique perspectives. If organizations recruit diverse members but subsequently pressure them to conform to the status quo and to act just like others in the organization, the visible diversity will have little impact.

All of these things will lead to greater parity that will make the U.S. more globally competitive. What is the United States missing out on by not having greater parity? What are the required policy steps to ensure that the U.S. reaps the benefits from such transformation? We need to remind White men of the changes that are required to make greater equality of opportunity and diversity work and pay for America, its organizations, and their members so that the nation can remain competitive.

For example, while there have been steady improvements in the quantity of education—such as expanded enrollment and more years of schooling— the quality of education, especially for girls and other relatively disadvantaged groups, needs to be improved. Because people of color and women are still disadvantaged relative to White men, poverty alleviation policies should give special attention to them. Promoting equality and inclusion will serve as tools to improve living conditions of the poorest populations.

A second way of capitalizing on diversity is by resisting reactionary attempts to reverse diversity efforts. It has only been within the past few decades that the nation has begun to realize that its success will be tied to issues of diversity and inclusion. It is important to demonstrate to organizational members that diversity is institutionally beneficial. In the business world, diversity produces positive outcomes over homogeneity because growth and innovation may depend upon people from various backgrounds working together and capitalizing on their differences. Although such differences may lead to some communication barriers and group conflict, diversity increases the opportunity for creativity and the quality of the product of group work. Diversity provides a competitive advantage through social complexity at the firm level when it is positioned within the proper context. In addition, linking diversity to the idea of parity makes it easier to see that diversity pays because organizations that draw on more inclusive talent pools are more successful. Diversity is positively related to organizational success because it allows organizations to "think outside the box" by bringing previously excluded groups inside the box, thereby enhancing creativity, problem solving, and performance.

Government can respond to diversity by encouraging it, discouraging it, or by ignoring it. Ultimately, leaders in this nation—in the corporate sector, in the government sector, in education, and in the non-governmental sector—need to be sensitive about the issues at stake and informed about the implications of their choices. Doing so will require honesty, good faith, and mutual respect. The process is important. It will call for openness, consultation, dialogue, and participation. Those working through such processes must be willing to confront the hard issues, and they will need to recognize distinctive historical and cultural experiences that have set the different paths for various groups. They will need to continue to enact policies and programs—even when they are met with resistance—so that America can reap the benefits of diversity.

As this chapter has suggested, we can and should reduce bias in organizational settings through programs meant to improve intergroup relations in diverse environments. This can be accomplished, in part, by using programs and initiatives that explicitly seek to make critical diversity legitimate in the eyes of various members. Such programs should be aimed at helping various kinds of members understand critical diversity. They should also help members see that their organizations are committed to critical diversity. And they should help members see the tangible benefits of critical diversity—for themselves, for those traditionally who have been left out, for their organizations, and for the nation—while also reducing diversity-threat among those who feel that they have much to lose with the implementation of diversity initiatives.

Notes

1 Roosevelt, 1991
2 Kalev, Dobbin, and Kelly, 2006
3 Collins and Herring, 2006
4 Collins and Herring, 2006

References

Collins, Sharon M. and Cedric Herring. 2006. "Managing Diversity to Improve Employees' Understanding of Diversity Initiatives in the Workplace." Unpublished manuscript.
Kalev, Alexandria, Frank Dobbin, and Erin Kelly. 2006. "Best Practices or Best Guesses? Assessing the Efficacy of Corporate Affirmative Action and Diversity Policies." *American Sociological Review* 71: 589–617.
Roosevelt, Thomas, Jr., 1991. "The Concept of Managing Diversity." *The Best of the Bureaucrat* 2: 41–44.

13
Accountability in Diversity and Inclusion Strategies

Increasingly, organizations are seeking ways to quantify the effectiveness and efficiency of their diversity efforts. In the current economic climate, senior management in many organizations insists, perhaps more than ever, that diversity initiatives are cost effective. Diversity officers want to comply, but they are often faced with two unpopular choices: invest time, resources, and energy into collecting significant amounts of data about their organizations and their diversity efforts while learning how to scientifically analyze them to calculate the organization's return on investment in diversity; or hire outside firms to generate return on investment (ROI) reports.

In this book, we have presented evidence that diversity pays. We trust that this point is abundantly clear. However, it is one thing to show that diversity pays for business organizations, and yet another to demonstrate that diversity pays for a particular organization. We understand that the typical reader of this book may be more concerned with accountability in his or her own organizations than the link between diversity and business performance more generally. They may want to know what diversity success looks like for their organizations. What are some of the most effective methods of measuring the progress of their initiatives? Are there different measures for different stages of the diversity journey?

This chapter provides guidance to those who are attempting to gauge the level of success in their diversity initiatives. It does so in a rigorous but non-technical way. It identifies ways in which organizations can begin to hold their managers and teams accountable for diversity practices that achieve their desired results. We discuss the diversity ROI determination process. We provide an overview of Edward Hubbard's "diversity scorecard" approach. And we offer a brief look at Craig Clayton's "diversity profit equation." We provide these discussions in ways that are accessible to the non-specialist.

Measuring Diversity Return on Investment

The return on investment (ROI) measures the monetary value of results and cost for a program or initiative. Normally, this is expressed as a percentage. Measuring the diversity return on investment has become a critical issue among those concerned with diversity. The subject appears regularly on meeting agendas and at professional conferences. Journals and books regularly embrace the idea with ever-increasing print space. Even top executives who have expressed unwavering dedication to diversity have stepped up their appetite for diversity ROI.

Even though interest in the topic has heightened and much progress has been made, it is still an issue that challenges even the most sophisticated and progressive diversity officers. Some professionals argue that it is not possible to calculate the ROI in diversity, while others quietly and deliberately proceed to develop measures and diversity ROI calculations. Regardless of the position taken on the issue, the reasons for measuring returns still exist. Almost all diversity professionals share a concern that they must eventually show a return on their organization's investment. Otherwise, sooner or later, funds for diversity initiatives may be reduced or the diversity department may not be able to maintain or enhance its influence on the organization.

The dilemma surrounding the diversity ROI process is often a source of frustration with many senior executives and even within the diversity field itself. Most executives realize that diversity is a basic necessity when their organizations are experiencing significant growth or increased competition. In those cases, diversity training, for example, can prepare employees with the required skills at the same time that they are fine tuning skills needed to meet competitive challenges. Diversity is also important during business restructuring and rapid change where employees must learn new skills and often find themselves doing much more work in a dramatically downsized workforce.

While many executives these days intuitively feel that there is value in diversity, they still want the hard data. They want to be able to logically conclude that diversity can pay off in important bottom-line measures such as productivity improvements, quality enhancement, cost reductions, and time savings. They also want to know that diversity can enhance customer satisfaction, improve morale, and build teamwork. Yet, they can feel frustrated by the lack of concrete evidence to show that their investment in diversity is really paying off. While the payoffs are often assumed to be there and diversity appears to be a plus, more evidence is required or money and other resources for diversity initiatives may not be allocated, especially in times of economic uncertainty. The diversity ROI process represents a promising way to show this accountability in a logical, rational approach.

Although much progress has been made, the diversity ROI process is not without its share of limitations and drawbacks. The mere presence of the process creates a dilemma for many organizations. When an organization embraces the concept and implements the process, the management team is usually anxiously awaiting results, only to be frustrated when they are not easily quantifiable. For a diversity ROI process to be useful, it must balance many issues such as feasibility, simplicity, credibility, and soundness. More specifically, the process needs to meet the needs of three major audiences: diversity managers and practitioners; executives, senior managers, and clients; and researchers.

Diversity managers and practitioners. For several years, many diversity managers and practitioners have presumed that diversity ROI could not be measured, or at least not in a very straightforward fashion. When they examined a typical diversity ROI process, they found long formulas, complicated equations, and complex models that made the process appear to be too confusing. With this complexity, they could foresee the incredible efforts required for data collection and analysis. They could also see that validating diversity ROI could substantially increase their costs. Because of these concerns, diversity managers and practitioners are seeking a diversity ROI process that is simple and easy to understand so that they can easily implement the steps and strategies. They also need a process that will not take an excessive timeframe to implement and will not consume too much staff time or too many additional resources. With growing competition for financial resources, they need a process that will be user friendly, save time, be cost efficient, and help them to validate the effectiveness and efficiency of their diversity initiatives and efforts.

Executives, senior managers, and clients. Executives, senior managers, and clients also have a strong interest in establishing the diversity ROI. They want a process that provides quantifiable results, using a method similar to the ROI formula applied to other types of investments. Executives and senior managers often want to have a diversity ROI calculation that can be boiled down to one number or percentage. Like diversity officers and practitioners, they also want a process that is easy to understand. They want the assumption made in the calculations and the methods used in the process to reflect their point of reference. Usually, they do not want or need a string of formulas or complicated statistical models. Instead, they want a procedure that they can explain to others if necessary. They need a process that is sound and realistic enough to engender confidence.

Researchers. In contrast, researchers will typically want a rigorous process that stands up to scrutiny. Researchers usually insist on including models, formulas, assumptions, and theories that are sound and based on commonly accepted methodological practices. In addition, they want methods that produce accurate values and consistent results. If approximations are necessary, researchers usually want procedures that can be replicated and that provide the most accuracy within the constraints of the situation. They want to make explicit what approximations and adjustments analysts used when there were uncertainties in the process. The challenge is to develop acceptable requirements for a diversity ROI process that will satisfy researchers and, at the same time, please diversity officers and practitioners, and executives and senior managers.

Calculating the Diversity ROI

The diversity return on investment is calculated using the program benefits and costs. The benefit-cost ratio is the program benefits divided by cost. In formula form it is:

$$BCR = \text{Program Benefits} \div \text{Program Costs}$$

The return on investment uses the net benefits divided by program costs. The net benefits are the program benefits minus the costs. In formula form, the ROI becomes:

$$ROI\ (\%) = (\text{Net Program Benefits} \div \text{Program Costs}) \times 100$$

This is the same basic formula used in evaluating other investments in which the ROI is traditionally reported as earnings divided by investment. The ROI from some diversity initiatives and programs can be quite large, as they can often exceed 100 percent.

Identifying Intangible Benefits

Most diversity programs will have both tangible monetary benefits and intangible nonmonetary benefits. The diversity ROI calculation is based on converting both hard and soft data to monetary values. Other data items are identified that are difficult to convert directly into monetary values. These intangible benefits include items such as increased goodwill, increased organizational commitment, improved teamwork, improved customer service, reduced complaints, and reduced conflicts. During data analysis, we should make every attempt to convert all data to monetary values. All hard data such as output, quality, and time are converted to monetary values. We should try to do the same with each soft data item, but if the process used for conversion is too subjective, then the resulting values lose credibility. In such cases, it is better to list intangible benefits separately with appropriate explanations. For some programs, intangible and nonmonetary benefits are extremely valuable, and they may carry influence much like the hard data items.

Below, we provide an overview of the "Balance Scorecard" approach. In particular, we focus on the "Diversity Scorecard" method developed by Edward Hubbard.

The Diversity Scorecard Method of Evaluating Diversity

Edward Hubbard defines the diversity scorecard as:

> a balanced, carefully selected set of objectives and measures derived from an orga-
> nization's strategy that link to the diversity strategy. The measures selected for the
> diversity scorecard represent a tool for diversity leaders to use in communicat-
> ing to executives, managers, employees, and external stakeholders the diversity
> outcomes and performances drivers by which the organization will achieve its
> diversity mission and strategic diversity objectives.[1]

Hubbard suggests that there are six perspectives that organizations can use in assessing their diversity performances within the diversity scorecard approach:

1 financial impact;
2 diverse customer/community partnership;
3 workforce profile;
4 workplace climate/culture;
5 diversity leadership commitment; and
6 learning and growth.

All of these indicators link to the organization's diversity strategy. The specific make-up of indicators will vary by industry and types of goods or services the organization provides. Moreover, some indicators are forward-looking and can only be assessed after the fact, and others provide information on past performance. Overall, this method provides a way of tracking, measuring, and forecasting the organization's progress in managing its diversity in relation to its overall organizational strategies.

The financial scorecard category is concerned with the monetary return on diversity. This is an indicator of how the amounts of economic resources invested in diversity initiatives relate to increases in revenue due to these initiatives. In particular, the financial performance dimension is concerned with bottom-line activity such as profitability, return on investment, economic value added, and sales growth. Indeed, several companies are using a wide range of finance, customer, process, and employee measures that yield hard data on the effectiveness of their diversity initiatives. Indeed, these companies must be experiencing direct payoffs from their investments in diversity because even during the recent economic downturn, many diversity programs remained intact or even saw increases in funding.

The customer category focuses on diversity market segments. It also involves market share of customer market segments. It includes measures of the organization's effect on its customers in areas such as customer satisfaction, customer retention, acquisition of new customers, and market share of targeted market segments.

In the internal business process category, companies can measure progress in many ways, from benchmarking to representation to supplier diversity. These diversity scorecard dimensions cover quality, response time, cost, and new product development.

Learning and growth is the final diversity scorecard category. One indicator of how diversity affects the growth of the organization is measured by its ability to attract talented, diverse employees. Many companies pursue the public relations value of winning diversity prizes that are awarded by local and national diversity group organizations. In addition, several diversity-oriented magazines rank companies on their diversity initiatives. Thus, the learning and growth dimension examines long-term growth and improvement through employee self-improvement and technological advancement.

The diversity scorecard approach offers a number of important variables, measures, and examples of hard data that can prove the value of diversity programs and initiatives. More categories and measures can and should be developed. In the financial area, for example, sales growth for new diversity group customers could be measured. In the customer category, the number of new customers from diversity groups and the number of diversity group customers who stay with a product (a variation on brand loyalty) could also yield valuable data. Internal business processes could include the number of new products and services developed for diversity group customers. In addition, a measure of internal process could be the number of problems resolved, the number of ideas for improvement, and the number of ideas for cost containment, all submitted by teams with diverse members. Finally, in the learning and growth area, new measures could involve the self-improvement efforts of members of diversity groups—the number of new skills acquired by diversity group employees, the number of internal courses and workshops completed by diversity group employees, and the number of external courses, specialist certificates, and even college degrees completed by diversity group employees.

Originally, the scorecard was created to link strategy and performance. Now, rather than being just a way of categorizing measures of organizational effectiveness, the diversity scorecard links organizational structure, processes, and results through strategy. The scorecard sets performance measures that track how well the goals are being met. Recent research shows that the effectiveness of diversity programs often depends on the strategic approach of the organization. Diversity can enhance proactive strategies by using creative problem solving.

Hubbard's diversity scorecard method offers several key advantages to those who want to provide a way of tracking the efficacy of diversity initiatives. A major disadvantage of this approach, however, is its level of complexity and the amount of resources it takes in order to provide an assessment of diversity ROI. While there are now software programs that will cut down on the amount of intellectual capital, time, and confusion, many practitioners will find this approach something less than accessible. Indeed, we suspect that most people will find his method far too technical in accomplishing their objective of demonstrating diversity's link and contribution to bottom-line performance.

Diversity Profit Equation

Craig Clayton provides a more accessible, though less detailed, approach to measuring the diversity ROI. He refers to his approach as the "diversity profit equation."[2] Clayton suggests that the:

> d/PE (diversity profit equation) is an internal comparative metric that allows companies to establish goals and targets based on fiscal metrics and models that impact earnings. Using these metrics can give organizations a process-oriented approach to eliminating inappropriate behaviors from the workplace while linking to organizational strategic goals. The diversity profit equation, shown below, can also give companies an idea of where they stand with key constituents.[3]
>
> Diversity Profit Equation d/PE
> d/PE = $dR/RI + $dR/OC + $dR/PLI
> dR/RI: Diversity Related Revenue Increase
> dR/CR: Diversity Related Opportunity Costs
> dR/PLI: Diversity Related Pipeline Impact Costs/Savings

The diversity profit equation is supposed to "measure the fiscal impact of diversity programs on organizations' profitability. The purpose of these measurements is to provide a snapshot of the strategic and fiscal significance of managing diversity as a business strategy."[4] Unlike the diversity scorecard method, it takes into consideration the negative impact of not having diversity present. Although this is somewhat difficult to quantify, Clayton's approach does suggest that the absence of diversity has costs that also need to be taken into account. His framework provides a straightforward way of identifying, quantifying, and monetizing such potential costs and, thus, linking them to diversity costs savings. For example, Clayton provides an example of the costs of "derailing behaviors" that result from insufficient diversity training or initiatives that can be linked directly to lower corporate earnings. In particular, he talks about employees' discretionary effort or slacking behavior. He shows how lack of effort, especially when self-reported, can be quantified and converted into organizational costs. Similarly, he suggests that many organizations calculate the costs of member turnover when members quit and leave their organizations. He suggests, however, that far more insidious is "turn-under" when members "quit and stay" (i.e., they stay with the organization but do not put forward their best or even a good effort in their duties).

Clayton's observations are insightful. As he suggests, with his diversity profit equation, organizations "will be able to see the impact of not cultivating the right programs and/or environment." Still, because measuring the impact of the absence of something is difficult, knowing exactly how to use the diversity profit equation approach in a step-by-step manner in order to measure the diversity ROI is not altogether clear.

As we mentioned at the beginning of this chapter, executives are taking an increased interest in diversity ROI. Executives and senior managers who have watched their budgets shrink during times of economic uncertainty have become frustrated and, in an attempt to respond to the situation, have demanded a return on their investments. Developing the ROI for diversity programs is challenging but increasingly necessary. In an era of accountability, the ROI issue can no longer be ignored. It must be implemented with a rational, transparent, and efficient approach that is useful to diversity officers and practitioners, executives and senior management, and evaluation researchers. We believe the diversity ROI model outlined in this chapter meets the criteria for an effective ROI process.

Notes

1 Hubbard, 2004: 132
2 Clayton, 2010
3 Clayton, 2010
4 Clayton, 2010

References

Hubbard, Edward E. 2004. *The Diversity Scorecard: Evaluating the Impact of Diversity on Organizational Performance*. Burlington, MA: Elsevier Butterworth-Heinemann.
Clayton, Craig B. 2010. "Measuring Diversity Return on Investment (ROI)." *The Diversity Factor* (Fall).

14

Critical Diversity: Where We Are Headed

In this book, we have defined critical diversity as the equal inclusion of people from varied backgrounds—especially those who are considered to be different from the traditional members because of exclusionary practices—on a parity basis throughout all ranks and parts of the organization. We suggested that critical diversity also refers to inclusive cultures that value and use the talents of all would-be members and includes them throughout all ranks of the organization. It acknowledges real and perceived differences among people in race, ethnicity, sex, age, physical and mental ability, sexual orientation, religion, work and family status, weight and appearance, and other identity-based attributes that affect their interactions and relationships. These areas are differences that are based on power or dominance relations between groups, particularly "identity groups," which are the collectivities people use to categorize themselves and others.

We believe, however, that focusing on all individual differences, rather than those differences that have important personal meanings and significant implications for power differences among groups, would render the concept of diversity impotent. Thus, throughout this book, we have used the idea of critical diversity to refer to group-based inclusion that requires equal access and parity.

People's group memberships affect their outcomes, opportunities, and experiences in society and in organizations. Such things as employment, compensation, advancement, retention, participation, and competitiveness are a few of the outcomes that are related to demographic background. In the United States, for example, those who are White, male, heterosexual, and do not have a disability generally have higher organizational ranking and earn higher salaries than do people of color, women, members of the lesbian, gay, bisexual, and transgendered (LGBT) community, and those who have disabilities. The categories of race, gender, age, physical ability, sexual orientation, and religion are not mutually exclusive. Some of these categories are fairly immutable. Others change over one's lifetime. Some groups face more barriers and organizational discrimination. It would, therefore, be disingenuous to ignore the fact that membership in some groups has more negative effects on access and opportunities for success than others. Therefore, critical diversity requires a concerted effort to recognize, acknowledge, and address historical discrimination, differential treatment, and unearned advantages rather than undermining efforts to address inequities in the name of inclusiveness.

In this final chapter, we provide some concluding remarks about critical diversity. We also point to the future and discuss what diversity must become. We take a look at critical diversity in American society in the Obama era. We also provide guidance on some diversity issues that we believe will become even more important in the future, such as religious diversity, immigration and globalization, disability, and generational diversity in the workplace. Finally, we conclude with advice about how to improve cultural competency, and how to be in the forefront of organization culture change.

Diversity and President Barack Obama

Forty years after the National Advisory Committee's report declaring that the United States was moving toward two separate and unequal nations, the first person of African ancestry was elected to the office of the Presidency of the United States of America. Barack Obama's election has been hailed as marking a fundamental change in race relation in America. How else can one explain this event that was believed by most people of all races as inconceivable in the U.S. even a few years before it occurred? Many people have concluded that the election of Obama is proof that we have reached the post-racial, color-blind society that so many have struggled to attain for over 400 years. Obama's candidacy, as well as his electoral success, was based on the premise that the United States had undergone an enormous transformation in racial attitudes among its citizens.[1] "The single most consistent trend from more than six decades of national studies of racial attitudes in the United States is a repudiation of the Jim Crow racism of an earlier era and the emergence of new norms calling for racial equality, non-discrimination, and integration. A clear illustration of this point has been the unabated decline in the number of White Americans who say they would not support an African American candidate nominated for president by their own party."[2] The percentage of White American who say they would not vote for a "qualified" African American fell from 60 percent in the 1950s to less than 10 percent in the 1990s.[3]

While it is tempting to take Obama's election as proof of the closing of the racial divide and validation of a growing trend of racial liberalism in America, the talk of a "post-racial" politics may be premature. Such

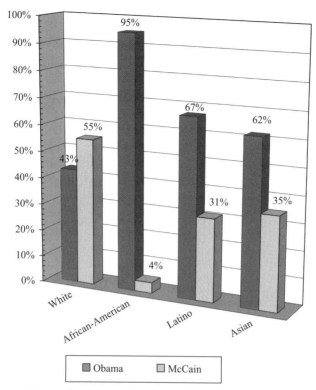

Figure 14.1 2012 Presidential Vote by Race

optimism appears to be challenged by the facts. Barack Obama won the election with 53 percent of the popular voter compared with 46 percent for John McCain. However, when the voting is analyzed by race, a strong pattern becomes visible. As Figure 14.1 shows, Obama received only 43 percent of the White vote compared with 55 percent for McCain. On the other hand, Obama received 95 percent of the African-American votes compared with just 4 percent for McCain. Obama also received 67 percent of the Latino vote and 62 percent of the Asian vote. This means that Obama won the election primarily because of the extremely high percentage of African Americans, Latinos, and Asians who voted for him. The vote in the 2012 presidential election was even more racially polarized, as an even lower percentage of Whites voted for Mr. Obama. This means that his victories were the result of the votes of minorities, especially votes from African Americans. Therefore, rather than indicating a developing inter-racial unity, the results may highlight just how racially polarized we still are as a nation.

Moreover, Eduardo Bonilla-Silva and David Dietrich challenge the idea that the presidency of Barack Obama is evidence that racism has declined in America.[4] Rather, they suggest that President Obama's election has made it more difficult to confront "color-blind" racism because of the symbolic

importance of the Office of the Presidency of the United States. Many people will view such a victory as a triumph over racism and discrimination;
however, Bonilla-Silva and Dietrich examine how the election of Barack
Obama was not an example of America becoming a "post-racial" country.
Rather, they argue that it reflects color-blind racism. They argue that the
Obama phenomenon as a cultural symbol and his political stance and per-
sona on race are compatible with color-blind racism. They forcefully argue
that, under the Obama administration, the tentacles of color-blind racism
will reach even deeper into the crevices of the American polity. In other
words, discussions and even critical analyses of racism will become much
more difficult to address.

Arguably, the election of Barack Obama moved racism from its color-
blind status back to its more overt form. For example, President Obama
regularly faces attacks from Whites, especially those who align themselves
ideologically with the Tea Party. It is clear that there are segments of the
White population who are beside themselves about the results of the 2008
presidential election. They still find it incredible that millions of people
voted for Obama to become president and, thereby, threatened the racialized social structure in America. There are still people who not only question his legitimacy to be president, but also question his citizenship, his
religious beliefs, and his loyalty to the nation. Routine courtesies that are
normally granted to all presidents have been denied to President Obama,
arguably because of race. Yet, many people cling to the notion of colorblindness in the Obama era.

Did 2008 signal a fundamental shift in the Black–White racial divide? Do
Whites—especially more educated ones—now have a more positive view
toward African Americans? Have the views of African Americans changed
in light of the Obama election? Have racial differences in perceptions of
racial inequality and justice converged, widened, or stayed the same? Are
differences in perceptions of racial inequality and justice race driven, class
driven or both? And how has the relative impact of race and social class
upon perceptions of racial inequality and justice changed over time? If we
use possession of a college education as a rough proxy for middle-class status, we are able to provide some answers to these questions. In particular,
Figure 14.2 shows that between 1986 and 2008 there was a slight convergence between Blacks and Whites in their beliefs about whether Blacks get
less than they deserve. The racial gap closed by 9 percentage points from a
46.3 percent gap in 1986 to a 37.3 percent gap in 2008. It should be noted
that this closing of the gap did not occur because Whites became more
sympathetic to the plight of Blacks; rather, this slight convergence occurred
because a smaller percentage of Blacks agreed with the idea that Blacks get
less than they deserve (down from 64.7 percent in 1986 to 56.3 percent
in 2008). And both of these numbers are lower than in 1992 when more

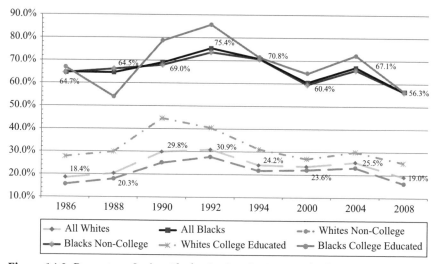

Figure 14.2 Percentage Saying Blacks Get Less by Race and Education

than three in four (75.4 percent) of Blacks reported that they believed that Blacks get less than they deserve.

Is the slight Black–White convergence due to class-based changes? Figure 14.2 shows that racial differences continued to be much greater than differences by class (education level). In 1986, there was virtually no gap between college-educated and non-college-educated Blacks. The same was true in 2008. And while there was a 10 percent gap between college-educated and non-college-educated Whites in 1986, this gap became even smaller (8 percent) in 2008. These patterns do not suggest that class was an important motor for the slight racial convergence that occurred in beliefs about the opportunity structure for Blacks. It is also clear that race remained far more important than social class in shaping perceptions about racial inequality and justice over this time period, at least for this indicator. In short, between 1986 and 2008, there was some convergence between Blacks and Whites with respect to their beliefs about opportunities for Blacks. This convergence does not appear to have been driven by class-based similarities in beliefs; rather, it appears to be driven by Blacks' decreasing belief that Blacks get less than they deserve.

Do these patterns hold true for other indicators? Figure 14.3 shows that between 1986 and 2008 there was a divergence between Blacks and Whites in their beliefs about whether slavery and discrimination have made life harder for Blacks. The racial gap grew by 7 percentage points from a 19.7 percent gap in 1986 to a 26.5 percent gap in 2008. The gap grew despite the fact that between 1986 and 2008 a lower percentage of Blacks came to believe that slavery and discrimination have made life harder for Blacks (75 percent in 1986 down to 63 percent in 2008). The decline in such beliefs

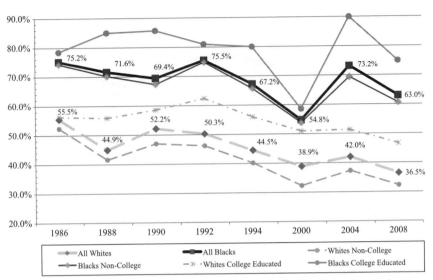

Figure 14.3 Percentage Saying Conditions Make It Difficult for Blacks by Race and Education

was even more precipitous among Whites in this timeframe (56 percent in 1986 down to 36 percent in 2008). Figure 14.3 also shows that racial differences continued to be much greater than differences by class (education level). These patterns do not support the polarization thesis, nor do they suggest that race became a less important determinant of beliefs about the opportunity structure for Blacks. Race remained a far more important factor than social class in shaping perceptions about racial inequality and justice over this time period for this indicator.

Our final indicator asks about affirmative action. Figure 14.4 shows that between 1986 and 2008 there was a slight convergence between Blacks and Whites in their beliefs about affirmative action. The racial gap closed by 13 percentage points from a 53 percent gap in 1986 to a 40 percent gap in 2008. Again, it should be noted that this closing of the gap did not occur because Whites became more favorable toward affirmative action—they became less favorable; rather, this convergence occurred because a smaller percentage of Blacks supported affirmative action by 2008 (down from 68 percent in 1986 to 50 percent in 2008). Whites' levels of support for affirmative action declined from 14 percent in 1986 down to 10 percent in 2008. Again, there is no evidence that the slight Black–White convergence was due to class-based changes. Among Whites, there is little variation in levels of support for affirmative action by educational levels; among Blacks, there is no systematic pattern that varies by education. These patterns do not suggest that class was an important factor in the racial convergence in levels of support for affirmative action. Although Blacks became somewhat

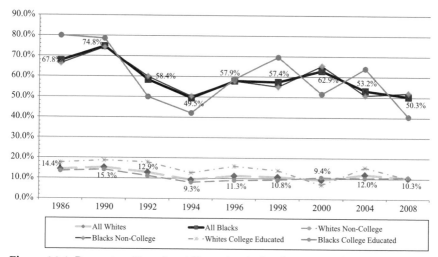

Figure 14.4 Percentage Favoring Affirmative Action by Race and Education

less supportive of the policy, they remained far more supportive than were Whites.

Overall, our results suggest that:

1   With respect to racial inequality and justice attitudes, race continued to be an important determinant of outlooks.
2   Blacks at all educational levels continued to be more similar to other Blacks with different educational attainments than to Whites with educations similar to their own.
3   The Black community did not undergo social and political polarization.
4   Socioeconomic standing did not become more important than race as a determinant of the social and political attitudes and outlooks examined.

The results reveal very strong racial effects with very little race and class interaction. Blacks are much more likely than Whites to perceive discrimination as a problem and much less likely to view the position of Blacks in society as having improved by a great deal. This supports the idea that there is a divide between Blacks and Whites with respect to their perceptions of racial justice and fairness. Whites tend to believe that the disadvantaged position of African Americans is deserved because it reflects their actual effort (or lack of it). Because of this, Whites tend to believe that African Americans should not receive any special treatment or government-sponsored assistance. The solution to the racial problem is for Blacks to try harder, stop being lazy, and stop looking for handouts. Whites, therefore, tend to see themselves as superior—not necessarily in term of biology or genetics but in the possession of superior character—especially in terms of work ethic. Black disadvantage, therefore, is a result of Blacks not possessing "White" characteristics such as being hard working and having perseverance, self-reliance, intelligence, and strong moral values. Basically, discrimination is believed to be a thing of the past and, accordingly, the position of Blacks has "greatly improved." African Americans tend to take the opposite view. They believe that far from being fair, their disadvantaged position is undeserved and unjust. Racial discrimination limits their opportunities and advantages Whites. Therefore, Blacks tend to feel that their situation is not due to their lack of effort, but to the fact that they get less than they deserve for their efforts. Blacks also view their "improvement" in less positive terms.

On some dimensions, the views of Blacks and Whites did begin to converge. But by no means did socioeconomic standing become more important than race as a determinant of the social and political views examined. In short, the predictions derived from Wilson's "declining significance" argument have not been realized even in the Obama era, and predictions consistent with his "polarization thesis" appear to be inaccurate, at least to this point in time.

There is very modest support for the idea of Black–White convergence in beliefs about social justice and equality during the Obama era. In such cases, it is not because Whites have become more sympathetic to the plight of Blacks; rather, it is because Blacks have come to see their situation as improving somewhat. Still, there is a gaping divide. Because Blacks have continued to endure conditions that differ from those of other Americans, they continue to apprehend the world in terms that differ from those of the mainstream even during the Obama era.

The (Re-)Emerging Issue of Religion

As we alluded to above, some conspiracy theorists openly questioned the religious beliefs of Barack Obama. They alleged that he is not Christian but rather secretly follows the beliefs of Islam or some other non-Christian religion. A 2008 survey conducted by the Pew Research Center found that 10 percent of respondents believed that Obama is a Muslim. This is despite his repeated declarations that he is "Christian by choice." We believe these false claims and rumor mongering against Obama, nevertheless, point to a larger issue: many Americans are not as religiously tolerant as we once hoped or believed.

The question of religion also emerged during the candidacy of Mitt Romney for President. Romney is a member of the Church of Jesus Christ of Latter-day Saints, whose members are commonly called Mormons. During his Republican primary race, supporters of his rivals openly stated that Mitt Romney is not a Christian and is in a cult because he is a Mormon. A supporter of then-presidential candidate Governor Rick Perry of Texas, Robert Jeffress, who is the senior pastor at First Baptist Church in Dallas, said, "Mitt Romney's a good moral person, but he's not a Christian. Mormonism is not Christianity. It has always been considered a cult by the mainstream of Christianity." A 2011 American Values Survey by the Public Religion Research Institute suggests that Jeffress is not alone in his assessment, as nearly half (49 percent) of White evangelical Protestant voters do not believe that the Mormon faith is a Christian religion.[5]

Whether Mormonism is part of Christianity is not consequential in and of itself. That so many Americans question the content of others' religious beliefs, however, suggests that Americans are not as religiously tolerant as we once hoped or believed. Because of the tendency for people to be hostile to those who are different from themselves is so strong, the implications for religious differences are great. Religious diversity is an important component of cultural diversity that we need to take seriously. Yet, religious diversity is often evaluated quite differently from other forms of diversity. In American society now, there is usually at least a polite agreement that racial and gender diversity are here to stay and that they enrich life. Minimally, most people realize that racial bigotry and gender chauvinism create problems and are inappropriate. Unfortunately, however, many people use quite different thought processes with regard to religious diversity. Many people feel that their religion is, indeed, superior to others. Not only do they value such beliefs, but also they regard such religious chauvinism as a necessary component of religious commitment. They see it as a virtue that should be cultivated among the faithful.

Although the ideals of religious faith are supposed to unite people across the great chasms carved by race, gender, and class, church attendance is perhaps the most highly segregated activity in the United States. In 2008, in a campaign interview, President Barack Obama reiterated this observation by saying, "The most segregated hour of American life occurs on Sunday morning."[6] But even within the White population, different religious groups tend to attract people of similar educational and occupational levels. Few factory workers are Episcopalians, for example, and few professional people and company executives are Baptists or members of Pentecostal groups. Some groups, such as the Roman Catholic Church, have working-class as well as wealthy members; but the data generally show that occupation and income vary with religious affiliation. Religious affiliation is related to class, and many social controversies result from perceptions that differ according to social class. Opinions on such issues as prayer in the schools, the teaching of creationism, abortion, women as clergy, the Equal

Rights Amendment, and homosexuality vary both by class and by religion. The conservative positions are generally supported both by fundamentalist and Pentecostal churches and by people who have lower incomes and less education.

Although there are more than 1,500 religious denominations in America, the big divide in American religion is between those who identify themselves as Christian and all others.[7] These religious differences have implications for organizations, especially the workplace. In particular, difficulties occur when employees are told they are not allowed time off from work to observe their particular religious holidays. Similarly, some employees are afraid to ask for time off from work to observe their particular religious holidays or they are led to believe that they cannot take breaks for prayer times. Other issues include dress codes that forbid beard or facial hair, even those worn for religious reasons. Also problematic are policies that prohibit employees from wearing clothing that expresses their particular faith. Even more troubling are unwritten rules that prevent people from receiving deserved promotions because of how they dress to reflect their religious preferences. Worse yet is when employees are fired or penalized in other ways for expressing their faith through the way in which they dress.

In the Christian versus others divide, anti-Semitism is an issue of concern. Historically, anti-Semitism is one of the oldest forms of discrimination. Unfortunately, it remains profoundly enmeshed in many societies. In America, it has flourished even in communities where Jews have never lived, and it has been a harbinger of discrimination against others. The rise of anti-Semitism anywhere is a threat to people everywhere. Hence, it requires constant vigilance and the strongest political will in order to be eradicated. It is hard to believe that more than 60 years after the tragedy of the Holocaust, anti-Semitism is once again rearing its ugly head. But it is clear that we are witnessing an alarming resurgence of this phenomenon in new forms and manifestations.

According to the 2011 American Values Survey, Americans strongly affirm the principles of religious freedom, religious tolerance, and separation of church and state.[8] Nearly nine in ten Americans agree that America was founded on the idea of religious freedom for everyone, including religious groups that are unpopular. Still, nearly half of Americans believe that the values of Islam are at odds with American values.

Junaid Rana argues that the historic relationship of Islam to America has increasingly placed Muslim communities in an ambiguous position within the United States.[9] The tragic events of September 11, 2001 have led to the racialization of Muslims through a logic that connects them to violence and religious othering. Rana argues that Muslims are racialized as threats, criminals, foreigners, and outsiders. In short, they are the victims of Islamophobia—the hatred of, prejudice against, or irrational fear of Islam or Muslims. It includes the belief that Muslims should be excluded from the economic, social, and public life of the nation. It also includes the perception that Islam has few values in common with other cultures and is a violent political ideology rather than a religion.

Former Under Secretary-General of the United Nations Shashi Tharoor identifies eight things that must have a place in any strategy to combat Islamophobia.[10] He discusses laws and norms; education; limiting the power and influence of hate media; leadership; two-way integration of cultures and peoples; dialogue (particularly interfaith dialogue); understanding the policy context; and combating terrorism and violence carried out in the name of Islam or any religion. He says that terrorism and bigotry both emerge from blind hatred of an "Other" and that, in turn, is the product of three factors: fear, rage, and incomprehension—fear of what the Other might do to you, rage at what you believe the Other has done to you, and incomprehension about who or what the Other really is. These three elements fuse together to ignite the deadly combustion that assaults and even destroys people whose only sin sometimes is that they feel none of these things themselves. The ends to both terrorism and Islamophobia are to be found in the same place. If they are to be tackled and ended, we will have to deal with each of these factors by attacking the ignorance that sustains them. We will have to know each other better, learn to see ourselves as others see us, learn to recognize hatred and deal with its causes, learn to dispel fear, and, above all, just learn about each other.

Immigration, Race, and Diversity

The United States is undergoing a transition that is characterized by changing demographic, economic, and political patterns that, in turn, raise critical issues with respect to governance, fair and just public policy, and the meaning of citizenship. Between 1990 and 2010, the foreign-born population in the United States increased from 19.8 million to 38.5 million. This 18.7 million increase in immigrants represented a 94 percent increase and reflected the historic rise in international migration over the past 40 years that brought a tide of new immigrants to the United States from Asia, Latin America, and other parts of the globe.

Despite the notion that America is a country of immigrants, the dramatic growth in the number of foreign-born residents concerns many native-born White Americans. Xenophobia, the intense dislike or fear of strangers or people from other countries, is on the rise.[11] This xenophobia describes attitudes, prejudices, and behaviors that reject, exclude, and often vilify people based on the perception that they are outsiders or foreigners to the community, society, or national identity. A growing number of Americans believe immigrants are a burden to this country. Moreover, a majority of native-born White Americans believe that immigrants take jobs and housing and put strains on schools and the healthcare system. Some are also concerned about the ethnic and cultural impact of the expanding number of newcomers. According to the 2011 American Values Survey, more than four in ten Americans say that the growing number of newcomers from other countries threatens traditional American customs and values. Ironically enough, however, the overwhelming majority of Americans believe immigrants are hardworking (87 percent), have strong family values (80 percent), and strengthen American society (53 percent).

By the year 2010 in the United States, immigrants, people of color, and women comprised the majority of new entrants into the labor force. The job market prior to the Great Recession of 2007 was expanding sufficiently to absorb them without driving down wages significantly or preventing the native-born population from finding jobs. Immigration has not led to welfare dependency among immigrants, nor is there any compelling evidence that welfare is a magnet for immigrants. Studies show that most other immigrant groups have attained sufficient earnings and job mobility to move into the economic mainstream.

Overall, immigration has been beneficial for the United States. Immigrant success stories represent the fulfillment of the American Dream. In contrast, the persistent inequality suffered by native-born African Americans demonstrates the limits of that dream. While recent immigrants have unquestionably brought economic and cultural benefits to U.S. society, the costs of increased immigration may fall particularly heavily upon those native-born groups who are already disadvantaged. While the experiences of Blacks and immigrants in the United States are not directly comparable, their fates are connected. The arrival of large numbers of immigrants of color in recent decades has transformed relations between minority populations in the United States. In many instances, it has created new kinds of competition between native-born people of color and immigrants of color. In particular, recent immigrants have secured many of the occupational niches once dominated by Blacks. In many instances, these immigrants now pass these jobs on through ethnic hiring networks that exclude African Americans. These patterns demand that we pay renewed attention to the entrenched problems of racial disadvantage that still beset native-born African Americans who have struggled to overcome the legacies of racism, ethnic intolerance, and destructive policies.

Immigration is one of the driving forces behind social change in the United States. It continues to restructure the way in which Americans think about diversity, race, and ethnicity. The complex politics of immigration have become intertwined with economic perceptions and realities, racial and ethnic divisions, and international relations. With recent immigration at high levels, there is speculation that the increased presence of immigrants will intensify the competition for housing and educational opportunities among minority groups. Within predominantly African-American neighborhoods themselves, the establishment of small immigrant businesses has raised concerns that these may hinder local residents from starting up similar ventures.

How have these demographic transformations affected the relationship between the two largest racial and ethnic populations in the United States: Latinos and African Americans? African Americans and Latinos are encountering each other in work settings, schools, neighborhoods, and other places. While some interactions have gone smoothly, many have been fraught with misunderstanding, competition, suspicion, hostility, and conflict. Prior research has documented that many members of both of these groups face some common obstacles: difficulties in finding higher-paying jobs, housing discrimination, inadequate educational opportunities, lack of quality healthcare, and police harassment. African-American and Latino communities, therefore, have much to gain by collaborating to solve mutual problems, make connections, start dialogues, and act in cooperative ways to transcend the rather deep divisions separating them.

On the question of whether immigrants are taking jobs away from African Americans, one is tempted to deny the existence of this competition. But more recent research by Abel Valenzuela, Jr. and Paul Ong found some adverse effects for African Americans with the impacts coming from the presence of low-skilled Latino immigrants.[12] Their study showed that increased joblessness for African Americans is connected to increases in Latino immigration. More precisely, their analysis focuses on the impact of immigration upon the joblessness and earnings among Black males between the ages of 18 and 24, and those between the ages of 18 and 64 with no more than a high school education. These populations were chosen because they are the most susceptible to job competition, primarily due to their concentration in the low-pay and high-turnover secondary sector. Ong and Valenzuela estimate that there is a small positive impact of Latino immigration on earnings, which is produced by two offsetting effects. The presence of immigrants appears to have a direct complementary effect in increasing the earnings of African Americans who are employed; but, on the other hand, the larger flow of immigrants works indirectly, through joblessness, to depress earnings.

Ong and Valenzuela argue that immigrants have a complementary effect for African Americans in public-sector employment due to the increased demand for public services and agencies as a result of the growth of legal and undocumented immigration. As the demand for public services, programs, and personnel has grown due to the population growth, a large part of which comes from immigration, African American employment in this sector has increased. In other words, even Valenzuela and Ong found that not all aspects of immigration are bad for African Americans. Immigrants appear to have a positive, or net complementary, effect on African Americans. The presence of Asian and other non-Hispanic and non-Asian immigrants is not related to higher Black joblessness, but is positively related to higher Black earnings. More recent research by Frank Bean, James Bachmeier, Susan Brown, and Rosaura Tafoya-Estrada also suggests that low-skilled immigrant workers play increasingly important and necessary roles in the U.S. labor market that are largely complementary to the roles played by natives, including African Americans.[13] Even as immigration rates have begun to slow, these complementary roles are likely to continue.

Disability and Diversity

Most perceptive organizations understand the value of having diversity in their memberships. As we have argued throughout this book, organizations' memberships should mirror their diverse marketplaces if they expect to be successful. However, what many organizations overlook in their diversity efforts is the population of people with disabilities. According to the 2010 U.S. Census, there are nearly 50 million Americans with disabilities. Disability affects one in five people. People with disabilities constitute a minority population that crosses all other diversity dimensions. From a marketing perspective, disability experts suggest that this population has an annual aggregate spending power of US$1 trillion, with $220 billion in discretionary spending.[14] This is a vast, largely untapped marketing opportunity, especially as the population continues to age, and aging increases the potential of living with disabilities.

The disabled have several skills that employers and the labor market need. Unfortunately, these skills are often overlooked and underutilized. With technological advances and greater insights into overcoming physical limitations, organizations should become more cognizant of the value of adding disability to their diversity outreach by recruiting and retaining talented people with disabilities. They should also become more involved in outreach and marketing to disabled customers.

Employers seeking talent often overlook people with disabilities largely as a result of misconceptions and fear. Only 39 percent of disabled people between the ages of 18 and 64 are employed. People with disabilities confront several marginalizations that add to their oppression, discrimination, and segregation. Living with a disability not only means managing limitations, it also means dealing with complex social and environmental forces that place the disabled in socially disadvantaged positions. Fears of increased costs, inflexibility in considering necessary accommodations, and outright prejudice all contribute to a reduction in job market opportunities for people with disabilities. Even when included, people with disabilities often work fewer hours and in lower-paying or lower-skilled positions.[15]

More than one quarter of people with disabilities live below the poverty line. People from diverse ethnic and racial backgrounds who have a disability, including Latinos, African Americans and Native Americans, are more likely to live in poverty than White people with disabilities.[16] People living in poverty are more likely to be unemployed, have limited education, and often lack access to healthcare and insurance. Indeed, research has demonstrated that living in poverty puts people at increased risk for developing a disability.[17] Impoverished people are less likely to eat sufficient amounts of healthy food. Moreover, they are more likely to live in conditions that expose them to dangerous and hazardous working conditions and unsanitary living conditions. Such risk factors increase the poor's chances of developing impairments and secondary disabilities.[18]

Being disabled also often leads to living in poverty. People with disabilities are three times more likely to live in poverty than the population as a whole.[19] From the perspective of distributive social justice, people with disabilities, particularly low-income minorities, have been excluded when it comes to the acquisition of wealth.[20]

To protect the rights of people with disabilities, the United States government passed the American with Disabilities Act (ADA) in 1990. The ADA was intended to protect the rights of the disabled in terms of accommodations at work, in gaining entrée to government facilities and services, in accessing businesses and public accommodations, and in protecting their rights to assistive communication devices. Passage of the ADA signaled a new era for independent living among the disabled. Still, people of color with disabilities lag behind in deriving benefit from this legislation. This is true particularly in the areas of employment, housing, and community integration.[21] Two decades after the passage of the ADA, racially diverse populations are still experiencing violations of their rights. They continue to experience discrimination and related barriers to becoming productive members of society.[22]

For several reasons, the number of people with disabilities is increasing.[23] There are several reasons for the steady increase in disability rates: the emergence of new diseases and other causes of impairment; increases in the life span and increasing numbers of elderly people with impairments; increases in the number of disabled children because of malnutrition, diseases, child labor, and other causes; and increases in survival in armed conflict and violence. With the growth in the number of people with disabilities, this is a critical diversity issue that is likely to become more visible in the years to come.

Generational Diversity

Another type of diversity that is commonly overlooked but of growing importance is generational diversity. Historically, it was rather difficult to find more than two generations working side by side within the same organization. Typically, older employees retired as younger ones entered the workforce. Today, however, in many larger organizations, there are likely to be work teams or divisions composed of people from distinct generations. Indeed, it is not uncommon to find three or even four generations working together. At times, the differences among the generations can lead to misunderstandings, tensions, and conflict as these people from different cohorts approach work, the family/work balance, organizational loyalty, authority, and other central issues from different vantage points. These generational differences may become of growing importance to organizational performance as traditional ideas about retirement change.

We can think of a generation as a cohort of people born during a particular era who shared common life experiences that took place in their formative years and helped to shape their values and attitudes. If we divide them by roughly 20-year time slices, we can define at least four generations that are currently active in the workplace and other kinds of organizations:

1 *pre-baby boomers* who were born before 1940;
2 the *baby boomers* born between 1940 and 1960;
3 the *echoes* or *Generation X* born between 1960 and 1980; and
4 the *Millennials* born between 1980 and 2000.

Of course, such cut-off years are approximations, but they do help to illustrate how millions of people across the nation can share common experiences mostly because they were alive and tuned in to the same cultural, social, political, and economic phenomena of an era. Although members of particular generations have differences among themselves, they do share commonalities that are useful to keep in mind as we attempt to implement critical diversity initiatives.

Pre-baby boomers, also commonly referred to as "the Greatest Generation," were born before World War II. They lived through the Great Depression. This generation is often characterized as being hardworking, dedicated, and making great sacrifices. They are, however, known for their conformity and respect for authority. Their formative years included an era in which there was unquestioned racial segregation and discrimination in much of America. It was a time when gender inequality was the norm. They came of age before the advent of social security and much of the social safety net that most Americans now take for granted. The vast majority of members of this generation are now retired, but it is estimated that more than 5 percent of them are still active in the labor market, and even more are still active in other types of civic organizations. Because this generation is more comfortable with stability than change, getting them to warm up to critical diversity can be more difficult than for members of other generations.

In contrast to their parents, members of the baby boom generation came of age during a time of general economic prosperity and plenty. These prosperous times gave way to a period of rapid social change, upheaval, and strife and conflict. This generation witnessed the modern civil rights and Black power movements, the women's rights movement, and anti-war protests. They were generally nonconformists who are at times described as being self-absorbed, usually hardworking but for the benefit of the individual rather than the collective or the company. They tend to be more focused than their parents on personal gratification, health and wellness, and personal growth. They came to see things such as access to education as a right rather than a privilege as their parents had. With this generation, society also started experiencing instability in institutions such as the family. Because many baby boomers came of age during an era of social movements geared toward greater equality, many of them embrace the tenets of critical diversity, but there are regional and class differences that make this generalization a bit more problematic. They make up nearly half of the workforce. While they are not opposed to diversity, they are suspicious of affirmative action and quotas that they believe may harm their opportunities.

Members of Generation X (or the Echo) came of age during the 1980s and 1990s. This generation entered the labor market during waves of economic recession and corporate downsizing. They came to view corporations as unreliable in terms of providing job security and with suspicion in terms of what they value. Arguably, these factors affected how members of Generation X approach the workplace. Rather than being loyal to a particular firm, they came to see themselves as being entrepreneurial even if they worked for a corporation. They felt little need to be loyal to a company that they felt would not be loyal to them. Unlike their parents, they usually work to live and enjoy life rather than deriving pleasure from work itself. They tend to strive for balance between work and the rest of their life. Many members of this generation were the children of divorced parents. They are more nimble with respect to adjusting to social change. This generation has techno-literacy and harnesses technology for information, business, and fun. Rather than challenging authority with an eye toward replacing it, they are more likely to appear to go along with decisions from higher ups while cynically ignoring such dictates. While many members of this generation attempt to determine what is politically correct and what they are expected to say, it is often difficult to determine when there is true buy-in from them. Still, this generation genuinely embraces diversity and thinks globally. Generation X comprises about 40 percent of the workforce.

Millennials are the most recent generation to enter the labor market. Many of them are still coming of age during this era of economic uncertainty. They have already lived through the Great Recession, and their employment prospects for the future look rather grim. They are concerned about how they will gain access to the job market and launch their careers, as previous generations appear to be staying on the job longer and unemployment rates remain high. They are often saddled with student loans that exceed their ability to repay them. There is fear that Millennials will be the first American generation to be worse off than their parents. This generation is tech savvy, as they have known the PC, email, texting, and the Internet their whole lives. They stay connected around the clock. They have taken Generation X's notion of the work/life balance a step further by integrating recreational activities into their education and work. They are known for their flexibility, and they are usually more comfortable with diversity than previous generations. Despite the appearance of a bleak economic future, Millennials tend to be optimistic and confident. They are achievement oriented and street smart. Currently, they make up approximately 10 percent of the labor force, but their numbers will grow dramatically over the next decade.

What do these generational differences mean for organizations? When members of these different generations work side by side, their core differences in values may come into conflict and get in the way of efficiency, work team cohesion, and morale in the workplace. Conflicts may erupt. Values differences may become especially problematic when members of one generation come to view those of another as apathetic or caring only about instant gratification. Any negative generational stereotypes will make communication difficult. Again, such difficulties will tend to sap productivity and morale in ways that undermine organizational goals.

Effectively dealing with generational differences and conflicts will require the same kinds of diversity management skills and training as other types of diversity that can yield discord. Members of organizations may not even be aware of the kinds of biases and prejudices they have against their colleagues who are from other generations. Even more, they might not understand the lived experiences of those from different generations. Through critical diversity training, members of organizations will be more capable of identifying negative assumptions they have about members of other generations. They can also become more skilled in not only accepting such differences, but also capitalizing on them for the greater good of a more unified team.

Toward Cultural Competence and Critical Diversity

Throughout this book, we have touted the virtues of critical diversity. We have pointed out that today, many organizations and the clients they serve have become so diverse that organizations and managers must effectively deal with greater numbers of cultural and lifestyle differences. How they understand and manage these differences will have an impact upon their success. They must move beyond being clueless with respect to diversity.

It is critically important for managers and leaders to improve their cultural competency and that of their members. Whether they are seeking new clients, motivating their members, communicating to students, or taking care of patients, they need to be willing to become more familiar with and fluent in the cultures of others with whom they interact. Understanding the cultures of others, however, does not need to be reactive. Organizations and their leaders can cultivate climates that champion diversity by actively demonstrating that they know that proficiency in interacting with people with different cultures and lifestyles helps their organizations.

Organization leaders should communicate with their members about how cultural differences affect their success. They should also talk about such issues in meetings and as they are devising strategic plans for their organizations. They should reinforce such messages by making personnel moves that demonstrate their belief in the benefits of diversity. They should engage in practices to ensure that they always have a diverse set of applicants to consider, as well as diverse recruitment and selection committees.

Leaders also need to include diversity considerations in their approach to customers and clients. This can be accomplished by using diverse teams to make presentations to customers and by including culturally sensitive marketing research to better understand how clients wish to receive their services. At the same time, they will also need to evaluate the impact of their organizational climate upon different group members. It is possible that some groups will see little impact of critical diversity upon performance, perceptions, or organizational climate.

There are some best practices in diversity that can be helpful in these efforts. For example, organizations can develop strategic diversity plans that are aligned with their general business plans. Organizational diversity plans help to set the tone for diversity-related outcomes. They should point out straightforward and measurable outcomes that are expected to flow from diversity efforts. For example, an outcome might be that members will better understand the organization's business case for diversity. Or, it could be announcements about hiring statistics by race, gender, and other characteristics and the organization's goals for change.

Companies have been looking for best practices in diversity training for many years. But company executives and diversity experts still wonder which of these practices work best to create effective and inclusive environments. Some additional best practices include things such as utilizing diversity scorecards (see Chapter 13), regularly reporting the diversity scorecard results to senior management, actively recruiting and promoting diverse candidates (see Chapter 4), engaging in ongoing diversity training, and creating and funding diversity resource and affinity networks (see Chapter 10).

In a perfect world, senior management will embrace critical diversity and be on board with bringing it about. In such cases, they should be asked to advocate for diversity initiatives. They may be effective spokespeople in championing diversity. In those instances where this is not the case, however, diversity efforts that are already under way may be a starting point and a learning opportunity for them to become more familiar with its goals and its accomplishments.

Key diversity personnel will need to clearly define their audiences and anticipated outcomes. After doing so, they will need to recognize and craft key messages for these audiences. This will also require that they decide the best methods and media for reaching their audiences. It is also best that they pilot their diversity plans on a small scale, if possible, before enacting them on a large scale. And as we suggested in previous chapters, it is important that they subject such initiatives and efforts to measurement, follow-up, and refinement.

Diversity will stop being an issue when diverse members feel valued and equally included. We believe that inclusion on a parity basis is the ultimate key to critical diversity. It requires proactive efforts to promote differences at every level and division of the organization—from race, class, gender, sexual orientation, and other emerging dimensions of diversity. Such inclusion will promote open disagreement and critical feedback in which no viewpoint is marginalized. The true power of diversity will be unleashed when inclusion becomes the catalyst and incubator for innovation. We believe such critical diversity is the ultimate business case for diversity.

Notes

1 Bobo, 2009
2 Bobo, 2009:16
3 Bobo, 2009
4 Bonilla-Silva and Dietrich, 2011
5 Public Religion Research Institute, 2011
6 National Public Radio, 2008
7 Bennett, 2001
8 Public Religion Research Institute, 2011
9 Rana, 2011
10 Tharoor, 2011

11 Herring, 2011
12 Valenzuela and Ong, 2001
13 Bean et al., 2011
14 McCary, 2005
15 Atkins and Guisti, 2004
16 Suarez-Balcazar et al., forthcoming
17 Elwan, 1999; Kielhofner, de las Heras, and Suarez-Balcazar, 2011
18 Elwan, 1999; Kielhofner, de las Heras, and Suarez-Balcazar, 2011
19 Saunders, 2006
20 Suarez-Balcazar et al., forthcoming
21 Fujiura, Yamaki, and Czechowicz, 1998; Fujiura and Drazen, 2010
22 National Council on Disability, 2009; Taylor-Ritzler, et al., 2010
23 Braithwaite and Mont, 2008

References

Atkins, Dan and Christie Guisti. 2004. *The Confluence of Poverty and Disability, in The Realities of Poverty in Delaware, 2003–2004.* Dover, DE: Delaware Housing Coalition.

Bean Frank D., James D. Bachmeier, Susan K. Brown, and R. Tafoya-Estrada. 2011. "Immigration and labor market dynamics," in E.E. Telles, M. Sawyer, and G. Rivera-Salgado (Eds). *Just Neighbors? Research on African American and Latino Relations in the United States.* New York, NY: Russell Sage Foundation: 37–60.

Bennett, Georgette F. 2001. "Religious Diversity in the Workplace: An Emerging Issue." *Diversity Factor* Winter (9): 2.

Bobo, Lawrence D. 2009. "Obama and the Burden of Race." *Focus Magazine* 37(4): 16–17.

Bonilla-Silva, Eduardo and David Dietrich. 2011. "The Sweet Enchantment of Color-Blind Racism in Obamerica." *The Annals of the American Academy of Political and Social Science* 634: 190–206.

Braithwaite, Jeanine and Daniel Mont. 2008. *Disability and Poverty: A Survey of World Bank Poverty Assessments and Implications.* Social Protection Discussion Papers. Geneva: World Bank.

Elwan, Ann. 1999. *Poverty and Disability: A Survey of the Literature.* Social Protection Discussion Paper Series 9932. Geneva: World Bank.

Fujiura, Glenn T. and Carlos Drazen. 2010. "'Ways of Seeing' in Race and Disability Research," in F.E. Balcazar, Y. Suarez-Balcazar, T. Taylor-Ritzler, and C.B. Keys (Eds). *Race, Culture, and Disability: Rehabilitation Science and Practice.* Boston, MA: Jones and Barlett: 15–32.

Fujiura, Glenn T., Kiyoshi Yamaki, and Susan Czechowicz. 1998. "Disability among Ethnic and Racial Minorities in the United States: A Summary of Economic Status and Family Structure." *Journal of Disability Policy Studies* 9(2): 111–130.

Herring, Cedric. 2011. "Combating Racism and Xenophobia on Both Sides of the Atlantic," in . C. Herring (Ed.). *Combating Racism and Xenophobia: Transatlantic and International Perspectives.* Chicago, IL: Institute of Government and Public Affairs: 1–13.

Kielhofner, Gary, Carmen Gloria de las Heras, and Yolanda Suarez-Balcazar. 2011. "Human Occupation as a Tool for Understanding and Promoting Social Justice." *Occupational Therapies without Borders* 2: Part 28.

McCary, Katherine. 2005. "The Disability Twist in Diversity: Best Practices for Integrating People with Disabilities into the Workforce." *Diversity Factor* 13(3): 16–22.

National Council on Disability. 2009. *National Disability Policy: A Progress Report.* Washington, DC: National Council on Disability.

National Public Radio. 2008. "Transcript: Barack Obama's Speech on Race," www.npr.org/templates/ story/story-php?storyId=88478467.

Public Religion Research Institute. 2011. *What It Means to Be American: Attitudes in an Increasingly Diverse America Ten Years After 9/11.* Washington, DC: Public Religion Research Institute.

Rana, Junaid. 2011. *Terrifying Muslims: Race and Labor in the South Asian Diaspora.* Durham, NC: Duke University Press.

Saunders, Peter. 2006. *The Costs of Disability and the Incidence of Poverty.* Wales: University of New South Wales/The Social Policy Research Centre.

Suarez-Balcazar, Balcazar, Ali Taylor-Ritzler, and Hasnain. Forthcoming. "Race, Poverty, and Disability: A Social Justice Dilemma," in J. Betancur and C. Herring (Eds). *Reinventing Race, Reinventing Racism.* Leiden, The Netherlands: Brill Academic Publishers.

Taylor-Ritzler, Tina, Fabricio Balcazar, Yolanda Suarez-Balcazar, Robert Kilbury, Francisco Alvarado, and Madelyn James. 2010. "Engaging Ethnically Diverse Individuals with Disabilities in the VR System: The Paradox of Empowerment and Oppression." *Journal of Vocational Rehabilitation* 33: 3–14.

Tharoor, Shashi. 2011. "Anti-Semitism and Islamophobia: Education for Tolerance and Understanding," in C. Herring (Ed.). *Combating Racism and Xenophobia: Transatlantic and International Perspectives.* Chicago, IL: Institute of Government and Public Affiars: 135–140.

Valenzuela, Abel and Paul Ong. 2001. *Immigrant Labor in California.* Berkeley, CA: University of California: University of California Institute for Labor and Employment.

Index